PENSÉES
CATHOLIQUES

VOLUME 1

Essais

EDWARD L. HELMRICH

Brilliant Books Literary
137 Forest Park Lane Thomasville
North Carolina 27360 USA

Dedication

St. Jude
St. Therese of Lisieux
Edward and Marian Helmrich
Timothy Gunnar Wohnson Coln
Jim Lonergan
Fr. Benedict Groeschel
Michael Sarro
Jack Erico
John Franklin Grogan
Badonna Hurwitz
Dr. Calvert Schlick
Mike Kearns
David Creedon
Robert Radcliffe
Tom S. Meyer
David Knopf
Prof. John Hodgson
Mr. John Genereaux
Dr. Ehrenhaft
Dr. Wolfe
Mr. Barney Gill
Mr. and Mrs. Patsy Mazzullo
Mr. and Mrs. Richard Mitchell
Dr. Daniel Cherico

MCzarnecki 2020

The Lord God took the man and put him in the Garden
of Eden to work it and keep it.

—Genesis 2:15, ESV

And this is what the Lord does for us when we receive the Eucharist:
he tills and defends the garden of our soul, through which he walks in
the twilight of the day.

Contents

Foreword

As a younger person, because of circumstance and inclination, I had to know if death was the end of human life - if we face unending non-consciousness. I have always had an experience of God. Was my experience just an imagination, as Freud suggests, no matter how real it seemed, or was it real? So, I read whatever I could find that might address this question. One might find an argument against God in any subject area. And then I sought responses to these arguments.

The last argument I addressed was one of the oldest: that the physical world has always been here. Daniel Taylor points out that even if something has always existed, it still needs an explanation for its existence, since it is possible for it not to be there.[1] So finally I could accept my experience as true, though now I have others reasons as well.[2] In the third book I try to look at evidence for the existence or reality of God, including evidence that at first glance seems to argue against the existence of God. This first book is a collection of literary and theological essays that address certain interesting literary or theological questions.

The first section presents a brief discussion of four classics from a Catholic point of view: <u>Moby Dick</u>, <u>Paradise Lost</u>, <u>Twelfth Night</u>, and <u>The Waste Land</u>, to show how rich this method of interpretation can be, and to argue that most authors of the classics wrote in dialogue with the religious tradition, and much is lost if this is forgotten. The second section begins with a discussion of the one natural example of infinite

---

[1]   Taylor, Daniel <u>Explanation and Meaning: an Introduction to Philosophy</u>, Cambridge: University Press, 1970. The other possibility is that reality is irrational, that things exist with no cause, but I don't find that likely, or possible.

[2]   Among them is the physical reality of the Eucharist.

things and how they work, and how this as a model solves certain problems in Eucharistic theology. It is followed by three related essays which conclude with what the world might have looked like if the Fall had not taken place. The third section includes essays on the structure of the Mass, on the rosary, and on the Apocalypse, concluding with what the Mass might have looked like if the Fall had not taken place. The fourth section has three unrelated essays, one on the dimensionality of the physical universe as an image of God, one on Marian apparitions, and one on suffering. The appendix includes sayings from Fr. Benedict Groeschel and by a friend.

There were three sparks that prompted me to write down these ideas. I read Milton's Paradise Lost and found theological problems, though admittedly the question he addressed is very difficult. Was another solution possible? Then, in 2011, Pope Benedict XVI authorized a change in the English translation of the Mass, which somehow was an occasion for me to study the Mass. Finally, Richard Dawkins and others presented the world with a bald and rude challenge that had to be addressed. These are the "New Atheists," who are eminently forgettable and are now largely forgotten. Their attack on all faiths, in his case motivated by personal circumstances, an attack which Scott Shay also addresses, calls for as many responses as possible.[3]

My hope is that a thought here or there might solve a question someone might have about the faith, a question or misunderstanding that is keeping the person from the faith. But it might be that now our situation is that of Revelation 22:11: "Let the one who does wrong continue to do wrong; let the vile person continue to be vile; let the one who does right continue to do right; and let the holy person continue to be holy." It might be too late to hope for change.

In general, it has to be acknowledged that our culture has recently moved beyond discourse and discussion, of which this collection is a part. We have moved on to simple conflicts of power. We might have

---

[3] The New Atheists are really very funny. They disdain religion, so they don't study it and know nothing about it, and so they don't see how unoriginal their comments and criticisms are.

even entered the world of James Joyce's <u>Finnegans Wake</u>, where there are no truths but all is shifting and changing. We might have entered Nietzsche's hoped for world, where the trammels of morality and the practices of religion have been "heroically" discarded. Perhaps, like Adam and Eve at the beginning, we are left with only love or hate.

Studying mathematics has made me laconic. As a result, these comments are brief, but at times I still manage to be prolix. Dr. Arnold Zucker, a psychotherapist and devout Conservative Jewish man, taught for many years at Iona University in New York. A wonderful man, he said he only wrote things when he had something to say. I hope I am following his guideline.

Thanks to Dylan Brown who typed up four notebooks of handwritten thoughts.

The saying are in memory of Fr. Benedict Groeschel, the saint; Jim Lonergan, sometimes unjustly called the saint of Christian hatred; and Timothy Coln, *il pensatore migliore*. Tim's favorite symphony was Beethoven's <u>Eroica</u>, and he enjoyed Burton's <u>Anatomy of Melancholy</u>.

I also acknowledge Jonathan Cahn, a convert from Judaism to Evangelical Christianity, who is a prophet for our time.

Four Literary Essays—Preface

In recent years, some literature scholars led by Joseph Pearce have interpreted literature through the lens of Catholic thought and history and theology. This approach has several advantages. For the Catholic, it is a reading of literature along the lines of absolute truth, locating the place of a work in an objective standard of truth and values. Also, in many cases, the writer of literature centuries ago wrote with the Bible and the Church in mind—either to support them, to deny them, or to ignore them—so it gives a more accurate view of the author's intentions. In some cases, the author's central interlocutor was the Bible and the Catholic Church, and this aspect is missed if not considered. In short, we've had Marxist criticism, Feminist criticism, Freudian criticism, Post-modern criticism, etc., and now we are starting to try Catholic criticism of classic literature. Apart from the claim to truth, being the oldest and largest body of learning in the world, the prospect of criticism from the viewpoint of Catholic teaching is promising. I would suggest that it might prove to be the definitive hermeneutic.

My approach to reading literature is to read the book carefully without reference to criticism or background information except as needed for basic understanding to try to see what the book means to me with the assumption that the author placed everything there intentionally and intended it to be understandable to the careful reader. Also, having read a lot of criticism of other works, I decided I wanted to know what I thought of a book before consulting the views of other people. What does it mean to me? As Chesterton says, reading the classic authors is easiest of all: his reason is that they illustrate truths which are known and recognizable and unchanging. My reason is that in a classic writer, one knows that nothing is there by accident. Everything has meaning. Every connection is intentional. I use the approach of reading the book without much criticism in part because, admittedly, it is the approach I am capable of using, but I think it is a justifiable approach.

Following are four short examples of the use of what one might call the Catholic hermeneutic that I, with Joseph Pearce, am promoting.

Moby Dick

I had an interesting time reading *Moby Dick* (*MD*). For some reason, on reaching the end and having taken eighteen pages of notes, I did not see the epilogue. I didn't feel something lacking, but I did have a few questions to answer. Of course, Ishmael had to survive to tell the story, and I guessed that he was the one who had fallen back when the three men were thrown off Ahab's boat, John-the-Apostle-like[1] (p. 817). I wrongly guessed that Ishmael had caught up to Ahab's boat and that he and maybe the others had rowed on until they found safety. And I didn't know why Ishmael found himself on Ahab's boat since he worked on Starbuck's boat earlier (p. 331). But the epilogue, which I found while looking up footnotes, provides a complete and perfect conclusion. For example, the ship's going down in the vortex now includes the entire ship, even Ahab's boat and crew, with the exception of Ishmael and the coffin.

Recently, Joseph Pearce in his book and DVD series, *Quest for Shakespeare*, made a strong circumstantial argument for Shakespeare's devout Catholicism and that of his family, a devotion that they couldn't reveal in Elizabethan England. These days, I'm not sure if such a conclusion would shock the Protestants more, who took him as a standard-bearer, or the secularists who can't believe that any serious thinker can believe in God. This essay is in the line of Mr. Pearce's book in making a case for the Catholic thinking (if not devotion) of someone not connected with Catholicism.

Of course, in *MD*, Herman Melville sets out to write a comprehensive novel. He starts with an etymology that mentions a collection of grammars of languages of the world and a collection of flags of the countries of the world. The second etymology lists the word for "whale" in different languages. Finally, a third piece of extracts tracks down references to the whale or Leviathan throughout history, secular or

---

[1]   Like John in his Gospel, the observer and writer toward the end speaks of himself in the third person. All quotes are from Herman Melville's *Moby Dick* or *The Whale* (The Modern Library, Random House, 1930).

sacred. And with a dedication to Hawthorne and an inscription from *Paradise Lost*, and including dramatic scenes in the text,[2] he includes all three forms of writing (prose, drama, and poetry) and writes in all three traditions. Additionally, the *Pequod* travels all over the globe—Nantucket, the Atlantic, Africa, Japan, the Pacific. Its sailors come from all over the globe-all parts of Cape Cod, Native Americans, a Manxman, African Americans, etc. And they come from different religions—Protestant, Quaker, heathen, cannibal, humanist (Starbuck), Muslim, or Hindu (Fedallah and his companions). At times, the narrative leaves the *Pequod*, and we find ourselves in the British Islands, in Peru years later, and even in the heavens (p. 395). We go forward in time with Ishmael to after the voyage is finished (p. 353), and we go back in time to the Ice Ages (p. 655). The description of Ahab is reminiscent of Julius Caesar: tall, dark, lanky, heron-built. (p. 679)

But the *Pequod* also represents American society in miniature, all of which it needs to survive the three-year voyage (p. 111). Craftsmen from different areas have representatives on the ship—a cook, a carpenter, etc.[3] Ishmael is the reporter. And the *Pequod* and its project, like the moon flights, is an epitome of American civilization. Perhaps the *Pequod* functioned like today's large corporations (AT&T, etc.) since many people own shares in the ship, even widows and orphans (p. 113). And the oil it brings back gives light to the country, and the country depends on it.

This comprehensiveness and inclusiveness give great power and importance to the story. Also, the events of the story slowly and carefully build up to the final confrontation, which adds more power as the story progresses (for example, the sailors kill other whales, building up to the attempted killing of Moby Dick, and the *Pequod* meets other ships that have encountered Moby Dick, leading to the *Pequod*'s meeting with him).

---

[2]   2   Chapters 38, 39, 40, and 108 give examples of scene directions and dialogue written as in a play.

[3]   3   Chapters 107, 112.

After I got over the introductory sections and absorbed the comprehensive intent of *MD*, my first impression was how close the structure of *MD* is to the structure of the New Testament. I can't think of another book where the chapters are not long enough to be short stories but function as markers in a continuous story. A few of the early chapters end with a crescendo and exclamation point, but that doesn't continue. Toward the middle of the story, a whale is killed (p. 449) and beheaded, and one can't help thinking of John the Baptist beheaded at some time during Christ's ministry. And another whale, an older one, is killed, and the gruesome but common method of putting the harpoon into the air hole until the purple blood of the heart runs out clearly brings to mind the Crucifixion and the lance of the Roman soldier. And Ishmael's description at the end, again, of the man falling back from Ahab's boat parallels John's anonymous description of himself at the end of his Gospel. So I quickly saw *MD* as a book about spiritual realities as well as about a riveting whaling expedition.

I found the epilogue because I decided to count the number of chapters in the New Testament after the Gospels. Acts, the letters, and the Apocalypse have 139 chapters in total. *MD* has 135 chapters, so I went back to look for another four sections. I found the two etymologies, one collection of extracts, and the epilogue: 139 pieces (this is the Catholic Bible; the Protestant Bible omits a few letters). This part of the Bible describes the actions of the apostles after the Ascension and in some sense describes the world from that time until the end of time, which is the location of Melville and his story and of us. Melville then clearly intends the reader to compare *MD* to the New Testament. And it seemed that at the end, we would see the gruesome death of Moby Dick, but he spared us.

The Old Testament references begin with the names of Ishmael and Ahab. Several Ishmaels appear in the Old Testament. The first is Ishmael, the eldest son of Abraham and Hagar in Genesis.[4] Ishmael lived 137 years, so with 135 chapters in *MD*, Ishmael must survive and go on for a little time more (telling people about the voyage). Ahab was

---

[4]   4 Ishmael in Genesis, son of Abraham and Hagar.

a king of Israel, the Northern Kingdom, "did evil in the sight of the Lord, more than all who were before him" (1 Kings 16:30 ESV), and his wife had Naboth killed. They tried to kill Elijah (1 Kings 19:19). So Melville intends us to use the Bible as a reference to understand *MD* and intends it to be as comprehensive in a similar way. To me, it doesn't seem that he wants to replace the Bible or to make a different Scripture, which so much current art does (e.g. *Lost*), but to present its mirror in another setting.

So there seems to be evidence that *MD* describes the spiritual and religious realities of human experience in the reflection of whale hunting. Melville constantly calls the whole sea-faring project "the fishery" (for example, in chapter 27), a concrete and modest word which keeps the reader from thinking of it as symbolic or legendary pursuit. On the other hand, Jesus tells the apostles that they will become fishers of men (cf. Mark 1:17). And the first symbol of Christianity was the fish because the first letters of the word "fish" in Greek match the first letters of the name and title of Christ. "The fishery" would be another name for Christianity.

Over and over, Melville refers to the "meadows of the sea" (e.g., p. 396), comparing the sea to a kingdom equal to or greater than the kingdoms of the land ruled by men. The masts of the ships, when taken together, look like the spires of the buildings of a city (p. 225). And Ishmael goes to sea periodically, previously on merchant ships because he becomes bored on land, full of ennui (p. 4). Perhaps he is bored with the material and hungry for the spiritual. If the sea is the kingdom of the spiritual, Melville intends the battle between Moby Dick and Ahab to be more than just the battle between a hunter and his prey—as dramatic as that battle is—but a battle between spiritual forces.

Having established the comprehensiveness of *MD* that the sea pictures the spiritual and religious realities of human experience and that it's closely related to the Bible and that we need to refer to the Bible to understand the author's meaning, I'll make a few unrelated sidenotes.

The story introduces the two main characters very late. We hear people speak of Ahab early on, and we see him from time to time, but we only hear a real conversation of his when he speaks with Fedallah late in the story (Chapter 117). I don't recall any conversation between Ahab and Ishmael. We don't see the other main character, Moby Dick, until the last three chapters, though we had heard about him. And this main character is a fish!

Several works take their names from *MD*, it seems. When Ishmael describes the man falling back astern from Ahab's boat, a man who turns out to be Ishmael, he refers to him as "the third man" (p. 817), the name of the short novel by Graham Greene and the great film by Orson Welles. Melville early on uses the phrase "as in time of the cholera" (p. 170), which calls to mind the novel *Love in the Time of Cholera*. One of the ships that meets the *Pequod* carries the name *Rosebud* (p. 583ff.) In chapter 100, Melville refers to the fishery as this "watery world" (pp. 634, 697), which Kevin Costner used to name a film. And another ship the *Pequod* meets has the name *Enderby* (p. 632) Starbuck's phrase to Ahab, "O captain, my captain" (p. 777) is the name of a later Walt Whitman poem about Lincoln. The Negro boy is named Pippin or Pip for short (p. 594ff). Ahab's moving up and down from the masts at the end reminds one of Mad Max in the *Thunderdome* movies.

MD clearly has a strong relationship to the Bible, but it also has a strong relationship with Shakespeare. Melville mentions Shakespeare (p. 502) in the phrase "Shakespeare and Melanchthon." Melanchthon was the taken Greek name of Philipp Schwarzerde,[5] the educational leader and assistant of Luther (could Melville mean here the Protestant and the Catholic?). Starbuck could have shot the sleeping Ahab, reminiscent of a more just Lady MacBeth (p. 736). The prophecy of Fedallah (chapter 117) functions like the prophecies of the witches in *MacBeth*. And "Tranquo," the name of the island king (p. 645), sounds like "Banquo." On the other hand, Melville often describes Ahab's mental strain in terms similar to those in *Hamlet*, for example, "unsleeping, ever-pacing thought" (p. 230) or "Hark ye yet again, the little lower layer. All visible objects, man are but pasteboard masks" (p. 236). And Ahab's speech to the dead hooded whale, admiring him for

---

5 *Wikipedia.*

his age, and having seen the depths that man had never seen sounds like Hamlet: "Of all divers, thou hast dived the deepest. That head upon which the upper sun now gleams, has moved amid this world's foundations" (p. 450).

Every so often, Melville slows down and includes a lyrical poetic description of the sea, which often sounds Shakespearean: "What a lovely day again! Were it a new-made world, and made for a summer house to the angels...a fairer day could not dawn upon that world" (p. 806). Another example is on page 703: "These are the times, when [the sailor] softly feels a certain filial, confident, land-like feeling toward the sea; that he regards it as so much flowery earth." The name Ahab means "brother of the father,"[6] which brings to mind Hamlet's stepfather.

But getting back to the argument, can we lay out the identity between the characters in *MD* and religious or spiritual figures and religions? They're not spiritual in the sense of not physical or denying the physical but in the sense of including all of human experience, the spiritual and the material. So this identity doesn't replace or remove the great story of *MD*. It gives it a second depth.[7] The identity with spiritual figures in a parallel with the enemies of Christ trying to kill him is brought to mind by the last three chapters of *MD*, which are titled "The Chase—First Day," "The Chase—Second Day," "The Chase—Third Day."[8] The reader anticipates finally meeting Moby Dick. Also, if one approached the pope in a formal ceremony before 1970 or so, one would from afar see his three-tiered tiara.

We later learn that the birds follow Moby Dick and form a sort of canopy over his head (p. 784), bringing to mind Mark 4:32, "So that the birds of the sky can dwell in its shade." At the very end, when Tashtego, wrapped in the flag of Ahab, nails a bird to the mast with the flag as he drowns, the bird is described as a "living part of heaven" (p.

---

[6]   Ibid.

[7]   Perhaps the instinctive attraction we feel toward *MD* comes from our sense that it includes all of human life and experience, the material and the spiritual, and that it even has the spiritual as the foremost without neglecting the material.

[8]   As each Gospel ends with the passion and death of Christ (and resurrection), *MD* follows that pattern.

822). When Ahab's boat is looking for Moby Dick, they know he is below the boat because the birds are circling above it (p. 340). Again, if one sees the pope in a formal ceremony or liturgy even today, he would have a canopy or baldachin over his head (and even people with fans, like the wings of birds).

Additionally, the title of the book is *Moby Dick or The Whale*. It is a picture of Moby Dick, in some sense the most important character in the story, and he is singular among sperm whales and identifiable as different. Among the dark brownish sperm whales, he is white, the same color the pope wears and no other bishop. In the title, he has two names, and the pope has two names. In 1851, Pope Pius IX and The Pope. One could guess that Melville took the name of "Mocha Dick," the historical whale, and adjusted it to meet his needs. Pope Pius and Moby Dick have the same number of letters. The abbreviation MD suggests a medical doctor, and healing is one of the tasks of the pope. Over and over, Melville refers to Moby Dick as the "White Whale," with capital letters, again a name similar to the name of Pope Pius with repeated first letters and of two words with the same length. Melville also often refers to Moby Dick's "wrinkled brow" (p. 233) as if he is thoughtful and knowledgeable and beset by care. His mouth from the front takes the form of a smile but from the side looks crooked (p. 233), perhaps indicating suffering and strain. His "sickle-shaped lower jaw" (p. 266) brings to mind harvesting and death. And his brow is called "snow white" (p. 264), which indicates purity and age. And he has three holes in his right fluke (p. 233).

Finally, there is the sexual connection. As far as I can tell, "Moby" is a proper name. Dick is the familiar for the male name Richard and part of the male anatomy, indicating manliness. And a priest, as we now know from current events, has to be a real man, a husband to his parish or diocese. The pope is celibate, but in Catholic terms, he husbands the largest bride, the church, and controls the life-giving sacraments which all flow ultimately through his jurisdiction and are under his control.

Also, Moby Dick seems to apply justice as in the Steelkit episode (p. 353ff). It seems, telling the story forward, that Ahab went to sea as a very skilled whaleman. He left behind his wife and child and really never spent time at home again (p. 777). Then he met Moby Dick, the first time in the Pacific, and Moby Dick took his leg. Perhaps he did it to try to get Ahab to go back to his wife and child as the other captain does later on after an attack (p. 629). Moby Dick seems to inflict punishment judiciously. At the end, Ahab still will not listen to Starbuck begging him to go back to his humanity (pp. 726, 777).

But Moby Dick seems to give him several chances: on the first day, he turns over Ahab's boat but doesn't hurt him. On the next day, he turns over another boat and kills Fedallah who had no hope of changing his purpose. Finally, on the third day, Moby Dick attacks the ship itself as Ahab watches, and then he eyes Ahab and waits. But Ahab, in a last attempt, throws his harpoon into Moby Dick who drags him off the boat and kills him (p. 821). It might even be the case that Moby Dick gave Ahab his wish of killing the great whale (though, mercifully, we didn't have to see it).

The only purely imaginative element of *MD* might be the character of Moby Dick himself, a whale with these many qualities, assuming the accuracy of all the whaling and historical details.[9] Melville had to choose them this way so that Moby Dick would make a suitable antagonist to Ahab. But they also seem to match the characteristics of the pope: the disposition of Moby Dick, even by reputation before we meet him, is sanguine, in control, powerful, unique. Could it be that Melville is writing an indirect description of the place of the pope in the world, a book with the pope as the main character?

The identity seems to extend to one between sperm whales and Catholics. We get a picture of whale society in chapters LXXXVII and LXXXVIII. The *Pequod* and its four boats chase several whales, but the whales look like they will escape. Then, inexplicably, they slow down, and the boats find themselves in the middle of a large herd. Thousands of sperm whales surround the boats. Around them are adolescent whales and adult whales, far underneath them are female whales with calves, some giving birth, and on the outside are the few that the boats have struck with harpoons. A sense of peace, tranquility, and unity pervades

---

[9]   PBS special on whaling, 5/2010.

the whole community to the extent that even the sailors on the *Pequod* feel a sense of awe. "Queequeg patted their foreheads; Starbuck scratched their backs with his lance" (p. 560). This community makes a beautiful picture of the Church: the young, the mothers, those older and adults, the suffering and dying, the martyrs, yet one community pervaded by peace. They seem to slow down to show themselves to the *Pequod*. On page 561, Melville writes:

And thus, though surrounded by circle upon circle of consternations and affrights, did these inscrutable creatures at the centre freely and fearlessly indulge in all peaceful concernments; yea, serenely revelled in dalliance and delight.

It is one of the most convincing pieces of evidence that Melville is writing about more than the whaling business (some say it's too much about the whale business, and it is if that's all he is writing about).

But individually, every sperm whale contains the spermaceti oil: it had been used to anoint kings and queens (p. 161); it provided light to the world at that time ("You are the light of the world" [Matthew 5:14]); it heals the sailors when they bathe their hands in it, and lifts their spirits (p. 600ff). They even use it to clean the ship (p. 615). And sperm, after which the whale is named,9 is the life-generating part of the male anatomy. It reminds one of the Holy Spirit who animates the life of the Church and of each Christian according to Catholic theology. And in the Sacraments that confer the Holy Spirit, the Holy Spirit is communicated to the person through oil.

Melville says that the membrane in their mouths looks like "bridal satins" (p. 479), which reminds us of the Church as the bride of Christ (Ephesians 5:22–33) and makes a comparison to the receiving of the Eucharist. When the whale dies, he turns to the sun or to the Son. Finally, the whale is Christlike in that he sees out of two eyes, one on each side of his head. Melville wonders how his brain can combine the two images (p. 477). In Christian terms, this parallels the two natures of Christ and the attempt to understand how the two natures interact. And it is reminiscent of the Christian who sees the physical world as it is but also with the "mindset of Christ" (cf. Phil 2:5). Ishmael calls himself in several places a "whaleman" (p. 97, etc.), at first in the sense of a hunter of whales, but then a student of whales and one attached to whales. The term is reminiscent of the term *Godman*, referring to Christ or Christian.

To my surprise, it seems that sailors weren't busy all the time but had lots of time to reflect. One can imagine Melville pondering as he stood on the watch at sea.

If the sperm whales are the Catholics, whimsically, maybe we can identify the right and Greenland whales with the Protestants who are not enemies of the Catholic Church. The right whales might be those very interested in morality; the Greenland whales might be those very interested in the next life. Melville calls porpoises "whales in miniature" (p. 204–205). The sharks defend the sperm whales from their attackers, and the birds do the same.

At the embarking of the *Pequod*, Captain Bildad[10] is seen reading the Bible, and there is a good sermon that describes the preacher as the prow of the ship (p. 57). Ahab has three first mates (Starbuck, Flask, and Stubb) and three harpooners (Queequeg, Tashtego, and Dagoo) in a parallel way to Jesus' taking the three apostles into the Garden of Gethsemane or to the Transfiguration. Perhaps we can identify those involved with the *Pequod*'s voyage with the Protestants who believe in the "Bible only," since the three-year voyage of the *Pequod* has many similarities to the three-year ministry of Jesus as reported in the Gospels. He even ends the book by saying that "the great shroud of the sea rolled on as it rolled five thousand years ago" (p. 822), five thousand being roughly the number of years recorded in the Bible since the creation of Adam.[11]

But why would Melville write a story with such a spiritual substructure? The substructure is like the whale swimming beneath the surface of the ocean. It could be that he had Catholic sympathies or at least embarked on an open-minded research into Catholicism. He certainly describes the spiritual world in a Catholic way, in a way

---

[10] 10 Of course, Bildad is the name of one of the three friends who visit Job.

[11] Counting back in years, Adam would have been created about 4004 BC or BCE (Source: Timothy Coln).

consistent with Catholic teaching and beliefs. His count of the chapters of the books in the New Testament is the Catholic count.

Ishmael, at the end, goes about telling the story of Moby Dick, so he's convinced of the goodness of the whale, like the apostles after the death of Jesus. Ishmael in the Bible is someone who repented, so Ishmael here repented of hunting Moby Dick. Now, instead of attacking whales, he studies them and promotes them. The sharks and birds refuse to attack him while he floats at the end, waiting for a ship to pick him up (p. 824). And the coffin, the strange life buoy, emerges from the sunken ship and saves his life, a very Christian idea. But we can't identify Melville with Ishmael. Still, he doesn't take a distant, cold, objective attitude. Perhaps some of his motivation comes from his appreciation of Catholicism, and perhaps, as a result, his book was unpopular in Protestant America.

But additionally, like the Wizard of Oz, which described the economic conflict in America in the late 1800s in allegorical form, Melville's motivation could come from a general desire to describe a present situation in an allegorical way. The Catholic hierarchy in the United States had begun with Bishop Carroll in 1789/1790 in Baltimore, but the Church in the United States was missionary territory until 1914 and reported to the Office of the Propagation of the Faith. In 1846, Pope Pius IX became pope, and in 1847, he appointed a nuncio or representative to the American government. Interestingly, the nuncio was here during the Civil War. But he only remained until 1867 when popular anti-Catholic sentiment required his removal. The members of the Know Nothings party were devout Protestants against all things Catholic.

I chanced to come across a website listing the ten greatest criminals in history, and Pope Pius IX made the list.[12] The accusations included benefiting and extending the American slave trade to make profit (though the Vatican had condemned slavery on the basis of race in 1451), being responsible for the killing of Abraham Lincoln, and of

---

[12] Internet.

engineering the Civil War. I had no idea he did all this. These charges give some idea of the charges of the Know Nothings in the 1850s.

Also, the first Vatican Council met in 1871 in Rome. It was the first council called since the mid-1500s, and it didn't get to address all the questions it hoped to address because of the 1870 war in Europe. The Council famously declared the infallibility of the pope when speaking about faith and morals. The Church had believed this for a long time, and many thought that the declaration unnecessary as a result, and one that would make interaction with the Protestants more difficult. But Pope Pius IX and the Council declared it, and the few who left early to avoid contradicting the pope were sought out and required to sign. But the issue of infallibility would have been under discussion in America, pro or con, in the decades before the Council.[13]

So Melville might have portrayed these current Catholic issues in *MD.*

It could be that in *MD,* Melville tried to give a fair and balanced view of the not only the Catholic Church and Catholicism but also the other branches of Christianity in America around 1850. It's amazing that he found such a clear mirror in the hunting of the sperm whale.[14]

Addendum: The Usher in MD[15]

After writing this essay, I still had the question of the relationship between the first part of *MD,* describing the usher, the older man dusting the grammars of the world with the flags of the world, and the rest of *MD.* This is indeed an introduction, a most beautiful and touching introduction, but is its relationship to the rest of the novel more than that?

---

[13] Hennessy, Paul K., C.F.C. "The Theological Influence of the Declaration of Papal Infallibility on the Church in the United States," Catholic University of America, 1977.

[14] In Thompson's *Lawrence Melville's Quarrel with God* (Princeton, 1952) the author identifies the central background of the end of *MD* to be the Crucifixion but misinterprets, in my view, the meaning of the Crucifixion.

[15] The usher carries no weapon, unlike the other characters in *MD.*

If we identify the whale, Moby Dick, with the pope for a moment, we could say that the usher is the human nature of the pope—older, dignified, learned in the languages and cultures of the world, interacting with the other countries of the world as a head of state (the flags). And as an usher, he holds the keys and "ushers" people into the Church through his delegated power.

In this reading, the human nature of the pope is beautiful but not intimidating. But then the rest of the novel would be the spiritual world of the pope, the spiritual world behind his calm exterior, the spiritual battle that isn't visible. And he is Moby Dick, the most powerful of all characters in the story and the focus of great hatred and violence. But they are the same person (I'm reminded of the sculpture that showed the meteor knocking over Pope John Paul II; while thought offensive, to me it shows the power of the pope—it would take a meteor to stop him).[16] In that way, *MD* is a diptych of the pope, the first panel is the usher, and the second is the whole story of Moby Dick.

---

[16] I know I run a risk by interpreting *MD* as an analysis of Catholicism since many authors have been convinced that *MD* is an exploration of a different topic, but the evidence just seems too strong and ubiquitous with no contradictions.

Paradise Lost

When I started to read *Paradise Lost* (*PL*), I had thought that *PL* would be a Protestant attack on the Catholic Church. It turns out that Milton intended *PL*, in 1660s England, facing the splintering of Protestantism occasioned by the printing press, as an effort to remind Protestants of their shared beliefs as an act of unity and unification.[17] It did not come into his purview to attack the Catholic Church. Milton doesn't even take time to attack different Protestant confessions (Milton was a Puritan) nor even plays up the differences with the Catholic Church.[18] And a Catholic can see, it as a legitimate attempt to read Genesis accurately and even as a gloss on the whole Bible and on Church history.

I had thought that *PL* would be a dark work, concentrating on the sinfulness of man, on man's complete depravity from the Fall, and man's inability to do any good work in this world as a result. These are traditional Protestant beliefs. It turns out that the main theme of Milton's work is the mercy of God, and the eternal salvific will of God. It could be that part of the Protestant Reformation erred not on the side of overstating the sinfulness of man but on the optimistic side: believing that God had redeemed man, and man had little to worry about (and so didn't need the Church). Perhaps part of the attraction of Protestantism was its optimism while at the same time believing in the total depravity of man. Milton does not mention total depravity at all. And Adam and Eve leave the garden full of hope in the future.

I had thought that *PL* would be weighed down with many classical allusions and that one might have to hunt them down to understand different passages, a hunting which might not always yield results. Milton does use classical allusions, but he uses them sparingly and in moderation. They add color and explanation to many scenes, but they are not dragged in, nor do they crowd out the narrative with allusions. When they did occur, if I didn't recognize the allusion, I found that I

---

[17]   John Rogers, Yale free online class, 2007: https://oyc.yale.edu/english.
[18]   Though the conferences of demons in the first few books might have overtones of Church councils. In two places, Milton even mentions the necessity of works to accompany faith.

could understand what was probably intended from the context. They added a lot of color but no obscurity. To some extent, Milton, like Saint Thomas bringing pagan philosophy into the Christian context, brought pagan mythology into the Christian context.

PL also contains, of course, many allusions to passages in the Bible. And I don't see how one can read *PL* without knowledge of the Bible; it is a commentary on the Bible. For example, when Michael tells Adam how to live after leaving the Garden, his words are very close to those found in St. Paul's letters. One hears these overtones many times, and though they are not intrusive, they add to the power and meaning of the verse. Milton is no doubt an expert on the Bible, on the geography of the Holy Land, and on biblical history.

I had thought that *PL* would tell the story of the fall of Adam and Eve and do so in elaborate and flowery verse.[19] But Milton writes simply. I read one page per day and rarely had to reread a page for lack of understanding. Perhaps his style is in line with Protestant clarity; it is written in almost a prose form which reads easily. I didn't find many phrases that arrested my attention, such as one finds on any page of Shakespeare; maybe it was just me. It was much easier reading than Shakespeare. But to me, the strength of the verse comes from its smoothness, and there are beautiful adjectives and descriptions.

One critic said Milton's strength was to make a dark scene very dark and good scene very good, and that is so. The verses were ten to twelve syllables in length, often exceeding the ten, but only on a rare occasion reaching only nine or stretching to thirteen. Many times, the last word in a verse could be extended while saying it, allowing verses to add a syllable or two as the reader desired. But it was almost as if what he had to say had importance, and he couldn't spend time hammering the verses into identical lengths.

The story of *PL* is by no means limited to the fall of Adam and Eve. That moment is really quite short and undramatic. The most dramatic

---

[19] It could be that the verse of *PL* and *PR* is not too difficult because Milton, having gone blind, was dictating it. In comparison, the verse of other works, like *Comus*, is very dense and intricate.

section is the one where Adam and Eve, having fallen, decide not to despair. And having chosen not to despair, the Archangel Michael comes to give them full encouragement and hope. It was a nice touch that they had to make the initial decision on their own on the basis of their reason alone.

The story begins with the fall of Satan from heaven. Then at the end, through the vehicle of Michael's encouraging, Adam, by telling him the future of his descendants (all mankind), it manages to go through all of biblical history and continues even to the end of the world. As the *Divine Comedy* is a comprehensive vision of reality at a given moment, this is a comprehensive vision of reality from the first moment to the last. And it proceeds in strict chronological order. This breadth of vision was a pleasant surprise for me, having wondered how Milton would go beyond the moment of the fall. Dramatically. Milton has the problem that every reader knows the story of the fall—how could he make it dramatic? Elaborate language alone could not do it, but Milton does not take that route.[20]

Milton solves this dramatic problem by expanding the scope of the drama to include the whole history of created reality, and it is successful. It is more inclusive than even the Bible in scope of time (in Catholicism, the Church Fathers filled in the earlier parts).[21] But he faced another dramatic problem: how to describe why Adam and Eve fell. Milton follows Aquinas's view, the view of the Catholic Church, and all Christians that Adam and Eve were perfect. They had no errant passions, they had no weakness of will, they had no obscurity of intellect, they had special gifts of grace, and they had no inclination or desire to disobey God (cf. Genesis 3:3). So why did they fall? What could have made them disobey God's direct order to not eat of the tree?[22]

---

[20] One senses that Milton's political prose writings influenced the prose-ish style of the poetry, and no doubt there are allusions to Milton's political views and causes, but I did not find them dragged into the story, nor is the story just a vehicle to vindicate them or showcase them.

[21] Perhaps for the Protestants, Milton functions like the Fathers of the Church functions for Catholics, explaining and expanding on the Scriptures.

[22] The other direct order of God was positive to go and fill the earth (Genesis 1:28).

From a Catholic point of view, I think Milton's solution is incorrect. Oddly, he blames Eve, and women should be rather annoyed at Milton (but only if they can come up with a better explanation). I think he is incorrect because as Presbyterian Minister Julie Faith Parker points out,[23] perhaps in response to Milton, that in Genesis 3:6 there is a Hebrew word that indicates that Adam was "next to Eve" when she ate the apple. That one Hebrew word completely undermines Milton's plot of Eve working alone, of Satan tempting overcoming her, of her seeking out Adam, and Adam eating the apple so as not to leave the wife he loves alone.[24] The whole plot is undermined, but it just points to the difficulty of trying to understand how they could have fallen.[25]

I didn't find in *PL* any hint of support for rebellion or support for Satan. Milton really believes in spiritual beings, i.e., angels and demons, and he shows Satan, admittedly anthropomorphized, completely and justifiably defeated. I suspect that the only way that Satan is seen as a hero is to assume that Milton did not really believe in spiritual beings, in which case Satan is just a human being without complete knowledge or great power. Then one can sympathize with him in that he has taken a position, even if it's wrong.[26]

---

[23] Julie Faith Parker, "Blaming Eve Alone: Translation, Omission, and Implications of המע in Genesis 3:6b," *Journal of Biblical literature*, 132 (4), 729–747.

[24] Milton's emphasis on Adam's fall—for example, having St. Michael explain the future to Adam and not Eve—seems to imply that Milton did believe that it was Adam's fall as head of the human race, not Eve's, which doomed the human race, which is the Catholic view.

[25] I think Scott Hahn provides the best explanation: the snake was no small snake but a monster and threatened Adam's life, and Adam didn't trust enough to die. So with Adam silent, the snake spoke with Eve who, unprotected, her own life threatened, acquiesced. I'll offer a solution later on, which can be duly criticized.

[26] 26 One would expect that Milton, who had rebelled against the king, would show support to the rebellion of Satan, but I don't sense echoes of Milton's political action and rebellion. Professor Rodgers explained that Milton had supported the rebellion against the king in favor of the Puritan Revolution and had been one of its primary supporters. But during the late 1650s, the Puritan reign had completely failed. It could be that having done his part and almost lost his life and now having lost his eyesight, he stepped away from political concerns and wrote for religious purposes. This could be if, as Professor Rodgers says. Milton

The other part of *PL* that a Catholic would disagree with, of course, is the appetites of the angels.[27] Angels can take on bodies and can eat (as we see in Genesis 19 with Lot), but the idea that they have the same physical appetites as we do, since they don't in themselves have bodies, is not correct. Finally, in *PL*, the Father looks around to try to decide whom he will send to rescue mankind from the Fall. From a Catholic point of view, Jesus is not another angel but the Son; he was the one intended to come into the world.

Paradise regained

In *Paradise Regained* (*PR*), Milton again addresses a difficult question not answered in the Bible: what was the conversation, not between Adam and Eve and Satan, but between Satan and Jesus? In both cases, we are given brief conversations in Scripture, but Milton seeks a fuller explanation. At only sixty or so pages, *PR* is a charming heroic story. As in *PL*, it begins with Satan's discussion with the other demons about what to do: they decide that lust isn't the route that will trap this great man, so Satan makes other plans. Satan knows that this person is greater than any angel or any man but doesn't know what "Son of God" means since all angels and men are, in a sense, "sons of God."[28]

As *PL* is largely a collection of conversations between angels and/or demons, spiritual beings, *PR* is a collection of conversations between

---

had lost hope in any state and had lost his desire to write a poem in praise of any country.

[27] The Eucharist is called the bread of angels: "Man ate the bread of angels" (Psalm 78:25, referring to the manna), and Milton seems to take this as meaning physical bread only. It can mean that angels have Communion with God in a way as intimate as the Communion we have with God in the Eucharist but not needing physical bread. For a Catholic, it's funny to see the angels heartily chowing down.

[28] One wonders how Milton will expand this event into sixty pages. At first, one thinks that he will do a parallel story of what the apostles and Mary will do while Jesus is in the desert for forty days, but they are not spoken of except that they don't know where Jesus is and they miss him. Milton unexpectedly gives a beautiful description of Mary in this section. The brief discussion of the demons on how to trap Jesus makes one think this might have been the source of C. S. Lewis's *Screwtape Letters*.

Satan and Jesus. In the Scriptures, Jesus is led into the desert by the Holy Spirit, so it is very fitting that he uses the Scriptures, the words of the Holy Spirit, to rebut the temptations of Satan. It is also fitting because he gives us an example: we can't argue with Satan and win (as Eve showed), but we can cite Scripture.

But Milton has long dialogues between Satan and Jesus. In the course of the speeches, one hears echoes of many places and events in the ancient world and many biblical events, past and future. The first temptation is that of food. Milton suggests, for some reason, that Jesus is not hungry or that he is hungry only for a few moments when he faces the temptation to eat of the banquet Satan places before him. Milton skillfully presents the first temptation silently in that it is never stated the food is just seen. As in the other temptations, Jesus' words not only overturn Satan's reasonable case, but they are on a higher level than Satan's words; they almost don't address Satan directly and defeat his argument completely (one hears echoes of Jesus in the Temple with the teachers of the Law at the finding in the Temple).

In the second temptation (Milton switches the second with the third temptations for dramatic effect), the main idea is that Satan knows that Jesus will become king, will rule the world, will destroy him, but the Bible doesn't say how Jesus will do it. Alone in the desert, without food, Satan suggests that if Jesus accepts kingdoms from him, he will have a route to gaining his kingdom. But Jesus replies that he will receive them when it is time and in the way he is meant to receive them and that he doesn't want to owe them to Satan. Oddly, Jesus also seems to state that he isn't interested in these kingdoms at all in any case. In addition, Satan tells Jesus that if he doesn't accept his offer, he has the power to make things difficult and painful for him, which he demonstrates in a violent overnight thunderstorm.

Milton places the second temptation, being thrown from the parapet of the Temple last, because he deals with it very quickly and dramatically. Jesus has no real desire to throw himself off the parapet, so the temptation fails. People will follow him when it is time for them to do so. After that, Satan flees, completely defeated at that time. And then another voice is heard: the angels who come to comfort Jesus.

From a Catholic point of view, one can only say that Jesus was indeed hungry and thirsty,[29] he did see the grandeur of the kingdoms he could gain (especially in that he could govern them and govern them with justice), he would have been troubled and hurt by the violent thunderstorm, and was aware of what gaining the adulation of the people would mean to him. These were very real temptations, and at the time of the temptations, he was physically as weak as is humanly possible on the edge of death. The only other objectionable element is Satan's stated admiration for the virtues and person of Jesus. This is not so: Satan hates God and hates Jesus as is seen in Jesus' Passion and Death, which is caused primarily by Satan. Because Satan hates him, Jesus does not engage in reality does not engage in dialogue.

Similarly, while Milton's Jesus condemns and criticizes Satan, in reality, Jesus would not do this: Jesus criticizes people to spur them to repent and change, but the demons cannot change, so there is no point.[30] Also, Milton's Jesus speaks ill of the average sinner, but Jesus would not speak disparagingly of people in this way. In addition, Milton's Satan acknowledges that Jesus is the Son of God in some sense and is greater than angels and men, but he didn't know what this meant. But Satan knew who Jesus was (cf. Mark 1:24).[31]

Samson Agonistes

I found the verse in *Samson Agonistes* more intricate and beautiful than the verse in *PL*. The poem shows Milton's general purpose: to flesh out the events in the Bible. He did so not by exfoliating their theological implications—as St. Thomas did, for example, certainly a valid approach—but by exploring them dramatically. One thinks of the Venerable Mary of Agreda's *Mystical City of God*, a four-vol-ume work, where her visions (perhaps combined with devotional thoughts at times)

---

[29] As the Israelites were in the desert.

[30] The spiritual beings are outside of time and have complete knowledge, so they cannot change their minds as human beings can.

[31] I'm only commenting on where these works intersect with Catholic theology, of course.

from her sickbed flesh out the details of many biblical scenes from the New Testament.[32]

Milton introduces the interesting idea that Samson wasn't supported or helped by the Israelites in fighting the Philistines, that the Israelites almost preferred Philistine rule; I'm not sure that was the case. Again, as in *PL*, the actual dramatic moment of the fall of the Temple of Dagon takes but a moment; actually, it takes place "off screen." The visits of the Danites, Manoah his father, and his wife remind one of the visitors of Job, though these are sympathetic.

In recent decades, our view of Jesus is as a friend, a gentle friend, even effeminate at times. But Jesus fulfills all the great men of the Old Testament or they are a prefigurement of him, so Samson, the strongest of men, is a prefigurement of Jesus. Jesus refers to himself as "the strong man" (cf. Mark 3:27, etc.) in one of his parables. And Samson's long hair, since he was a Nazarite, prefigured Jesus' long hair, though Jesus probably also used his long hair as a pillow when he had "no place to lay his head" (Luke 9:58, NIV).

Most of all, and one thanks Milton for drawing this out, Samson destroyed the evil kingdom of the god Dagon by knocking out the two supporting pillars of the temple, while everyone was there celebrating their conquest over their greatest and most dangerous enemy. And Samson accomplished this feat by allowing himself to be killed. This event clearly prefigures Jesus, nailed to the Cross between two criminals, perhaps the two pillars of the evil kingdom being murder and blasphemy, and willingly giving up his life to bring down the kingdom of Satan and of evil.[33]

---

[32] Ven Mary Agreda, *Mystical City of God*, vol. 4 (Corcoran Publishing Co., 1914).

[33] In *Paradise Lost*, we see both Adam and Eve tempted. In *Paradise Regained*, we see Christ tempted and his victory over the three temptations. But where is the temptation of Mary that corresponds to the undoing of the temptation of Eve? Mary is not faced with a temptation by Satan because Jesus, unlike Adam, guarded the garden and wasn't silent in the face of Satan. But where is Mary tested or tempted, it must be there. The temptation of Mary is indeed seen. It is seen in the Annunciation. The angel could have asked Mary to do anything for God, and she would have done it without question. There was only one statement the angel could have made that would have troubled or confused Mary. And it was

Twelfth Night

On starting to read *Twelfth Night* (*TN*), I expected a romp, the twelfth night being the last night of the celebration between Christmas and Epiphany. And certainly, it is. But it was presented first on February 2, 1602,[34] Candlemas, the Feast of the Presentation, the final end of the Christmas season. Elizabeth I died in 1603; could Shakespeare in this play anticipate the death of Elizabeth and the return of Catholicism to England or at least a loosening of the laws against Catholics (it was treason punishable by death to be Catholic).

Like other Shakespearean plays, taken as a drama in itself only, it is so rich and multifaceted, so rich a commentary on the human condition that it hardly needs a background meaning to justify its writing. But on the other hand, it does not rule out such a background, especially one that would have to remain hidden. Also, without a background, even though it is so rich, doesn't it just blow away in the wind? Also, where does the intensity and urgency it contains come from? It can't come from just trying to hold "the mirror up to nature."[35]

I started to look for clues as I read and quickly found quite a few. In this essay, I plan to suggest that Shakespeare was speculating on the coming death of Elizabeth, making a final plea to her to return to Catholicism and was a surreptitious part of the effort of Catholics to bring England back to the Church. This is quite a claim, but there seems to be lots of evidence that it might be so.

---

just the statement the angel did make that she would be asked to have a son and by implication give up her perpetual virginity, which was the central sign of her devotion to and union with God (Gabriel does not explain how this will happen until Mary asks). Also, previous to the Annunciation to Mary, we see Gabriel announce to Zechariah the conception of a son, and he fails the test and is struck dumb until John the Baptist is born. Mary does not doubt that what the angel says would come true but asks how her vow of perpetual virginity could be reconciled with this reality, so she overcomes the temptation or test and undoes the failure of Eve.

[34] Elizabeth Story Donno, ed., *Twelfth Night* (New York: Cambridge University Press, 1985), p. 1. All quotes come from this edition.

[35] *Hamlet*, act 3, scene 2.

The evidence begins with the title: *Twelfth Night* indicates a period of celebration in the Catholic Church, also in Anglicanism, and begins the theme of feasting, which is a contrast between the thorough joy of Catholicism and the muted restrained joy of Anglicanism. It is a reminder to the audience of what the English gave up or lost when they left the Catholic Church. The alternate title, *What You Will*, would then mean that this is a picture of the Catholicism that the English viewer really does want.[36] The alternate title, also introduces the idea of a choice, reading it as "What do you will?" or "What do you choose?" Anglicanism or Catholicism? This choice, of course, is not just a choice of a confession since the turn to Anglicanism had dismantled the culture of England to that point,[37] which could be returned. It was also a consequential choice because England would soon rule most of the world and would carry its religion with it. (The subtitle could also be read "What you, Will?" implying that Shakespeare engaged in something disreputable or unacceptable, perhaps Catholicism).

But before going on to more evidence, let's describe fully the claim. As stated, Shakespeare wrote *TN* in 1601/1602 when the death of Elizabeth was clearly in the near future. The character of Olivia certainly looks like Queen Elizabeth: the names Elizabeth and Olivia, for one thing, have the same number of syllables. And the action takes place around Olivia's palace[38] in the land of which she is the ruler. Orsino, in contrast, is also a ruler in this land, but his palace is never located, though Viola does know where to find him. And the central theme of the play, peeking over the secondary plot of the confusion of identity of Viola and her twin brother, Sebastian, is whether or not Olivia will accept the love of Duke Orsino. If Duke Orsino represents the Catholic leader, it makes sense that his location is never known since to be Catholic was illegal. But then the question of whether Olivia will accept

---

[36] Perhaps Shakespeare was careless with his written texts because if studied too carefully, they could be used as evidence against him as a Catholic or Catholic sympathizer.

[37] Eamon Duffy, *The Stripping of the Altars* (New Haven: Yale University, 1992)

[38] This circumstance makes one think of G. K. Chesterton's play, *The Surprise*.

Orsino translates to the question of whether Elizabeth will accept the Catholic Church.

Viola and Sebastian, apparently Spanish and maybe French, both Catholic countries, shipwreck on their way and end up in Illyria. At that time, it was a capital crime to be Catholic in England, but Jesuits and others would cross the channel from France to minister to the Catholics in England, risking their lives, and would adopt disguises to avoid capture. Viola and Sebastian were not headed to Illyria; perhaps they were headed back to Spain or on a mission to the New World but ended up in Illyria after the shipwreck, thanks to the kindness of the captain and of Antonio who rescued them separately (their ship or boat had been scuttled near Illyria; the ship is often a symbol of the "bark of Peter," the Church).

To elaborate the thesis further, let's consider the cast. If the Catholic/Anglican struggle underlies the drama, we can divide the cast into two camps: the Catholic and the Anglican:

Catholic	Anglican
Orsino	Olivia
Court of Orsino:	Court of Olivia:
Valentine	Sir Toby Belch
Curio	Sir Andrew Aguecheek
Viola (Caesario)	Fabian
Sebastian	Maria
Feste	Malvolio (Puritan) Sea Captain
Antonio	
Priest (Anglican)	

We're told that the scene is Illyria, and that "Viola" is pronounced with an emphasis on the first syllable. But now let's identify each character with the person he or she could be associated with:

Catholic	Anglican
Orsino—Cardinal of England	Olivia—Queen Elizabeth
Valentine—secretary to the Cardinal	Sir Toby—minister/relative
Curio	Sir Andrew Aguecheek—minister/relative
Viola (Caesario)—missionary	Fabian—minister/relative
Sebastian—missionary	Malvolio—Puritan (and Sir Topaz)
Feste—Catholic layman	Sea Captain—in Elizabeth's navy
Antonio—in Elizabeth's navy	
Priest—Anglican priest	

The name Illyria, Olivia's domain, indicates that the place is a combination between being idyllic (Elysium—"This sceptered isle," etc.) and a place besieged by an "illness," perhaps England under Anglicanism.[39] Illyria is also described in 3:3:10–11 as a place of pirates, which makes sense as a reference to the plundering of the English Catholic Church by the rulers.[40]

There are four levels to the plot: the first is between Orsino and Oliva. The central issue of the play is whether or not Olivia (England) will accept the love of Orsino (the Catholic Church) for her. Not to spoil it, but she says no and says no through the end, marrying no one.

---

[39] Or perhaps Illyria is a combination of Achaia, where like Viola and Sebastian, Odysseus had to return in disguise to expel the usurpers and Elysium (mentioned by Sebastian in Act I).

[40] William Shakespeare, Elizabeth Story Donno, ed., *Twelfth Night, The New Cambridge Shakespeare* (New Rochelle: Cambridge Press, 1985), note to 3:3:9–11. The notes in this edition are excellent.

The second level of the plot is what happens to Viola and her twin brother, Sebastian. They are from Spain or France, travelling by sea (the ship being an image of the Church), and on their way to some place other than Illyria, perhaps the New World. They are shipwrecked (perhaps shipwrecked by Elizabeth's navy that stopped ships bringing Catholics from the Continent to England). Somehow, though, Viola doesn't know what she will do in Illyria (1:2:3), she knows of Orsino and where to find him. And she dresses as a man, as her brother dresses, and enters into Orsino's service. Eventually, not to spoil it, Viola does marry Orsino, though the term *mistress* has an ambiguity about it and could indicate a nonsexual partnership.

The third level of the plot is what happens with the ministers, courtiers, and relatives of Olivia. They have their troubles: Sir Toby drinks, Sir Andrew is a coward, and they spent their time engaging in practical jokes and schemes, even against each other. It's not a flattering picture of Elizabeth's court, if our analogy is accurate. The court accepts Viola under her disguise as a man.

The fourth level of the plot involves the people who saved the lives of Viola and Antonio: the sea captain and Antonio. There is no indication they are anything but strangers to the captain and to Antonio (in our analogy, many people in England were no longer familiar with Catholics). Antonio had fought against Orsino's people and had taken much from him (3:3:33–4), and the sea captain is later put in jail by Orsino, which would indicate that they are Anglicans working for Elizabeth.

In the first act, we see Orsino surrounded by his attendants, speaking of love, specifically his love for Olivia. The early 1500s was a tremendously difficult time for the Catholic Church: the Muslims came very close to attacking Italy from the south and conquering it; Luther split Christendom with the introduction of Protestantism and took half of Europe away from the Church; King Henry VIII took England out of the Church and declared himself its head in England. The Catholic Church, at its best, aims at love (of God and neighbor) and knowledge. These two are nicely shown in the words of Orsino in act 1, scene 1, and in the names of his attendants, Valentine and Curio. But after the first scene, we don't see Orsino again until act 5 where he is met by Feste, which indicates that Orsino has joy and humor as well.

But in between these two points, we follow the path of Viola and Sebastian in this strange land. Viola as a man takes the name Caesario—what could point more to Rome and the Catholic Church? And that a Catholic priest smuggled into England would have to go under a disguise to avoid being killed by the government. We follow the practical jokes and pranks that the ministers of Olivia (Elizabeth) play against each other, all of which disappear once the identity of Viola and Antonio is known, leaving the main questions of what should happen to Malvolio (the Puritan) and whether Olivia (Elizabeth) will accept Orsino (the Catholic Church).[41] I think it really can be seen as a religious drama or a drama of religions.

Let's look at each character to see if there are clues there that also support this thesis (I'm using *TN* to argue that religious or spiritual thought is often at the center of what great authors write since it's at the center of human experience and that looking at works from this viewpoint, in particular from that of Catholicism, is very fruitful; *TN* is an example).

Duke Orsino—This is an Italian name which supports the idea that he is Catholic. It means "little bear," which fits. If the pope is "the bear," the Catholic Cardinal in England might be "the little bear." And it's a common Italian baby name, and Catholics are taught to be like children before God. Though he is the Duke of Illyria, his location is never specified, which works if he is in hiding or has been exiled from the country (if the Church is removed from an area and the diocese closed, the exiled bishop is still the bishop, though not resident, as was the case with the bishops of Northern Africa when that area was taken over by Islam). He starts the play with a beautiful hymn to love which is the

---

[41] Malvolio kind of has the last laugh since the Puritans ended up leaving England and founding the colonies, and they would take over the English government (with disastrous results for the Irish Catholics) about sixty years later. On the other hand, the Puritan government under Cromwell starved Ireland and so sent Catholic missionaries around the whole world.

central reality of Catholicism. His magisterial presence suggests that he has complete command in some sense and reminds one of Shakespeare's Oberon and Trollope's Duke of Omnium. His name can be broken up as Or ("Now" or "Gold" in French); Si ("yes" in Spanish); No ("no" English): Now gold, yes or no. A choice had to be made about Catholicism (Gold) as Elizabeth (1602) neared her death.[42] Since England would soon take colonies around the world, whether they were Anglican or Catholic, was of international moment (how did Shakespeare find such a perfect name?).

Viola—the name Viola is close to the name "Olivia:" it is a scrambling of letters. But her name is also connected to that of Orsino in that both have three syllables. And "Viola" is close to the French *voile* or "sail," again connecting her to the Church where each person can be considered a sail of the ship of the Church. She has a sterling character throughout the play, and because she has such a sterling character, she is fit to serve Duke Orsino. The stage directions indicate that Viola's name is pronounced "Vie-o-la:" "vie" meaning "life" in French; "ola" meaning "hello" in Spanish, tying her to the Catholic French and to the Catholic Spanish.[43] If Viola is trying to return Catholicism to England, from a Catholic point of view, that could be described as "Hello life." Throughout the play, her part is labeled "Viola," but she is known in Illyria as Caesario. She doesn't know about Illyria (1:2:3) but knows where to find Orsino. She disguises herself as a boy and presents herself for service to him as a eunuch,[44] reinforcing her connection with the Catholic priesthood.

---

[42] Italy, France, and Spain of course being Catholic countries.

[43] Catholics smuggled themselves into England from France to bring the Sacraments to the Catholics in England. When Viola speaks to Olivia and learns that Olivia will not entertain men because of the death of her father and brother, Viola suspects she might be attracted to women. This isn't the case, but is it a play on the Virgin Queen?

[44] At 1:2:56, it's interesting that Viola originally wanted to serve Olivia (1:2:42).

Sebastian—Viola's twin brother after whom Viola dresses so convincingly as a man. He is also on this missionary voyage on which they are shipwrecked. Perhaps he has the earlier alias, Roderigo (2:1:11–12) so that he, like Viola, can have two names. Antonio, who rescued him from the sea, can't go into the town for fear of being arrested for what he had done previously to Orsino (does the taking of goods refer to what the nobles had taken from the Church and the monasteries?). So Sebastian isn't in the town until act 4. His sterling character is attested to by his dealing with Sir Andrew Aguecheek in the duel, which he is forced into, and in Antonio's great affection and concern for him. If Antonio is part of the Queen's navy, his attraction to Sebastian might indicate the attraction of the English people for the Catholic Church. Viola and Sebastian are from Messaline. If taken as the name of a silk fabric, it might explain how Viola was able to dress so convincingly as a man by copying her brother's attire. It might be Marseilles (France) or Messina (Italy), both Catholic. But even more in line with our argument, it might be from the Greek *messalianoi* meaning "those who pray."[45]

Feste—a jester in Olivia's household, his name is Italian, of course, meaning festival or feast day or holiday or birthday, all appropriate for the twelfth night, the end of the celebration between Christmas and Epiphany. He has been away awhile, and no one knows where (1:5)—in Catholic Italy or France? Like other jesters, he can speak openly where others cannot. His jesting and humor might represent a part of Catholicism that was now lacking in Anglican England, though Olivia does appreciate and enjoy his jesting to a point. As there are different kinds of clowns and jesting, his jesting is purely fun, and his jesting style of speech almost threatens to take over the play as other characters participate in it.

Sir Andrew states (2:3:17–18) that Feste can dance and sing well, better than he can. But the members of Olivia's court are often annoyed

---

[45] *Webster's Third New International Dictionary of the English Language, Unabridged* (Springfield, Mass., G. & C. Merriam Co., 1966).

by his singing (as the Anglicans would be annoyed by the festive activities and singing of Catholics), for example, Maria in 2:3:74, "For the love of God, peace!"

In 2:3:10, we are told Olivia's father took much delight in Feste's jesting—a reference to King Henry VIII's early joy as a Catholic? Feste even says "he lives by the church," a criticism of Catholics. Of course, he clarifies that his house is next to the church (3:1:2).

He often refers to Olivia as "Madonna," which points to her place as head of the Church in England. But it could be ironic, a jab, reminding her that the real Madonna is Mary.

In 2:3:55, Feste responds to Sir Andrew, "Some dogs will catch well," changing Sir Andrew's meaning of dog; the "dogs" is a reference to the Dominicans, the dogs of God. There are spiritual and ecclesiastical references throughout the play.[46]

In 1:5:31–2, Feste has a dialog with Olivia. Olivia says, "Take the fool away." And he replies, "Take the lady away." In terms of the Anglican/Catholic struggle, this was the question if Feste represents the Catholic side, which side would be taken away, especially at the nearing death of Elizabeth.

In 2:3:33, Feste sings a song (and the songs in this play are excellent):

> O mistress mine, where are you roaming?[47]
> O stay and hear, your true love is coming,
>> That can sing both high and low.
>> Trip no further, pretty sweeting;
>> Journeys end in lovers meeting,
>> Every wise man's son doth know.

---

[46] 46 A very long paper could be written on the spiritual and ecclesiastical references in *TN*. If *MacBeth* is a picture of the reign of Elizabeth from the inside, blaming much on Elizabeth I, *TN*, if taken as a picture of the reign of Elizabeth, blames more on her ministers and even hints at Elizabeth having an affection for the Catholic Church.

[47] The term *mistress* here allows its later use between Orsino and Viola to have other meanings than marriage. The phrase "can sing high and low" that follows can refer to high or low Mass, which is "sung."

This song could be, in the religious analogy, a summary of the whole play: will Olivia (Feste's mistress) accept Orsino's love and end her past mistake of refusing it? Will Elizabeth I accept the Catholic Church's love and be reunited (or England after her death) and end this time of error? That would be the wise conclusion, Feste as jester is able to suggest (if Shakespeare is a recusant Catholic, one wonders if Feste is a bit of a self-portrait).

Valentine, Curio—attendants on Duke Orsino; perhaps they represent the search for love and for knowledge that is at the heart of the Catholic Church at its best.

Olivia—Olivia's father and brother have died, and she has decided to mourn and to remain single for seven years, though her attempt to marry Caesario suggests that this position isn't ironclad. These deaths remind us of Queen Elizabeth in that her father, King Henry VIII, and her brother, King Edward VI, had died. Olivia does refuse to marry Orsino, even to the end, but she loves Caesario who, unbeknownst to her, is a woman and who is (in this analogy) a Catholic. Perhaps Shakespeare suggests that Queen Elizabeth would have an affection for Catholicism if it weren't for her ministers. "Olivia," from the olive, is a reference to the Benedictines whose symbol is the olive and who brought Christianity to England. And one notices that the names Orsino and Olivia are close in form as Catholicism and Christianity, but there is a difference. In 1:5:256, Olivia won't accept the ring Orsino has left behind; the ring is part of the symbols of office of a Catholic bishop.

Sir Toby Belch—kinsman and minister of Olivia, a heavy drinker. He likes to play pranks and eventually marries Maria who also plays pranks. None of the kinsmen or ministers of Olivia have the character of Viola, Sebastian, or Orsino. He is lots of fun.

Sir Andrew Aguecheek—kind of a fop and a coward, a companion of Sir Toby, very proud of his position. He participates gladly in the pranks, but then the only one where someone gets hurt is played on him. Instead of saying Malvolio is "the devil incarnate" in 5:1:169, he says he is "the devil incardinate," which is the word used for a priest being accepted into a diocese—incardinated—which places Sir Andrew on the Anglican side of the ledger.

Fabian—part of Olivia's household, Fabian doesn't appear very much in the center of the play, except as an onlooker, and one wonders at his purpose. But when Olivia has important messages to delivery in act 5, she can trust them to Fabian. Fabian is also the name of a pope.

Maria—also a member of Olivia's household, she is a major lead in the pranks along with Sir Toby whom she eventually marries. Smart and lots of fun.

Malvolio—Olivia's steward, not on the level of her kinsmen and ministers. Sir Toby, with the others, plays a prank by convincing Malvolio that Olivia is in love with him and encouraging him to abuse the nobles. When he acts on this knowledge, he is considered out of his mind. When Olivia later finds out about the letter written by Maria, she quickly and painfully disabuses him of the idea. In our analogy, Elizabeth had no affection for the Puritans.

If Feste is the fool in the Catholic line of characters, Malvolio is the object of laughter in the Protestant line of characters. And Feste has a chance to abuse him as Sir Topas.

Christianity was brought to England by the Benedictine St. Augustine of Canterbury in 597, and the symbol of the Benedictines is the olive. "Malvolio" is another one of the many names that is a variation of the word olive—Olivia, Viola, Malvolio—but his name starts with "Mal," which indicates that his version of Christianity is particularly bad. He is a Puritan. If Shakespeare is a Catholic recusant, he would disagree with the Protestant doctrines, but he would disagree most with the Puritans who pushed Protestant doctrines to the limit. Placing Malvolio in a dark room as a madman, having him tell Sir Topas it's as dark "as hell" (4:2:29), and having Feste as Sir Topas call him a lunatic

(4:2:19) support this bad opinion. Presumably Sir Topas was a respected Anglican clergyman; even the Anglicans disapproved of the Puritans.

Sea Captain and Antonio—they rescue Viola and Sebastian respectively and separately from their shipwreck. The sea captain is later jailed by Orsino, and Antonio can't go into the town for fear of being jailed by Orsino since he earlier had participated heartily in taking many of Orsino's goods, so they are on the Anglican side of the divide. They both admire Viola and Antonio greatly and help and care for them in this unknown island.

Priest—he is brought in to perform the marriage of Olivia and Caesario (Viola) who is really Sebastian, to Sebastian's confusion. But it isn't carried out, so in our analogy he would be an Anglican priest. There is a second priest in the play, sort of, when Feste pretends to be the priest Sir Topaz and speaks to Malvolio who is shut up in a dark room. This second priest in our analogy would be a Puritan.

In the plot, the effort of Orsino to have Olivia accept his love— in our analogy for Queen Elizabeth I to accept the pleading entreaties of the Catholic Church to return—fails. Olivia (not to spoil it) does not back down from her stern refusal of Orsino's suit, though she falls in love with Caesario. When Caesario is revealed as Viola, Olivia does not turn to Duke Orsino.

The plot begins with Duke Orsino expressing his ardent love for Olivia, but then he is not seen again until Act V when he enters with Feste, the fool. In between, we see the humorous consequences of Viola's deciding to dress as a man so she could serve at the court of Duke Orsino. The complexity of the misidentifications come just to the edge of being too complex, though it might be easier to follow if seen rather than read. We see the ministers and relatives of Olivia's court play pranks on each other, and especially on Malvolio, the Puritan, and we hear about the captain and Antonio.

But once Viola's identity is revealed, all these plots are resolved or fall away, and we are left with only two problems. We are left with Malvolio finding out that Olivia did not write the letter that led him to believe that Olivia loved him and which asked him to act superior and ridiculous: Maria wrote it. But she is protected from harm because she marries Sir Toby, Olivia's uncle, who has the same taste for pranks as Maria.

The other problem is Olivia's continued refusal of Orsino, even though Viola is not available, and Orsino marries (in an ambiguous sense, perhaps as a coworker) Viola. So the conclusion is that in the analogy, Queen Elizabeth has continued to refuse the overtures of the Catholic Church and will probably continue to refuse them, leaving England Anglican, separated from the Church.

In summary, it's not that the story is a placard for the underlying analogy. Hardly so; it is complete in itself. But in great masters, every detail has meaning and is not accidental, and they all point in the direction that behind *TN* is a religious argument and a religious history. This observation suggests that religious and spiritual concerns might be the first motive behind Shakespeare's writing and writing from a Catholic point of view and that these concerns need to be considered first when interpreting the writings of great authors: the Catholic hermeneutic.

"The Waste Land" in General[48]

T. S. Eliot was born in 1888 in St. Louis, attended Harvard, and moved to England. From his boyhood in St. Louis, he was a devout Christian (Evangelical?), and his poetry can easily be read in the tradition of Christian poetry. He ended up in the High Anglican Church. And it could be that part of his motivation in poetry was evangelization.[49] It is not surprising then that the first impression of "The Waste Land," considering its five divisions, is that it forms a beautiful historical life of Christ. In order, they are

- "The Burial of the Dead"—Is there a more beautiful description of the transition from Judaism to Christianity? And it is a phrase that is used not only by Jesus but often in the Old Testament.[50]
- "A Game of Chess"—Is there a more beautiful and laconic description of Jesus' early life where he was hunted by Herod, etc., and chased into Egypt and then back north to Nazareth, and how he was chased during his public ministry?
- "The Fire Sermon"—Is there a more beautiful description of Jesus' public ministry, which included preaching having power not seen before? The half-length verses seem to me to suggest that the Gospel of Jesus, in spite of its power, is given in humility and simplicity.[51]

---

[48] These three essays were written at different times. My essay on James Joyce's *Ulysses* was lost; it argued that *Ulysses* has similar structures to "The Waste Land"; for example, both present a history of the world.

[49] As Vincent Van Gogh, who wanted to be a preacher (Protestant) and then preached through his paintings. His *Café Terrace at Night*, for example, can be read as a Last Supper—thirteen people, one in white.

[50] I use "Hebrew Scriptures" and "Old Testament" interchangeably.

[51] It could be also that the Gospel is sung in solemn Masses, and in poetry, when a song is inserted, its verses are usually half the length of the usual verses of the poem.

- "Death by Water"—Is there a more exact description of the death of Christ with the common thinking that Jesus died of asphyxiation, where water fills the lungs and one can't breathe?
- "What the Thunder Said"—A perfect description of the Father's response to the killing of his Son, the same voice heard at the baptism, heard at the moment of Jesus' death with hints of Emmaus and stretching until the end of time.

Eliot is not mocking or distancing himself from the Bible at all, nor from the life of Christ, but just the opposite: the poem can be seen as an homage or even a stepping-stone to the Bible, to the Gospels in particular, a kind of junior Bible[52] or junior Gospel. And since the Mass is the life of Christ, it can be seen, from a Catholic point of view as a Mass.

That being said, "The Waste Land" is a very rich poem, written from 1917 to 1922 during and in the aftermath of World War I or The Great War, and has at least five contexts that all play out independently throughout the poem. They form a kind of structure of five intersecting planes where the line of intersection is the narrative, the simple words Eliot uses in the poem. And this is one reason for their simplicity that they have to carry many meanings at once (the other reason is, I think, that he wants again to imitate the Gospels: he uses simple words to carry important truths).[53]

Here are the contexts, all of equal importance, and meant to be all-inclusive, giving a framework for a world that had lost its framework:

1. A day in a German park with his wife, James Joyce and Gertrude Stein.
2. A life of Christ/as a Mass.
3. A summary of World War I from beginning to end.
4. A summary of the history of the world including sacred history from Adam.[54]

---

52 "The waste land" is, of course, a phrase often encountered in the Old Testament.
53 Unlike Milton, who seldom uses the articles *a* or *the* and often skips simple words.
54 The first stanza echoes the creation and the fall in Genesis 1–3.

5. A summary of the history of Western Christianity.[55]

To flesh out these contexts with a few suggestions, let's start with 3 above. "A Game of Chess" can refer to the strategies of the different countries as they start to fight the war. Different events can be seen in different verses; for example, "That corpse you planted last year in your garden" (line 71)[56] clearly refers to the death of Pope Pius X in August 1914, just as the war began; the verse "Mr. Eugenides, the Smyrna merchant" (line 209) could point to the disaster in Turkey; and the last three words, "Shanti, shanti, shanti," meaning "peace," would mark the end of the war. Toward the end of World War I, the Civil War in Ireland took place, and the Russian Revolution took place; perhaps this is why toward the end, we see the word *da*, which means "good" in Irish and "yes" in Russian.[57]

In regard to 2 above, to speak of part IV, in particular "Death by Water," in the Life of Christ listed above, we have a meditation on Christ's Passion. Christ identifies with Phlebas, the Phoenician (line 312), a non-Jew and a common man and a sailor; and Christ is the head

---

[55] The epigrams at the start of the poem, one in Latin, one in Greek, and the last lines of the poem being in Hindi suggest that the poem traces the history of Western culture from the beginning to the end. The second epigram, in English reading, is from *The Satyricon*: "With my own eyes, I saw the Cumean Sybil, hanging in a basket." When the boys asked her, "Sybil, what do you want?" she replied, "I want to die." The Sybil had done a favor for Apollo, and in return, he granted that she would not die, but he didn't grant (or forgot to grant) her not to age. So at 115 years of age, she was very old and incapable and wanted to die. And this is how Eliot felt after World War I—very old.

[56] If the poem is a history of the Western world, this event, coming shortly before the advent of Christ in Part II, would be the death of Julius Caesar. If the poem is thought of as a history of World War I, perhaps this corpse is the change in President Woodrow Wilson to decide to enter the war, the burial of his earlier position of staying out of the war.

[57] Of course, for a Catholic, the greatest event during the years of World War I was the appearances of Mary at Fatima. One wonders if that appears in the poem. It doesn't seem to. Perhaps it was too early, and T. S. Eliot didn't know about it or its status hadn't been determined at that time. Or, being Anglican, he had not heard of it.

of the Church which is pictured as a boat. In the rest of line 312, "a fortnight dead," Eliot tells us that Christ was reconciled to His Passion and was detached from this world, his life already given up at the Last Supper before his Passion began. He has forgotten the things of this world. And he encourages us to consider our own death and to be prepared for it.[58]

As a Mass, on which so many symphonies are based, one has the rite of penance ("The Burial of the Dead"); the reading from the Old Testament and the Letters showing the struggle between good and evil ("A Game of Chess"); the Gospel ("The Fire Sermon"); the Eucharistic Prayer ("Death by Water"); and the result of the Sacrifice, including peace ("What the Thunder Said").

In 1 above, we can identify each person in the first section of the poem. The first stanza begins with Eliot's voice, but each person speaks; it is a polite introduction. Line 17, "In the mountains, there you feel free" sounds like James Joyce echoed a little later in Eliot's speaking to Joyce in line 33–34, translated "Where are you going, my Irish friend?" as Joyce heads away from Christianity. Lines 19–34 all seem addressed by Eliot to Joyce. In the section beginning with line 13, "And when we were children, staying at the archduke's," and ending with line 17, we seem to hear the voice of Mrs. Eliot, echoed later in lines 35 and 36: "You gave me hyacinths first a year ago; They called me the hyacinth girl." This is followed by Eliot's voice describing how he felt after what sounds like the birth of a child (though they had no children).

The fourth person, with the words in line 12 translated as "I am not Russian but Lithuanian, real German," I identify tentatively as Gertrude Stein. She would also be Madame Sosostris in line 43, the famous clairvoyante. The first part ends nicely with Eliot in reflection, reflecting on busy London in lines 60–61: "Unreal City, Under the brown fog of a winter dawn"; reflecting it seems on the scholarly background he has with Joyce in line 70: "You who were with me in the ships at Mylae"; recalling for Joyce his Catholicism and what he has lost in lines 71–2:

---

[58] Phlebas's "a fortnight dead" gives a spiritual lesson: to prepare for death, think as if one has already died.

"That corpse you planted last year in your garden, Has it begun to sprout? Will it bloom this year?"; and closing in line 76 with a concluding plea, it would seem to Joyce, though it could be addressed at the same time to all scholars or thinkers to return to Christianity and to sanity but said with compassion, "You! Hypocrite lecteur!—mon semblable,—mon frère!"

Speculatively, the outing of these four starts with getting ready for the trip and arriving at the garden in Munich ("The Burial of the Dead"); a discussion, which becomes heated at points ("A Game of Chess"); sunbathing ("The Fire Sermon"); going into the water ("Death by Water"); and getting out of the water because of thunder ("What the Thunder Said"), leading into the evening.[59]

In regard to 4 and 5 above, the hints that "The Waste Land" is a summary of sacred history, we start with the first word, *April*, a word of time, and time started everything—in the beginning. The first seven lines are sort of a brief evolution from the start of time to the emergence of plants, and finally, in line 8, of man. And if this part parallels the creation story in Genesis, it allows us to surmise that we are reading also the story of salvation along the lines of the Bible. Both the history of the world and salvation history end with peace,[60] which we see in the last line of the poem. At the start of the second section, line 43, the breath-taking entrance of "Madame Sosostris, famous clairvoyante" would point to the advent of Mary at the pinnacle of the Jewish faith. At the end of the second section, the three voice "Goodnight," a phrase appearing ten times in three verses, point to entering darkness and the darkness of section 4, which we identified as the Passion of Christ. The ladies mentioned could be Martha and Mary, with whom Jesus dined

---

[59] Perhaps Eliot's poem ("Shantih Shantih Shantih") and Joyce's *Ulysses* ("Yes," I said, "yes, I will. Yes.") both end with the marital embrace of husband and wife.

[60] "The world will end with peace, not annihilation"—summary of Pope Francis' talk on Nov. 24, 2014, https://www.ncronline.org/blogs/francis-chronicles/world-will-end-peace-not-annihilation-pope-francis-says.

just before going to Jerusalem. Even in a history of the world, the life of Jesus gets central billing.[61]

These indeed are just suggestions and hints. They are supported by James Joyce's *Ulysses*, which has the same five contexts, though taken from an opposite motive (see appendix).

In the process of following these five plot lines, Eliot has the following purposes:

1. World War I having destroyed European culture, Eliot works to recall what he can and save it in the poem. Almost every line is a verse that is slightly altered, as if misremembered from a classic in world literature. It must not be totally lost.
2. Eliot works to preserve also the forms of the art of Western civilization and culture that is being and has been destroyed. So in a sense, the poem can also be seen, using clues in the text as:
   a. A novel;
   b. A drama;
   c. A poem;
   d. A statue (of Christ);
   e. A symphony with the usual five movements;
   f. A painting (a Renaissance painting of Virgin and Child).

There are also hints as to the for forms list above. For (a), (b), and (c), the poem has a plot and is an interplay of voices, so it can also be read as a novel or as a play.

As a statue, consider lines 19–20: "What are the roots that clutch, what branches grow, Out of this stony rubbish?"[62] which suggests that this is the base of a statue of the cross. Moving upward from the ground,

---

[61] T. S. Eliot also carefully makes this a European poem: he uses Latin, Greek, English, German, French but only puts Spanish in a footnote since it was ruled by the Muslims for seven centuries. It is a Eurocentric view; Europe is the source of things, after inheriting them from the ancient world, but toward the poem's end, the Hindu reference in line 396: "Ganga is shrunken" points to a sharing of this culture with the rest of the world.

[62] This paragraph also seems to be addressed specifically to James Joyce who had smashed his Catholic background.

by the time we get to section 4, "Death by Water," we see the face of Christ on the cross and the last line 434: "Shantih shantih shantih" acts like a three-pointed crown or tiara.

For (e), we can list the five parts of the poem as: overture ("Burial of the Dead"); the first movement ("A Game of Chess"); the second movement ("The Fire Sermon"); the short bridge ("Death by Water"); the third movement ("What the Thunder Said"); the coda (last stanza in this section).

For (f), a painting, considering lines 79–80: "Held up by standards wrought with fruited vines/From which a golden Cupidon peeped out," and the rest of the section: it sounds like the description of a Renaissance painting of Jesus and Mary. And one sees a ceiling that is very common in Renaissance paintings in line 93: "Stirring the pattern on the coffered ceiling." So T. S. Eliot is not only preserving the content of the art of the destroyed civilization but the forms of their great art.

In "The Waste Land," T.S. Eliot uses astonishingly simple words; seldom does a verse contain more than one word of multiple syllables. As suggested, I think he is doing homage to the Bible, to the Gospels in particular, which are written not in technical language but with simple straightforward words.

Another motive of T. S. Eliot, I think, is to show that Judeo-Christianity is embedded even in the shapes of the letters of the language we write. For example, in many great poems, the word *the* appears infrequently. But in "The Waste Land," the word *the*, probably the most common word in English, is all over the place. It makes us consider the word *the* and to examine its shape.

First, it begins with the cross. Even if the "t" is capital, it begins with the cross (if capitalized, the Tau or Franciscan Cross). Then comes the letter *h*, which in Irish is an aspirant—it changes the pronunciation of the letters around it but doesn't have a sound by itself. It brings to mind the Holy Spirit. As the tallest letter, it points to heaven, to the spiritual. The letter *e*, the most common letter in English, is one of the most important constants describing the physical world. So the word *the* is comprehensive in its reach from the spiritual to the physical. But also, if the first letter is the cross, what remains, *he*, a man, is up against the cross: the word *the* itself is a picture of Christ on the cross.

The word *that* has a similar form; it begins and ends with the cross, the symbol of God from the beginning and in the end. And in between—perhaps what was intended in a world without sin—is the word *ha*, a laugh, joy in life in this world. Creation begins and ends with God, and in the middle was meant to be delight (the word *Eden* in Hebrew can mean "delight").

Another example is the word *to*, a word that contains the symbol of Western religions (*t*) and the symbol of the eastern religions (*o*). T. S. Eliot's frequent use of these words, and others, invites us to examine them carefully, and there are many others.

In terms of punctuation, each comma in the middle of the verse has the shape of an oar as we work to travel through the poem. Or, at the end of a verse, it has the shape of a ladder that we climb down to the verse below. And each verse can be read on its own as well as part of the poem, so its structure is like that of the rungs of a ladder, perhaps Jacob's ladder, as we move in this world toward heaven.[63]

In addition, words often have harmonics that add meaning. As one example of many, the sound of *world* has the same sound as *whirled*, which is a good description of our planet, both physically and spiritually. So each word has to be investigated in each of these ways beyond its first meaning.

To conclude, James Joyce's *Ulysses* has these same contexts, except for the summary of World War I:

1. A novel or story; in this case, over one day.
2. The life of Christ; in this case blasphemous, and so a Mass also but a black Mass.[64]
3. The course of the world history.
4. The course of Salvation history.

---

[63] In an autobiographical piece, T. S. Eliot attributed his flat plank-like verse to his midwestern background.

[64] A black Mass doesn't have a specific form; any "Mass" that is a desecration of the Mass is a "black Mass."

But Joyce's aim is not to praise the Bible or God, as Eliot does, but to try to get this reality out of his being. The fight between Eliot and Joyce is like the Frazier-Ali fights—epic.[65]

Finally, beginning with the verse: "April is the cruellest month, breeding," the poem places itself self-consciously in the line of the great epics, *The Canterbury Tales,* beginning with "Whan that Aprille with his shoures soote" or "When in April, the sweet showers fall."

No doubt, "The Waste Land" is the most important poem in English or generally in the twentieth century in the line of the great epics. Like Leopold Bloom in *Ulysses,* the narrator of "The Waste Land" is an average man yet the hero of an epic poem. Here, the hero is a Christian (just to endure in this world at this time is heroic). But the poem, of course, must be read in light of the earlier epics. Without looking at the poem through the Judeo-Catholic lens, its central meaning would be lost.

"The Waste Land" as a life of Christ or a Gospel

I decided that T. S. Eliot's poem, "The Waste Land" (1922) must be accessible on some level to the average reader and that it must make sense on its own without knowledge of all its uncited references. The meaning I found was not socioeconomic, a meaning which several authors point out in footnotes, but religious and historical-religious.

Maybe this list of notes and contexts will be helpful to those looking for footholds into this poem. It was encouraging to find that the poem was decidedly religious. The poem seemed to require a word-for-word reading, the close reading of French literary criticism, and that more than a verse a day was too much. At the same time, the verses could not be read in parts; each verse is a unit. I saw the footnotes as part of the poem,[66] like a bass-line in a song, clarifying meaning, adding emphasis or background, and pointing to contexts that might be overlooked, somewhere between poetry and prose.

---

[65] At one point, T. S. Eliot listed the talented poets of his time; Joyce appeared late in the list, and one could hear his reluctance at having to include him.

[66] T. S. Eliot originally, of course, did not include footnotes.

The poem seems to take in the entire world and its history as its subject, if only by omission. It is told from the viewpoint of Western European Judeo-Christian civilization. Mr. Eliot acknowledges this Western viewpoint when he writes modestly in the first footnote that the structure of the poem comes largely from a book by Ms. Jessie Weston.

Following is a list of some notes and contexts.

1. The poem feels like an introduction to and an invitation to the Bible (it reminds me of Charles Dickens's *A Child's History of England* but for the Bible.) The poem's intent is not to replace or to compete with the Bible. On the contrary, its attitude is reverential and, to me, like a sapling leaning against a great oak.

2. Although the words are often simple, the meaning of each verse is not obvious at all. Like Moses in the desert, the reader has to patiently tap each word until the many meanings fall out, and finally, the meaning of the verse becomes evident.

3. Unlike many poems, each verse seems able to stand on its own, having its own independent meaning. In this way, reading it felt like climbing a ladder one rung at a time. And each verse then is also like a Communion Host which one ingests one a day at most (and it's not a replacement for the Host but a compliment and complement to it). It is also intended that the poem be eventually understood; it isn't inherently self-contradictory or forever shifting between incompatible meanings.

4. Many times, nouns are followed by adjectives as they are in French. Many times, noun-adjective or adjective-noun pairs can be read in either order as adjective-noun or noun-adjective. Sometimes the shape of the letters is suggestive, like the many "o's" which signify completeness or wholeness.

5. The poem is a pastiche of pieces from other works of literature and an introduction to many writers (I found the song from *The Vicar of Wakefield*, cited in a footnote, particularly beautiful). Most pieces are slightly modified. For example, the verse in part one: "Or did the sudden frost disturb its bed?" might come from

Trollope's *Is He Popenjoy?* "I think it was the suddenness of it that disturbed her" (v. 2, p. 361). A pastiche or collage is to me the most inauspicious or modest form of art, but of course, it succeeds here.

6. Footnotes are used in "The Waste Land," not in the original but as a result of popular demand. But they make a link between this work and other religious works. Footnotes are used in Anthony Trollope's *Dr. Thorne* (one or two) and in John Bunyan's *The Pilgrim's Progress* (many). In the former, the notes are words directly from the writer to clarify a religious point or practice. In the latter, most are scriptural references. This suggests T. S. Eliot's spiritually salutary respectful intentions.

7. On the whole, the poem seems to form an interface between English literature and the Gospels, making the passage from one to the other possible, and showing that they are not contradictory. By making a bridge between these literatures and Judeo-Christianity, the poem performs a missionary act, an act of connection.

8. The poem seems to reach a climax in Part IV: "Death by Water," then pauses a little and ascends to perhaps a larger climax at the end of Part V: "What the Thunder Said." The last stanza of the poem is like a coda, almost coming after the poem has ended, as if the poet steps out of the poem and addresses the reader directly in a sort of sonnet.

9. The poem is also visually complex. In Part III: "The Fire Sermon," the verses are roughly half-length compared to the verses in all the other sections. If we regard the poem as a life of Christ, and this section as his public ministry, the impression is that Jesus' teachings—while the most powerful and can be understood by the average person— are like a song. The last eight verses of Part III are clearly the beginning of the Passion— Jesus mentions his humble people, the reference to Carthage (the city under foreign rule), and "I came" hints that this person

is on the level of Caesar or greater; the "burning" and "pluckest"[67] hint at the suffering he is beginning to endure, which reaches out to his death on the cross in the following "Death by Water."

10. Part V seems to divide into three parts with the third part having three speakers. This multiple use of the number three brings the Trinity to mind (as does T. S. Eliot's constant use of ordinary three-letter words). As a whole, Part V has ten block-like stanzas plus a conclusion, almost like a string of small sonnets or even a decade of the rosary. The word *DA* in Part V, used three times, suggests the three Persons of the Trinity and both letters being capitalized suggest the word *LORD* or *YHWH* in the Old Testament. The word *da*, at the same time, is even shorter and more intimate than *dad*. The three-time repetition of the word *shantih* ("peace") at the poem's end could be the response from each Person of the Trinity. It could be that Part V is in brief a summary of Christian theology.

The conclusion is that "The Waste Land" is an example where the use of the biblical and Catholic hermeneutic is very helpful in understanding the poem; in fact, it seems to provide its central context.

One verse of "The Waste Land"[68]

The 289th verse of "The Waste Land, "White towers," occurs at a high point in the poem and is a good example of the kind of reading the poem requires. The verse has no punctuation and no footnotes and has only three syllables. It appears at the end of the second part of the three-part indented "song" which itself appears within the poem's third section, "The Fire Sermon." The verses of this song are half the length of the poem's other verses and have minimal if any punctuation. The effect is that of directness, simplicity, and even childlikeness, also a kind of

---

[67] Which brings to mind Oedipus and his tragic suffering because of sin. The word is mentioned twice, perhaps once for each eye.

[68] T. S. Eliot, "The Waste Land, *Oscar Williams' Master Poems of the English Language World* (New York: Trident Press, 1966), p. 950ff.

shimmering. At first, this makes these verses feel weak, a letdown, but by their position at roughly the poem's center, they use brevity and simplicity to convey power, importance, and to an extent a sense of otherness. The first part of the song is a kind of build-up and the third part a high-level dialogue or confession; but the second and in one reading is a majestic, imperial, leisurely, untroubled ride down the Thames, and "White towers" appears at its conclusion as London Bridge is seen and passed under, and the government and city buildings pass by.

As any verse in the poem, "White towers" can be examined on its own. Its lack of punctuation, even at the end of the song's second section, indicates that the song is not over, and the lack of need of punctuation implies a kind of perfection. As probably every verse in the poem, it can be seen as the alteration or misremembering[69] of a phrase from another literary work or from several. "White towers" might come from *White Nights*, the title of a short story by Dostoyevsky in which a man has a terrifying dream/vision where he sees his own sinfulness as causing the disorder and unhappiness in the world. Upon awakening, he rushes out to serve the poor.

Also, as can be said of many verses in the poem, "White towers" gains a multiplicity of meanings from the ambiguity of which word is the noun and which is the verb, if any. With *white* as the noun, white reaches a pinnacle of success as it "towers." This has meaning in particular in the context of the "Game of Chess," the title of Section II.

If *towers* is the noun, then the adjective tells us that either they are literally white or they are beneficial. In the context of the life of Jesus, perhaps this verse represents Jesus' entrance into not London but Jerusalem for the Passover, and the towers are the religious authorities of the time, the "whited sepulchers" that he earlier referred to where the whiteness is only superficial (cf. Matthew 23:27).

If "White towers" is a compound noun, it could refer mystically to agents that work for goodness, like angels, or more prosaically, agents that promote decency or morality. All these meanings coexist, but the context one chooses points to one or other as dominant.

---

[69] Which displays T. S. Eliot's attitude of humility.

Throughout the poem, especially toward the end, T. S. Eliot again and again uses words with three letters—*the, and, not, but,* etc.—as if telling us that the Trinity is embedded in our language. "White towers," having three syllables, fits into this scheme. Perhaps another purpose of using three-letter words is to point to the Trinity in a different way than Dante in the "Comedia," where Dante uses a three-verse rhyme scheme.

Progressing in a different direction, "towers" contains the verb *owe*, which can be read in several ways. Negatively, it could mean stealing or taking wrongfully. Positively, it would mean acknowledging indebtedness and thankfulness. In the related title, *White Nights,* if *nights* is spelled *knights*, it brings to mind heroic battles and the Middle Ages. These harmonics are vaguely present to the mind as the poem is read aloud. A kind of context-limited word association again and again seems to be an intended road to uncovering the additional meanings of a verse. I found that these meanings are either distinct or harmonious and are not in conflict with each other: the poem is at once rich and challenging but not at all shifting, unstable, nor endlessly puzzling[70]—quite the reverse. The words are simple, so they can carry many meanings.

"White towers" appears in the second section of this song at the start of which appears a footnote that recalls a ceremonial parade of Queen Elizabeth down the Thames (perhaps it is a parallel, in England, of Jesus' entry into Jerusalem). That footnote, appearing at the start of the section, can be seen as governing the entire second part of the section. At the commencement of the whole song, a footnote refers to the Thames' maidens, which brings to mind the Rhine maidens and can be seen as governing all three parts of the song, even identifying it as a song. One footnote suggests the place, and the other identifies it as a song.

"White towers" appears in the section titled "The Fire Sermon."[71] As part of a sermon, it takes on moral and religious meanings, including perhaps the admonition that "goodness succeeds" or has in the past or

---

[70] As is Joyce's *Ulysses.*

[71] The use of *the* as opposed to *a* indicates the uniqueness of this sermon, supporting its identification with the public ministry of Jesus which, of course, is unique.

will soon in the future. Chapter 9 of *Moby Dick* is titled "The Sermon," and it's a "fire and brimstone" sermon, so this verse might have a basis there (does "White towers" refer to the whale?). If the "Game of Chess" in section 2 is a battle between white and black, this verse indicates that white, the good, has or is about to conquer, to succeed.[72]

The verses of "The Waste Land" very much stand by themselves, consistent with the poem as a recollection of cultural shards, imperfectly remembered, from a no longer existing, destroyed, cultural tradition. When the word associations of "White towers" and the other routes to meaning are put together, they suggest the overall contexts of the poem, e.g., the history of the world, which are hidden but can be uncovered.[73]

---

[72] White seems to die in the next section, "Death by Water," but like Jesus, he conquers in his death.

[73] Both Joyce and T. S. Eliot explore and display the richness of language but in two totally different ways. In "The Waste Land," T. S. Eliot invites us to look at a common word and to consider other words that sound like that word, creating valences of meaning. In *Finnegans Wake*, Joyce doesn't leave words alone but deforms them, taking the first part of one word and the end of another word to make a third word. So the valences of meaning come from the several words that make up the single new word.

Four Theological Essays 1—Preface

As an amateur in theology with a background in mathematics and philosophy, I can only hope to make a few suggestions in the area of Catholic theology. The first essay addresses a problem posed by Protestant theology. We Catholics celebrate Mass every day and could say that we want to unite ourselves mystically to the cross every day and that this act wins grace for us and for the world. But we also claim that this offering is a new but equal offering by the Church and by Christ to the offering of Christ on the cross in an unbloody manner. Yet the Passion and Death of Christ was sufficient for the salvation of the world, so how is this possible or necessary? Additionally, how can our suffering add to Christ's suffering when His suffering was sufficient? How can we add to his Passion? Why do we try? I suggest that an excursion into Cantor's infinite arithmetic might offer a solution to this collection of related problems.

The other three essays form a piece and build on each other. Starting with many of the ideas presented by the wonderful and prolific Scott Hahn, I try to sketch what might have happened in the world if the fallen angels and man had not sinned. But I have to begin with two preliminary essays. Then we can see how far the world has or has not strayed from God's plan and in what ways and where we are now in God's plan. As a side issue, if successful, it might vindicate God as not being the source of evil things in any sense. With Dr. Pangloss,[1] we might even conclude that this world is indeed the best of all possible

---

[1]   Leibniz.

worlds (Milton tried to vindicate God in *Paradise Lost*, but his theology is so flawed that its power to convince is mostly lost).

Theology, moral and biblical, is kind of out of fashion at this time when the stress is on freedom, acceptance, and pastoral practice, but I'll try it anyway. Actually, it looks like we've turned away from reason completely (which has happened a few times since the Enlightenment) and have turned to sheer power to answer problems. One important trend in theology, not part of these essays, is the conversion of a number of the Jewish people by God. This event, according to the Catholic Catechism, has to take place before the Lord's return. Roy Schoeman even suggests that it might make up for the falling away from the faith in the West. In this line, one also notes the work of Rabbi Jonathan Cahn.

After the first essay, which stands alone, there are some questions that still arise to which the last three essays might offer some solution:

- Why did God allow Satan to tempt Adam and Eve so severely?
- Why does God allow evil to remain in the world?
- Is God punishing us? Is God a punishing God? Is suffering required?
- Why did Jesus have to die so terrible a death on a cross?

Cantor and Theology

In the late 1800s in Germany, Georg Cantor (1845–1918) discovered a new branch of mathematics within set theory called Transfinite Arithmetic. It was so unusual that some mathematicians refused to regard it as mathematics. Transfinite Arithmetic is an investigation into the different sizes of infinite sets and the establishment of the rules of addition and multiplication of sets of finite or infinite size. It is very beautiful.

The important thing for us lies in the theological implications of this theory, how it models the interaction of the finite and the infinite, and how the properties of infinite sets and their arithmetic suggest answers to some theological problems. God's interaction with us itself is an interaction between the infinite and the finite.

First, I have to list some properties of infinite arithmetic; the proof of a few of these ideas can be found in the appendix:

1. Every number is either finite or infinite. An infinite number can be defined as a number, such that given any finite number n, the infinite number is greater than it. Or it can be defined as the size of set which is strictly larger than any set of finite size.
2. The smallest infinite set is countable (can be counted), and is the same size as the natural numbers {1, 2, 3, 4, 5, 6, etc.}.
3. There are different sizes of infinity; there are at least a countable number of infinities of different sizes.
4. There is no largest infinite number: given an infinite number, we can always construct a set that is infinite and strictly larger in size.
5. No finite number is closer to infinity than another other finite number: any finite number is an infinite distance from infinity. For example, one million is no closer to infinity than is one hundred: there is an infinite distance between any finite number and infinity.

6. If A is an infinite number, and B is a finite number, A + B = A where adding B to A doesn't change the size of the infinite number A.

7. If A and B are equal infinite numbers, A + B = A. Even adding an infinite number of the same size does not change the size of the original infinite number A.

8. This means that if we have a finite number of instances of the same infinite number A, adding them together A1 + A2 + A3 +...+ An equals in size A1, i.e., even adding them all to A1 does not change the size of the original number. Many of these results are counter-intuitive since they are different from what happens with finite numbers.

Now I can detail a few theological problems and some possible solutions suggested by using Cantor's theory as a model. In each answer, I refer to the numbers 1–8 above.

1. In the eleventh century, the monk Berengarius raised the sensible question, if we consume the Eucharist, which breaks down within us, do we decrease the size of the Body of Christ? When the priest confects the Eucharist, does he increase the size of the Body of Christ?

    Answer: In the finite natural world, there is no model that can explain how the answer can be no. But by number 8 above, noting that the very Host has the same infinite size and there are only a finite number of Hosts in the world, where each is the whole Christ, if a Host is designated by Ai, their sum A1 + A2 + A3 + ... + An still equals in size A1. Removing one Ai from the list by consuming a Host does not change the size of the sum. That one did not harm or lessen the Body of Christ by receiving the Eucharist was of course believed before Cantor's model, but there is no model for it elsewhere.

2. How can a Host contain the whole Christ, every part of a Host contain the whole Christ, when there are other Hosts and other parts of Hosts?

    Answer: The same argument applies as in 1.[2]

3. We receive the Holy Spirit in confirmation, we receive the whole Person of the Holy Spirit. But there were other confirmed with us. How can the Holy Spirit be wholly sent to me yet sent elsewhere at the same time?

    Answer: What is true of Jesus in the Eucharist (see 1.), that he is present entire in each Host, is also true of the Holy Spirit: when we receive the Holy Spirit, we receive the whole Holy Spirit, though he is wholly elsewhere as well. Cantor's theory of infinite numbers gives us a model for this reality.

4. At Mass after a piece of the Gospel is read, a "pericope," the priest says "The Gospel of the Lord" as if it were the whole Gospel. How can this be so?

    Answer: As with the Eucharist, a part of the Gospel can be considered as having the same size as the Gospel as a whole since it is infinite in nature (also the implied comparison of equality between the Gospel and the Eucharist is theologically accurate).

5. God is infinite; is there more than one infinite size?

    Answer: By number 3 above, there are different sizes of infinity, and given one, one can always construct a larger one.[3] Since

---

[2] While Cantor provides a model in our world where this is possible, another explanation is that we're speaking of Christ's risen body, which has different properties than bodies in this world.

[3] It is proven in set theory that if one has a finite set A and one takes the set of subsets of the set A, called A' or the power set, that A' must exist and that A' must be strictly larger in size than the size of the original set A. Cantor proved that

God has to be larger than the largest infinity, God is in a sense "infinitely infinite."

6. How is it possible that God loves all people but at the same time loves each person individually as if he or she were the only person?

Answer: Let's say that God loves each person with an infinite amount of love, A1. There are a finite number of people. So, by number 8 above, adding together all of these same infinite numbers, A1 + A1 + A1 + A1 + ... + A1, we get an infinite number that has the same size as the number A1 with which we started. So the size of God's love for one person is the same as the size of God's love for all people taken together.

7. The Trinity is the godhead, but we believe that each of the three Persons of the Trinity, if alone, would be God.

Answer: Indicating each Person of the Trinity as the same size infinite number A1, A2, A3, the sum of these three numbers— A1 + A2 + A3—is still A1.

8. How can we explain the Parable of the Day Laborers (Matthew 20:16) that seems so unjust?

Answer: First, it must be said that the landowner or God is not unjust because each worker agreed to his pay. But further, we note that the work each laborer did—whether it was eight hours or four hours or one hour—was a finite amount of work. But the payment that the landowner gave, the payment by God, was an infinite payment (eternal life). Even if looked at as a daily

---

this holds true even if the original set A is of infinite size. By repeatedly taking the power set of the original set A and of the resulting power sets A,' A", etc., the sets Ai are all infinite but of different sizes and always getting larger, which implies that there are many infinite sizes.

payment, it can be seen as the Eucharist, our daily bread, which is infinite. But by number 5 above, no finite number is closer to infinity than any other finite number, and any finite number is an infinite distance from infinity. Since the amount each worker did is finite, each worker is no closer to "earning" or "deserving" God's infinite gift, the landowner's daily pay, no matter how many hours the worker put in.

9. How can we understand better St. Paul's description of the man who was raised to the third heaven (which was probably Paul himself) in 2 Corinthians 12:2?[4]

Answer: By 4 above, there is no largest infinity. Referring to footnote 81, sets which have the sizes of the different sizes of infinity can be listed as A1, A2, A3, A4, A5, A6 (or one can use Aleph for "A"). These sets are all infinite in size, and each one is strictly larger than the preceding one. If this structure of sets is taken as a possible model of the infinite heavens, the third heaven is better understood. This model also suggests that the heavens can be numbered 1, 2, 3, 4, 5, 6, etc., i.e., that they can be counted or that there are a "countably" infinite number of them (at least). The third heaven would just be parallel to the third set in this list.

10. During the Protestant Reformation, the Protestants denied many of the central beliefs of the Catholic Church. For some of these denials, the Church had no model in the physical world to support its claim, although it, of course, had Church authority and tradition. But Cantor's theory might provide a model in the physical world that gives the Catholic more support. One objection was how the Host could be the entire Christ while there is only one Christ and there are many Hosts. We showed

---

[4] If it is Paul, his modesty parallels the modesty and inclusiveness of John where John refers to himself as "The disciple whom Jesus loved" (John 13:23 and elsewhere).

how Cantor's theory provides a model for this reality in number 1 above. A second objection was, how can our suffering be of value or add anything to Christ when the suffering of Christ was sufficient to save the world?

Answer: By number 6 above, considering that the suffering of Christ was of infinite value and that our suffering is of finite value, we see that while our suffering is not of zero value and does add to the suffering of Christ, it does not increase the size of the suffering of Christ. If A is the infinite suffering of Christ (infinite since he is God), and B is our finite suffering, $A + B = A$ because A is infinite and B is finite (what we also add, what is lacking in the sufferings of Christ, is our participation).

11. A third objection of the Protestants is the Catholics' practice of saying Mass daily? If Jesus' Passion was sufficient and unique, how can the Mass have any real value or significance? The Church claims that not only is the Mass significant but as a sacrifice is equal in an unbloodied manner to the sacrifice of Jesus on Calvary. But how can Jesus' Passion be sufficient yet repeated at Mass at the same time?

    Answer: Jesus' Passion is clearly of infinite value; call it A^1. Let's assume that the Mass has the same value; call it A^2. In the model of infinite numbers, by number 7 above, when we add these two equal infinite values, we still get A^1. And the number of Masses said from the death of Christ until his return is finite, so the Masses, even though each one is of infinite value and of the same value as the suffering of Christ on the cross, do not increase the size of Christ's suffering on the Cross: $A^1 + A^1 + A^1 + \ldots + A^1$ still equals A1 in size.

12. We believe that while Jesus walked the earth, he was, in his Divine Nature, still fully in heaven. How can this be?

Answer: Jesus as God in heaven is, of course, infinite while his human nature is finite. We can see from number 6 above that we have a model where adding a finite amount to an infinite amount leaves the original infinite amount unchanged, a result which we can apply to this problem: adding his human nature to his divine nature did not change the "size" of his divine nature. A similar statement would be that Jesus' taking on a human nature did not take anything away from his divine nature.

13. How can the Father beget the Son eternally and yet have them each be equal? Isn't a son always less than the father in some sense?

Answer: Infinite quantities give a model for this reality, showing that it is possible: if one has an infinite quantity, one can take away a subset of the original set, a subset that has the same size as the original set, and leave the original set as having the same size as it had originally.[5] For example, the set of natural or counting numbers—{1, 2, 3, 4, 5, 6, etc.}—has the proper (not the whole set) subset made up of the even numbers: {2, 4, 6, 8, 10, etc.}. Cantor showed that these two sets have the same size (see the appendix for the proof.) If one takes the subset of even numbers out of the original set of counting numbers, one is left with the set of odd numbers: {1, 3, 5, 7, 9, etc.} And Cantor showed that the set of odd numbers, the set of even number, and the original set all have the same size. So infinite sets provide a model for the reality that the Father eternally begets the Son and that the Father and the Son are of the same "size."

14. If the infinite and the finite are qualitatively different, and if the infinite overwhelms the finite, how can God, who is infinite,

---

[5] An infinite set can have a proper subset that has the same size as the original set. This can't happen with finite sets.

not overwhelm man, who is finite, in making contact with him or her?

Answer: By number 6 above, if we add a finite quantity to an infinite quantity, it is true that we are left with the original infinite quantity unchanged. If we add a finite size set to an infinite size set, it's true that the resulting set is the same size as the original infinite set. But the added finite elements are indeed still present in the new set. For example, if we take the infinite set, {1, 2, 3, 4, 5, 6, etc.}, of counting numbers and add three fractions, {1/2, 3/2, 5/2}, the resulting set, {1/2, 1, 3/2, 2, 5/2, 3, 4, 5, 6, etc.}, has the same size as the original set of counting numbers, but the added elements are still there. In this way, we have a model for the idea that stated differently, in joining our lives with God, we gain an infinity of things but lose nothing.

15. If I pray to Jesus or to Mary, and you pray to Jesus or to Mary at the same time, how can he or she hear us both at the same time?

Answer: This has to do with Jesus and Mary and heaven, which we can't understand at this point. But again, if the same infinite quantity is added to itself a finite number of times, the result is a number of the same size as the original infinite quantity. Using this as a model, it would imply that the many simultaneous "consciousnesses" of Jesus or of Mary, when added together, result in no more than a single consciousness of Jesus or of Mary if that consciousness has an infinite nature to it. The infinite numbers of Cantor might provide a model of how this can be possible.

St. Paul tells us that creation mirrors for us aspects of the Creator and of spiritual realities. In his poetry, Robert Frost, as one example, is always finding in a regular natural event or setting a reflection of spiritual realities and indirectly inviting us to think of these realities.

Theologically, one might say that it makes sense that God, who created spiritual realities, would have them mirrored in the physical world (including mathematics) which God also created (one wonders if there is any natural reality that doesn't reflect a spiritual reality). In Cantor's Transfinite Arithmetic, we find models for some difficult theological realities.

In her unpublished thesis, "Something New with St. Therese: Her Eucharistic Miracle," 2019, Suzie Andres suggests that a few saints have been allowed to have the Eucharist in their bodies between Communions as in a Tabernacle, St. Therese being one of them.[6] If one speculates that the end of human life is to have the Eucharist, God, in each one of us as if he were nowhere else, Cantor gives us a model as to how this might be possible.

---

[6] See the Msgr. Loughman Collection (of St. Therese materials) at Iona College.

God Always Intended to Become Man

Some time ago, I considered the idea that God became man to save humankind from sin and death. No doubt, he did. However, would an act of man lead God to take such a fundamental step? Without the *felix culpa* of Adam, would there indeed have been no Incarnation? Did man's sin inspire God's decision to become man? Could becoming man really have been God's backup plan? On the other hand, did God always plan to become man? Did God take on a human nature because man had sinned or in spite of the fact that man had sinned?

In this essay, I hope to present several arguments that support the idea that God always planned to become man and a few of the consequences. Historically, some Franciscans have supported this idea, but some Dominicans opposed it. St. Thomas opposed it on the grounds that he wanted to investigate what happened and not what might have happened.[7]

The first argument starts with creation. God chose evolution as the means to develop creation and evolution, which took place (mostly) before man's sin, might set the stage for the Incarnation in the following way.

As we all now know, the metallic elements on earth came from the explosions of distant stars eons ago. The most primitive life-forms absorb these physical elements and have cell structures. Plants absorb chemicals and have cell structures, so they have the characteristics of these primitive life-forms, but they also have other characteristics; for example, they grow and have differentiated cells. Animals eat plants and have many of the characteristics of plants; they grow and have differentiated cells, and they need light and water, but they also have consciousness and social behavior. Man, the final step in creation, has the characteristics of animals—for example, social behavior—but also other characteristics: self-consciousness, greater range of motion, and

---

[7] Interview with Bill O'Neill, Professor of Philosophy, Iona College, 2010.

greater mental capacity.[8] Moreover, all these different kinds of life participate in each other since plants absorb minerals; animals eat plants; man eats plants and animals.[9]

In each case, one can say that the later type of life contains the earlier one in both senses of evolving from the earlier one (at least in part) and of consuming the earlier one. Also, one can say that the earlier one participates in the later more complex one. Evolution, then, is not only linear but also cumulative. Man, the summit of creation, has the characteristics of all earlier forms of life,[10] and the earlier forms of life and matter itself participate in man. All this evolution took place, of course, before the sin of Adam and Eve.

This means that when God became man, because of what man is, he not only took on a human nature, but he also took on characteristics of and participated in all forms of life. Moreover, all forms of life and physical matter participate in him, in the nature he took on. In a real sense, he took on and participates in the nature of his whole creation. Since God intended this method of creation, one can conclude that God used evolution in creation so that he could participate in the nature of all of his creation, become in solidarity with it by taking on a human nature, and that all his creation could participate in him.[11] A non-evolutionary development would not allow this kind of interconnectivity and unity.

---

[8]   Just to give specific examples, an ape has a mother and a father, and a man or woman has a mother and a father; an anteater has a nose, and a man has a nose; bees live in communities, and men and women live in communities.

[9]   This line of thought provides one argument that God intended man to be an omnivore.

[10]   We see this also in the development of the human embryo, though it is human being at all points.

[11]   There could be other reasons why God used evolution to create the world: It is elegant and economical.

God allowed creation to participate in its own creation to the point where it might even look self-creating.

Creatures praise God by showing their desire to live in the struggle for life. It involves a majestic span of time and space befitting God's dignity.

Each person can see himself or herself to be physically the result of 13.7 billion years of cosmic/biological evolution.

One can conclude then that by using evolution, God intended to have all of creation participate in man, for man to be the culmination, the integral of all of creation, the summation of 13.7 billion years of evolution.[12] The creation account in Genesis supports this idea since man is not created on his own day; if he had been, we would see him as just another form of life. God creates man at the end of the sixth day after God creates the animals. So man has closeness with the animals, placed at the end of the sixth day, but like an exponent, he (and she) can also be the summation of all earlier forms of life.

If God had intended all along to become man, it was fitting that God would have made man the culmination of creation. In this way, by becoming man, God would participate in all of his creation. As God said in Genesis, "He saw that it was very good" (Gen. 1:31, NLT), so good that it was, as planned, suitable for him to actually take on its nature.[13] Evolution and the long development of man sets the stage perfectly for God to become man, so perfectly that one might conclude that that was his original intention. Evolution in this way gives an argument for the Incarnation and certainly has beauty and purpose.[14]

A second argument that God always planned to become man rests on a second purpose of the Incarnation. God became man to save mankind from sin to rescue man. But God, Milton's God in *Paradise Lost* notwithstanding, also became man to bring mankind into full communion with himself and to bring men and women into full communion with one another. As an illustration, let's say that a doctor

---

[12] That man is the culmination of physical creation and God became man might put the possibility of sentient life on other planets in some doubt.

[13] "Let us make mankind in our image, in our likeness" (Gen. 1:26, NIV): if Jesus was always to become man, this verse also refers to man physically.

[14] It is suggested that the fallen angels fell because God intended to become man, and these angels refused to serve a lesser creature. It is possible that was part of their reason, though the motive of power and the resulting hatred might have been more dominant. However, it doesn't make sense that the fallen angels fell if God did not always intend to become man; if God did not always intend to become man, why would the fallen angels tempt man to sin, forcing God to become man to rescue him (and her)? This is almost a proof that God always intended to become man.

plans to visit his mother who lives in another city. While planning his visit, his mother becomes very sick. The doctor then visits his mother as planned, but he goes now first as healer of his mother's illness. One would say that he visited his mother to save her from death but that his first purpose of fellowship, family relations, and communion still remained. As the doctor would not heal his mother and then leave, God did not come only to heal us but also to have communion with us. And this purpose would have been operative before the fall took place, it would have made even more sense before the fall.[15]

A third argument that God always planned to become man comes from the observation that, prior to Adam and Eve, all had gone according to God's will (excepting of course the fall of the bad angels). Elizabeth Kolbert[16] has pointed out the six cataclysms and the six epochs of world history, all of which took place before Adam and Eve, except for the current one (the Anthropocene). The six days of creation might have an echo in these six epochs. But one can ask, what was God's purpose over all this time?

As a start, in the Hebrew Scriptures, we see that the Temple of Solomon was a microcosm of the cosmos, a precursor of the cosmic temple.[17] Then we have the words of Jesus: "Destroy this temple, and in three days I will raise it up… But he was speaking about the temple of His body" (John 2:19–21).[18] One purpose of creation then, perhaps the central purpose, was for creation as a whole to become a cosmic temple of God and for man individually to become a temple of God. Both would praise him and give him thanks and be a place for his glory to reside. Scott Hahn speaks of the role intended for Adam as the high

---

[15] "For *the Son of* God became man *so that we* might become God," St. Athanasius, *On the Incarnation.*

[16] Elizabeth Kolbert, *The Sixth Extinction* (Henry Holt, 2014).

[17] God told the Israelites how to construct the temple in great detail; if the body of Jesus is the definitive temple, then God also very carefully constructed it over the billion years of evolution.

[18] The words of Jesus indicate that it wasn't meant to be torn down at all.

priest of creation,[19] and Jesus as above tells us that his body is a temple of God. If the purpose of creation is to act as a cosmic temple, how fitting for God to take on a human nature and to become, at the center of that cosmic temple, the focus of that temple, the perfect temple of God in his body.[20] But the body of Jesus could have been the most fitting temple of God, even if man had not sinned, and God clearly did not bring about this purpose because of man's sin. It makes more sense to say that God embedded this plan in creation, that it existed in God's original plan.

Finally, one can observe that if God were always to become man in Jesus, God had a built-in way to redeem men and women, his free creatures, from sin. If not Adam but another man had committed personal sin, God could redeem that person in Christ, perhaps with less suffering than took place at Calvary (unfortunately, the head of the human race gave in to sin and took the whole race with him).

The opposite idea of our thesis, the idea that God decided to become man only after man had sinned, also leads to at least three uncomfortable conclusions which seem to be resolved by our thesis. First, if God had not planned to become man, then God intended Adam and Eve to be the definitive head of the human family. When they failed and fell, Jesus (and Mary) came and replaced Adam and Eve, Adam and Eve never to be restored. But we know that Jesus came to restore all things: Jesus says "It was not this way from the beginning" (Matt. 19:8, NIV), pointing to his task of returning things to their original state.

Replacing Adam and Eve would not have restored things to the original plan of God.[21] It seems more beautiful and gives evil less success in the end to say that Adam and Eve were the head of the human family

---

[19] Scott Hahn, *Genesis to Jesus: Lesson Two: Creation, Fall, and Promise* (Steubenville, Ohio: St. Paul Center for Biblical Theology, 2011).

[20] What I call the Helmrich Rule of Theology that God does everything twice also holds here—if Adam were the first high priest of all creation, Jesus was always intended to be the second and definitive high priest of all creation.

[21] God could not restore Adam and Eve's innocence without denying their free will; he could not give to their descendants purity at conception because that would deny that Adam and Eve's leadership of the human family.

biologically and in time but that they were always meant to be the penultimate head, subject to the definitive head of the human family, Jesus and Mary.[22] This beautiful plan could have been the plan from the beginning: Jesus and Mary are sons of Adam, sons of Man, and owe their physical lives to Adam and Eve; but Adam and Eve existed not only for themselves but also to bring forth Jesus and Mary, the purpose of the human family. This allows Jesus not just to save Adam and Eve but to restore them to their original status and role.

A second problem involves Mary. One rightly says that God had to send his Son to save the world, that his Son had to take on a human nature so a man could undo what a man had done. In order to have him become man, he had to be born of a woman, so God chose Mary to be his mother and protected her from original sin. It sounds as if God looked around and chose Mary over other available women of the time. However, if God always planned to become man, then, from all eternity, God had chosen Mary to be Jesus' mother, and all was arranged for her to be his mother. There are three ways for one person to be united with another person—marriage, childbirth, obedience—and Mary is related to each of the three Persons of the Trinity to the highest degree in one of these ways. The person who would have this relationship eternally with the Trinity could not have been chosen hastily, at the last moment, and wasn't chosen at the last moment if God had always planned to become man.[23]

Finally, a third correction removes an uncomfortable aspect of the Immaculate Conception. One says that God intervened and prevented Mary from contracting original sin, which of course He did. But it seems unbalanced, a singularity resulting from God's power alone, not from justice or plan. What if Jesus and Mary were always the definitive head of the human family, and Adam and Eve the penultimate head? Then it is right and just that Adam and Eve's fall would affect us—they are our leaders, we go where they go.

---

[22] There are then two different heads of the human family—"The Helmrich Rule of Two."

[23] It also seems appropriate that those closest to Jesus and Mary—John and, in my opinion, Joseph—were cleansed of original sin.

But Jesus and Mary are greater than Adam and Eve in God's plan, and it would not be just for their mistake to injure Jesus or Mary in themselves, though they would have to live in a fallen world. It would be more just that they receive protection from Adam and Eve's mistake. Not only that, but it is right that Jesus and Mary, the definitive head of the human family, and not Adam and Eve, determine where the human family ends.[24] They, in justice, can act to win back the human family to its original destiny which as above even includes restoring Adam and Eve to their penultimate headship.[25]

This line of thinking also allows us to read the creation of man in another way: "God created mankind in his image; in the image of God he created them; male and female he created them" (Gen. 1:27).[26] The verse seems to speak of Adam and Eve and the rest of us who followed, and Jesus and Mary eventually. But if Jesus and Mary were already in God's plan, this verse speaks first of all of Jesus and Mary. In addition, we can see a threefold reading: "God created man" refers to Adam and Eve (immediately); "God created man" refers to us (through them); "God created man" refers to Jesus and Mary (as the definitive man and woman). And Jesus and Mary were created in thought before anyone else, and all else was created for them, though also for themselves. In thought, God created the head of the human family, the penultimate head of the human family, and the rest of the human family (later in Genesis, one can also see the punishment pronounced on Adam and Eve as addressed to each of these three groups with different meanings; Genesis 3:10ff). That God

---

[24] The devil, of course, did try to win over Jesus and Mary as he had Adam and Eve. This was the definitive temptation since they are the definitive head of the human family, though the attempt was doomed to fail. Since the devil failed, Jesus and Mary succeed in leading the human family back to its original state. Notice that since Jesus faced the temptation, unlike Adam who said nothing, Mary never had to face the devil. Man is to guard the garden.

[25] Adam in heaven in Dante's "Paradiso" holds a preeminent place. For Adam and Eve to retain their penultimate headship of the human family as God had planned, we have to inherit the effects of original sin.

[26] All biblical quotes are from the New American Bible (revised edition) (Philadelphia: American Bible Society, 2010). One can speculate that God had created the angels in his image but not male and female.

always intended to become man allows this verse to address primarily Jesus and Mary, which sounds right.

Having looked at three arguments that make it plausible to think that God would have become man even if Adam and Eve had not sinned[27] and at three problems that this idea solves, we have to consider an even more fundamental result of this idea. It is the delightful thought that if God had always planned to become man, then Christ was always meant to be not only at the center of heaven but also at the center of this world's reality in time. The phrases "For in him were created all things" (Col. 1:16, ESV) and "And for him are all things" (Rom. 11:36) gain even clearer meaning.

In addition, since man is the summation of physical creation and all participate in man, Jesus takes part in all of creation and all creation participates in him. God's creation always seems to be characterized by this substantial unity. In God's plan, man is the measure of all things,[28] if that man is Christ. Everything that exists was always meant to take its measure and meaning in relation to Christ. It is a beautiful idea, and its beauty to me argues for its truth.

In this case, then, Jesus did not push himself into this world to rescue it because it had (mostly) gone bad, and God did not devise a plan to send Jesus into the world after we had sinned (e.g., what happens in Milton's *Paradise Lost*). That plan was already made. There never was a time when we stood at the center of even this world or when we would have done so: everything was and always has been oriented toward Christ, gradually moving toward Christ, and then to God being "all in all."[29]

Ultimately, we don't have to struggle to work in the world in order to center it around Christ nor to drag Christ into the world: the whole universe does and always was meant to circle around him and him incarnate. It was

---

[27] Another supporting idea is that if there is a good to do, and God could do it, God would or did do it, and his always planning to become man is a good.

[28] Protagoras.

[29] 1 Corinthians 15:28.

made for him.[30] If man had not sinned, would man have had this world to himself (and herself) until the end of time? Not if God always planned to become man.

To list a few corollaries of the idea that God always intended to become man, one can say first that we were always meant to be God's and Jesus' brothers and sisters. Second, that our choice is not to whether to invite Jesus into this world or not but to decide whether we want to participate in the fullness of this world which is Christ's world or not. Another corollary is that the date of the Incarnation was fixed,[31] and the date of the Second Coming of Christ is probably fixed, set before the start of creation.

Another corollary to this idea, I suggest, is that we have to drop one of our complaints against God. We, or any being, could complain to God that we did not ask to exist and that we alone, not him, have to bear the fear and uncertainty of existence. We can't make that complaint if God always intended to become man and to face the same condition.

Perhaps also it is new to read the Bible from the point of view of God's becoming man (Jesus) and God filling a person fully with his Holy Spirit (Mary) as the point of all creation from the beginning. The kingdom of God, gradually achieved, was then always the purpose of creation with Jesus Incarnate as its center, making it sacred, hallowing it.[32] The Bible then is not the story of man's salvation only, or even primarily, but of the always planned Advent of the godman. It takes man from the center point in the drama of creation, salvation or damnation, and places it on the godman, which is a relief. Man is not the center of gravity of the Bible but God. Moreover, man's sin did not derail God's plan nor could it. Man's sin did not even substantially alter God's plan for his creation, except for making it more difficult.

---

[30] The only part of creation that Christ does not automatically inhabit remains the heart of the free person: the person has to choose, man or angel. How critical is the free choice of a person.

[31] Rick Larson, *The Star of Bethlehem* (Mpower Pictures; Spokane, WA: Distributed by Sound Enterprises, 1 videodisc (65 min.), 2009).

[32] And the purpose of creation is not Hegel's idea that God needed self-knowledge: God lacks nothing.

Genesis 3:15 is generally read as a promise from God that he would send a savior into the world. But before that, in Genesis 1:1– 3, we read:

> [33]In the beginning when God created the heavens and the earth—and the earth was without form or shape, with darkness over the abyss and a mighty wind sweeping over the waters—Then God said: Let there be light, and there was light.

We see God the Father and God the Spirit (the wind), but where is the Word? Could it be that the light, while of course meaning visible and invisible light, also means Jesus, "The light of the world" (John 8:12)? If so, it means that the first verse of the Bible is Trinitarian and that God always planned to come into the world since it occurs even before Adam's sin.[34] One might say that in this first sentence, God gives us the whole story of Creation: the light becomes physical light, and the rest of the Bible is just the story of how the light entered the world and how the world was prepared for his coming, up to the end of the Bible where his definitive entry into the world takes place.

---

[33] New American Bible (revised edition), 2010, Genesis 1:1–3.

[34] It also tells us that the person of Jesus (and Mary) is the purpose of creation, and all else is created to serve them and then for themselves.

Death Was Part of God's Original Plan

[T]he Christian faith teaches that bodily death, from which man would have been immune if he had not sinned.[35]

Part 1: Death was part of the natural world before man's sin

Some think death so horrible that death among the animals—chasing and killing and eating—could not have been part of the natural world before man and man's sin. It's too gruesome for God, too cruel, too violent. But one can see, of course, that death was indeed part of the world before man's sin. Darwin's Theory of Evolution depends on death as the element that allows a generation to improve on the generation before it.[36] And, surely, Adam and Eve knew what death was when God said of the tree, "When you eat from it you shall die" (Gen. 2:17). If they didn't know what death was, the command would not have made sense to them: they had seen death in the natural world.[37]

What then about death and man? Would man have been subject to death had he not sinned? It would seem not since why would God place death for man, a self-conscious creature, into his plan? What could terrify a self-conscious creature more than the possibility of eternal nonexistence or eternal nonconsciousness? It would seem cruel and a cruelty unmerited by man. And God is an enemy of death in any form, so how possibly could it have had a place for man in creation?

But then we are faced with one ambiguous and one curious quotation from Genesis and another curious verse from Hebrews.

---

[35] Austin Flannery, OP, ed., *Pastoral Constitution on the Church in the Modern World in Vatican Council II: The Conciliar and Post-Conciliar Documents* (Boston, MA: Daughters of St. Paul, 1975), p. 918.

[36] Even if one does not accept atheistic Darwinism (see David Berlinski's devastating critique at https://www.youtube.com/watch?v=Ec8lpcA5hls &list=PLDC24EE32111EB2B9&index=1), evolution even within a limited context still relies on death.

[37] The vision of Isaiah 11:6 where the lion lays down with the lamb might not describe what was true in Eden but might describe only an eschatological reality at the end of time.

Part 2: Genesis and the punishment of God

Following the fall of Adam and Eve, God delineates the punishment each would face, speaking to the serpent, then to Eve, and then to Adam in the order that they sinned. Completing his sentence on Adam, God states, "By the sweat of your brow, you shall eat bread Until you return to the ground from which you were taken; For you are dust, and to dust you shall return" (Gen. 3:19).[38] The ambiguous phrase comes from the above, viz.: "Until you return to the ground from which you were taken." Does this mean that they would die and be buried as part of their punishment? Or does it mean that at the end of their lives, they would die and be buried in the ground, as expected, and then also suffer decay and become nothing as well? In the latter case, what is added as punishment is not death but in addition to the suffering of illness and old age and futility in the toil of life—decay after death. Physical death itself in that case was part of the original plan.

The second verse from Genesis appears just a little further on in the expulsion from Eden: "Now, what if he also reaches out his hand to take fruit from the Tree of Life, and eats of it and lives forever" (Gen. 3:22)? God had made "The Tree of Life in the middle of the garden and the Tree of the Knowledge of Good and Evil" (Gen. 2:9). If man would reach out his hand to the Tree of the Knowledge of Good and Evil, which he knew was forbidden, why would he not reach out his hand to the other tree? But although the Tree of Life is a clear foreshadowing of the cross, the tree from which we eat eternal life,[39] it seems here that "lives forever" refers not to eternal life with God but endless life without death in this world. Then we have to conclude that the two trees God had established were related, the first giving knowledge and wisdom, which included perhaps knowledge of the location and meaning of the second tree. But it also implies that man as created originally was not

---

[38] All biblical quotations are from New American Bible (revised edition) (Philadelphia: American Bible Society, 2010).

[39] "Whoever eats my flesh and drinks my blood has eternal life" (John 6:54).

intended to live endlessly in this world (i.e., to the end of time); otherwise, why would God have created a Tree of Life?[40]

Finally, there is this verse from Hebrews 5:7–9:

> [W]ith loud cries and tears to the one who was able to save him from death, and he was heard because of his reverence.

Paul here refers to Jesus, of course, but what can this mean since obviously Jesus was not saved from death? We could say that he was saved from death, not from having to face it but by being raised from it. But that is not what is expected. Again, perhaps facing death was part of the original plan.

There are then three kinds of death, all called death: the death of the body without decay (falling asleep); the death of the body with decay and the death of the soul. Jesus is now our Savior from all three kinds of death, where in the original plan, Jesus would have only had to save us from the first. If death was part of the original plan, the first kind of death would have existed in the world, and Jesus would have still been our Savior from death.

The idea that death was part of God's original plan takes some getting used to. Didn't God specify death as the punishment if Adam and Eve ate of the tree of knowledge, meaning that it was not part of the original plan? "From that tree you shall not eat; when you eat from it you shall die" (Gen. 2:17). And death here is implied to be immediate, not far off the future.

But as Scott Hahn points out, Adam and Eve did not die physically at all when they ate of the tree. They did die spiritually and immediately as is shown by their loss of innocence and their hiding from God. So physical death is not part of the effect of the eating of the tree and could still have been part of the original plan.

---

[40] Perhaps the Tree of Life was there in case a man or woman died in an accident, but they probably would not have known where it was unless they ate of the tree of knowledge of good and evil, still meaning that it would have become operative only after a certain time.

Concerning the Tree of the Knowledge of Good and Evil, one might ask if God would have made a tree whose fruit was "good for food and pleasing to the eyes…and desirable for gaining wisdom" (Gen. 3:6) but which was not meant at some point in time to be eaten. Perhaps there would have been a time when man could have eaten of the Tree of the Knowledge of Good and Evil without sin. Perhaps if they ate of it at a time after God had allowed it, it would have indeed been good for food and the gaining of wisdom and would also have pointed out the Tree of Life (after God had allowed it, the two trees could have made a primitive Mass: the learning of wisdom from the Tree of the Knowledge of Good and Evil, while pleasing all the senses, and then the eating of the Tree of Life, giving endless life in this world[41]).

There are other instances in the Scriptures that point to the possibility that physical death was part of God's original plan. One is found in the parable of Lazarus and the rich man (Luke 12). In this parable, the wealthy man accumulates great riches with the hope of enjoying them, but he couldn't because "This night [his] soul [would] be required of [him]" (Luke 12:20). This could describe death in the original world, a "requiring of the soul" of a person.

Another image comes from one of the miracles of Jesus, the bringing of the young girl back to life. There is no doubt she was dead, but Jesus says, "The girl is not dead but asleep" (Matt. 9:24, NIV). Here, death is identified with sleep, a sleep from which one awakes. As in other places, Jesus refers to death not as a complete end of life but as a "falling asleep."[42] It implies no pain or suffering. The importance of these verses is that having one's soul "required of thee" [by God] or "falling asleep" could have happened to a person in a world without sin in God's original plan.

---

[41] This suggestion is an example of the Helmrich Law of Theology: God does everything twice. It happens so often that God does something twice that finding one thing, I always look for its pair. If God intended to establish a primitive mass with the two trees, giving the possibility of endless life in this world, God later established the full mass, giving eternal life with God.

[42] For example, at the death of Stephen: "And when he said this, he fell asleep" (Acts 7:60).

Finally, in the second Eucharistic Prayer, we pray, "Remember also our brothers and sisters/who have fallen asleep in the hope of the resurrection."[43] Here, death is again called "falling asleep." Jesus came to restore things to how they were in the beginning,[44] so possibly, death and its effects are also returned to what they were originally. One can think of several reasons why death as falling asleep would have a place for man in God's original plan. One reason for death is that the earth would then indeed not have too many people, and it would allow God to create more people. With death in the world, more people could be born and find a place. A second reason is that death gives drama to life. The prospect of life ending in this world at any time spurs man on to greater works right now. A third reason is that limited evolutionary factors—race, for instance— would shape mankind around the world only if death were operative. And death gives man the ultimate opportunity to show love for God and for others. In the Bible, we see that all the great men and women had to be willing to die.[45]

A fourth reason is given by Joy Davidman in *Shadowlands*, the movie about her marriage to C. S. Lewis.[46] As she nears death, she states that "she cannot think of a better way for God to teach a person that he (or she) is not in charge." In a world without sin, after a life of accomplishment and service to God and neighbor, there would remain one last lesson to learn that all depends on God. And death would teach this lesson perfectly. Having reawakened, the conscious creature would know for sure that his or her consciousness and existence rely totally on God's will and love. It is a powerful reason to have death even in a sinless world.

---

[43] *Daily Roman Missal: Complete with Reading in One Volume* (Woodbridge, Illinois: Midwest Theological Forum, 2011), p. 789.

[44] "[B]ut from the beginning, it was not so" (Matthew 19:9).

[45] On a side note, while Darwin showed the motive of survival, which dominates the natural world, Jesus shows the other motive: to give up one's life out of love which dominates the human world.

[46] Joss Ackland, Claire Bloom, *Shadowlands* (Worcester, PA: Vision Video, 2004), 1985.

Part 3: What would death look like in a sinless world?[47]

There are several events in the Scriptures and in the Church which suggest what death might have looked like in a world without sin in God's original plan. First, there is Melchizedek who seemingly has no beginning and no end. As such, Melchizedek, the King of Salem or "peace," gives us no doubt a preview of Christ, the High Priest. His seemingly "beginningless" and endless life in this world suggests that some people might have lived in this world until the end of time, presumably as a result of eating from the Tree of Life. And scientists do tell us that, theoretically, the human body is made to last endlessly if the self-destructive process of aging, which is an illness coming from the fall, could be stalled.[48]

Then there is Enoch, son of Cain, who "Walked with God, and he was no longer here, for God took him" (Gen. 5:24). Enoch is an example of a man taken out of this world, body and soul. This occurs again with Elijah: "A fiery chariot and fiery horses came between the two of them, and Elijah went up to heaven in a whirlwind" (2 Kings 2:11).

---

[47] The verse in Psalm 116:15, NIV, "Precious in the sight of the Lord is the death of his faithful servants" could still hold, even if it's only a temporary falling asleep.

[48] Another reason for the presence of death in the non-lapsarian world is that in the Trinity, there are at least three relationships between the three Persons all at the same time: absolute equality, absolute obedience, and absolute love. In terms of obedience, the Son obeys the Father, and the Holy Spirit obeys the Father and the Son while not compromising equality at all. And if we enter in relationship with the Trinity, we enter into these relationships also. In terms of obedience specifically, we and the angels have to learn total obedience to God (any of the three Persons). The angels, the Fathers tell us, were put to the test. Would they sacrifice their will to do the will of God? Some did not. The angels, pure spirits, cannot die physically of course. How does God teach and test our obedience? We would have to learn it even in a world without sin. This is another argument for death as falling asleep being part of a non-lapsarian world; while doing God's will in life would train us in obedience, death would train us in absolute obedience. We now learn obedience through suffering and death. It could be that death would teach obedience, poverty, and chastity—all aspects of heaven.

God also seems to have even given us physical examples of what death might have looked like: the incorruptible.[49] These are the over one hundred blessed and saints whose bodies, when disinterred for burial in a church, were found to be incorrupt. They did not and have not decayed, the most recent being Fr. Solanus Casey who was named blessed in 2017. Perhaps that is what death would have looked like: the body placed in the earth but lacking the disorder of creation caused by sin, no attacking or breaking down of the body by nature. Maybe in God's original plan, there would have been three possibilities for a person: to die without suffering and to be buried (without decay); to live in this world until the end of time (eating of the Tree of Life); or being taken up body and soul into heaven. There are at least two examples of the last case, adding Moses as a possible third example.

All these examples, taking place in the world after the fall, show that the question of death even in a fallen world is not a simple thing, which implies that other possibilities remain for how death could have functioned in a world without sin.

In Mary, preeminently we see death as falling asleep: the instant she died was the same instant she awoke in eternity; death never held her for an instant, not body or soul. And even she learned definitively that her existence depended entirely on God, a central reason for death in God's original plan. But even Mary did not reveal to us the final state of man, for that we have the death and resurrection of Jesus. As above, in a sinless world, we would see him as Savior from death since he would show that those who had fallen asleep, without decay, would rise again, body and soul. He would still have opened heaven, bringing souls from Sheol, a place where people waited for the coming of the Messiah, in a world without sin, not a place of pain but a place of peace, perhaps not even of darkness. Jesus uniquely would still have revealed the final state of man, the Resurrected Christ. Unknown until then, man would see

---

[49] Joan Carroll Cruz, *The Incorruptibles: A Study of the Incorruption of the Bodies of Various Catholic Saints and Beati* (Rockford, Illinois: Tan Books and Publishers, 1977).

that the bodies of those who had died, mysteriously waiting in the earth, would rise again and be transformed.

Additionally, death, even as falling asleep, would have given to each man and woman an opportunity to offer himself or herself completely to the Father in thanksgiving. Death would give each person an opportunity to offer himself or herself as a sacrifice to God.

Concerning the quote from Vatican II in the title above, one can say that the death they refer to is the death of suffering, death and decay that we know in this fallen world, a result of sin, and is not the death of falling asleep that could have existed in God's original plan. And so we should not fear death in itself; it is a falling asleep from which we awake.[50]

---

[50] 54 "When I awake, let me be filled with your presence" (Psalms 17:15).

The World without Sin[51]

In this essay, I will assume the conclusions from the two previous essays: that God always intended to become man and that death as a falling asleep was always part of God's plan for man in this world. The next question is what the world would have looked like; how would it have proceeded if the angels and man had not sinned if sin had not entered the world? In particular, what would the life of Christ have looked like in a world without sin?5[52]We see three archangels in Scripture: Michael, Gabriel, and Raphael. Lucifer, we are told, was one of the greatest angels, perhaps the greatest. Michael is God's defender, Gabriel is God's messenger, and Raphael is God's healer.[53] Perhaps Lucifer, by the evidence of his name, was intended to be the one that helped carry God into the world.[54] In any case, he had an important role. But, of course, to accept these roles required free choice, so Lucifer said no to the role and became a stumbling block to God's plan, Satan.[55]

---

[51] It is assumed here that the angels had fallen but that Adam resisted the temptation. Men and women would also be tempted by the fallen angels, but they would have had no inclination to sin. And if one sinned, it would affect only that person, not the whole human family. If the angels had not fallen, one might surmise that Lucifer ("light bearer") would have had a role with Adam and Eve, had a beneficent role with Jesus in the desert, and had a role in his death. It's just that the now fallen angels act badly in these places, disobediently, rebelliously, but their place in the world at certain moments was not taken away from them, even though they fell.

[52] It is thought that the spiritual beings did not have the vision of God until they passed a test, so the fallen angels never had the Beatific Vision.

[53] Other than the three archangels, the only named spiritual beings in the Bible are Lucifer/Satan and Legion, and Legion is and is not a name (we see the 3–1 pattern of the Trinity here).

[54] cf. The First Eucharistic Prayer "[C]ommand that these gifts be borne by the hands of your holy Angel to your altar on high" in *Daily Roman Missal* (Woodridge, Illinois: Midwest Theological Union, 2011), p. 779.

[55] It's interesting to speculate that like the Trinity, which is three and one at the same time, we see three archangels reflecting different aspects of God. Perhaps Lucifer had all these roles together; certainly a reason for pride.

As the three archangels had specific roles in history, perhaps the role of Lucifer involved the highest moments of human history. He would have appeared to Adam and Eve. He would have met with Jesus at the start of his public ministry. He would have appeared at Jesus' offering to the Father. And he would appear at the end of time as predicted in Revelation. But instead of doing what God intended him to do, at these moments as a fallen spirit, he did differently. Instead of serving God and his plan, he inspires things that harm creation and mock God.

So in those four moments, he tempted Adam and Eve, he tempted Jesus, he tortured Jesus, and he will inspire a battle at the end of time. But God, who is good even to the unjust (cf. Matthew 5:45) did not remove the role of Lucifer from creation but allowed him to appear where God's plan for creation planned for him to appear, even though he would act differently than planned. God willed his creation, and he would not change the plan for his creation in time, what we usually call fate or providence. It also could be that God, because he created the world over time yet created it all at once in idea, could not remove Satan from his plan.

While this took place outside of time, the next place to begin, not to be redundant, is Genesis. In God's punishment on Adam for the original sin, God tells Adam, "Thorns and thistles it shall bear for you...[and] by the sweat of your brow, you shall eat bread" (Gen. 3:18–19, NABRE). This sentence applies to Adam's work, to man's work, and preeminently to Jesus' work as all would become more difficult, fraught with pain, and even futility (the thorns mentioned, of course, bring to mind the crown of thorns of the Passion). But as a sentence applied to Jesus as Son of Man, what was Jesus' work that would now become more difficult? What was the work that already existed that was already planned out for Jesus?[56]

Similarly, God tells Eve, "In pain, you shall bring forth children" (Gen. 3:16). Eve, in giving birth, and all women would suffer more pain

---

[56] The punishments of God on Adam and Eve and the serpent can be read as directed toward three audiences: Adam and Eve; all their descendants; Jesus and Mary. And it is perhaps primarily directed to Jesus and Mary as to what they would face.

than God's plan originally included.[57] Similarly, this punishment applies to Eve, to all women, and preeminently to Mary and to her giving birth. At the foot of the cross, helping Jesus give birth to the Church, she suffered more than she would have suffered. And as Mother of the Church,[58] in bringing new members into the Church and to spiritual birth, she would suffer and struggle and sometimes fail since now people had a tendency toward sin. But in a world without sin, what would her work have looked like?

With these central questions posed, let's proceed chronologically to see how things might have been intended to progress. In the beginning, God created the universe, and it marched forward until the advent of man.[59] Through all this time, the cosmos evolved according to the laws of physics, and when life appeared, survival of the fittest ruled in biological evolution.[60]

At the high point, Adam and Eve were created. God intended Adam to become the high priest of all creation of the cosmic temple.[61] And God intended Eve to become the mother of all the living. In order to teach the first couple obedience and as a result of the nature of things, God gave them three commands: "Be fruitful and multiply and fill the earth" (Gen. 1:28, ESV); to "cultivate and care for it [the garden]" (Gen. 2:15); and to be free to eat of any tree in the garden except of the tree

---

[57] But this implies that women would have had some pain in giving birth, and men would have had to endure some suffering and effort in their work.

[58] A new title in the universal church for Mary added by Pope Francis in 2018.

[59] It can be argued that this took only six days, 144 hours, if looked at from the location of the big bang while being 13.7 or so billion years for us. See Gerald L. Schroeder, *Genesis and the Big Bang* (New York: Bantam Books, 1990).

[60] As a first example of what I call the Helmrich Law of Theology that God does everything twice, a second law, the law of Jesus, also ruled in a sense: "No one has greater love than…to lay down one's life for one's friends" (John 15:13). In a way, animals and plants followed this rule as they died to feed other animals. And all creatures acted on the will to live.

[61] Scott Hahn, *Genesis to Jesus* (Irondale, AL: EWTN, 2012).

of knowledge of good and evil: "You shall not eat it or even touch it" (Gen. 3:3).[62]

In what did happen, Satan appeared to Adam and Eve. Following Scott Hahn's suggestion convinces me the snake was not a harmless garden snake[63] but a great monster.[64] The monster gave Adam a choice: either eat of the tree or be slain. Adam had the choice of complete trust

---

[62] n Genesis 2:9 we see two trees among others in the garden of Eden: the tree of the knowledge of good and evil and the tree of life, the second being "in the middle of the garden." Adam and Eve know where the first tree was, since they were told not to eat of it or even to touch it, but they didn't yet know where the second tree was, though they had to leave because they would eventually find it. The prohibition "You shall not eat it or even touch it" (Gen. 3:3) sounds like the prohibition one makes to a young person about the sexual organs: "Don't touch that tree in the middle of your garden," one might say, though sadly, it might be "More honour'd in the breach than the observance" (*Hamlet* act 1, scene 4). But it's not the case that the Garden of Eden situation is a projection from man's sexual situation but that before sin and the misuse of sexuality, sex is a mild reflection of the situation in the Garden.

But more to the point, the prohibition on sexual activity for young people is not forever but only until they grow and marry. So if there is an analogy between these two realities, it implies that God eventually would have invited man to eat of the fruit from the Tree of Knowledge of Good and Evil, and at that time, it would not have been a sin. The situation of not being allowed to eat but later being allowed to eat can be seen in Leviticus 19:23, where they will only eat of the fruit trees for the first three years where pork, etc., is forbidden but then is allowed (Acts 10) and where blood cannot be eaten, but then Jesus commands them to drink his blood (cf. John 6:56), even if it's of his resurrected body.

[63] As Scott Hahn points out (video series *Genesis to Jesus*, EWTN, 2020), the word used for *snake* is *Nahash*, which is used again in Numbers 21:6 ("a venomous snake"), in Isaiah 27:1 ("gliding serpent"), Revelation 12:3 ("enormous red dragon"), and Revelation 12:9 ("great dragon").

[64] It convinces me for many reasons, but one is that Satan speaks to Eve. Satan would have spoken to Adam first, but if his threat cowed Adam, quite understandably, that left Satan to speak to Eve for whom a trick was more effective than a threat. In contrast, because Jesus resists Satan, we (gratefully) don't see Satan tempt Mary.

in God in allowing himself to be killed, trusting that God would raise him again to life, or to disobey.[65]

But as our speculative scenario progresses, with no fallen angels, Lucifer's test of Adam was different. He would have had a test, perhaps not to eat of the tree only, but Lucifer would have helped him to pass it. Remembering that death is just a falling asleep, over which God has command, if the test involved his death, Adam allowed himself to die (or at least, like Isaac, was willing to die). And Eve suffered in watching Adam die or contemplating death.[66] Having obeyed God, having learned his complete dependence on God, Adam, raised by God from the dead and restored to life, was ready to take on his position as the high priest of creation and preliminary spiritual head of the human race.[67] And Adam and Eve's descendants inherited all the gifts of original justice and grace with which God had endowed them.

After Adam and Eve, the head of the human family in time, God led the human race to accomplish two tasks. One was to grow and to fill the earth; the other was to build civilizations and to develop cultures, arts, and sciences. And the beautiful diversity of cultures and languages developed. Adam and Eve, as we see anyway, pray to God and make sacrifices. And as we see from the story of Cain and Abel (Genesis 4), they and their progeny would always offer to God the best of what they had in thanksgiving. After this time, men and women died—fell asleep—and were buried but did not decay.[68] The average life span

---

[65] Hebrews 2:15 speaks of everyone; those "who all their lives were held in slavery by their fear of death" might refer to Adam's fear of death, which led to sin and the slavery to sin of mankind.

[66] ere, Jesus was not only the second Adam, but Adam was the first Jesus, and Eve the first Mary. The Old Testament figures all prefigure aspects of Christ and Mary; Adam and Eve would have prefigured Christ in a spectacular way.

[67] Even after original sin, God did not take away Eve's role as mother of all the living nor did he take away Adam's role as penultimate head of the human family. And it's always instructive to see how Adam and Eve repented and still trusted in God and prayed to him after the fall. Jesus, of course, carried out this task by allowing himself to be killed.

[68] One might wonder also why God would give us the Eucharist if our bodies would decay. One could say, of course, that it is the most efficient way to get grace to

could have been longer than we know it. Throughout, there remained the initial blessing given to Adam by God, which traced its way through Adam's descendants.

Finally, at the appointed time, beginning the preparation for the advent of God into the world, God intervened and called Abra(ha)m in order to establish the Hebrew people and eventually the Jewish faith. In a world without sin and old age, perhaps having a child at ninety-nine was not difficult. And God made the first of seven covenants with man, the one with Abraham.[69] The Lord led the seventy-two down to Egypt where they learned service and obedience but without slavery. And the Lord led them out but without the obstruction of Pharaoh. Then the trip to Sinai to worship God, the Ten Commandments, and the short trip to the promised land.[70] They would still have the Passover rite.

The native peoples, having heard of this people and how God delivered them at the Red Sea, would have welcomed them as the favored of God and served them, a people intended to bring God to the world and to serve the world. The Jewish Scriptures were written, and the prophets taught what would happen in the future.[71] Perhaps everyone would marry.[72] The father of every family would also serve the family as priest of the family, giving it spiritual life, while the mother gave it physical life.[73]

---

our souls. But it could be that even though we would fall asleep in death, our bodies were not intended to decay, so the Eucharist was part of God's original plan.

[69] cf. Scott Hahn on the covenants of God with man as family covenants, establishing a family as the central theme of the Bible.

[70] In a w/w/sin, the peoples of Canaan would have ceded their land happily to the Israelites, who were the people through whom God would carry out his purposes.

[71] Brief retelling in a brief manner the great actions of God appear frequently in the Old Testament.

[72] Speculation of Fr. Benedict Groeschel, interview, May 5, 2010, "Without original sin, everyone would be married."

[73] As Scott Hahn points out, God limited the priests to the descendants of Aaron and the Levites after the sin of the Golden Calf at the beginning of the forty years, and God limited the High Priesthood to the descendants of Phineas after the sin at Moab at the end of the forty years. Scott Hahn, *Genesis to Jesus* (Irondale, AL: EWTN, 2012).

Hints of the Messiah abounded, and the world was ready when he came. Elizabeth and Zechariah were inexplicably without children for a long time when John was conceived. And Joseph and Mary[74]— Joseph bearing the blessing of God from Adam—did the unheard of and entered a celibate marriage. Then God, needing to provide male chromosomes for his Son's human nature, in the second act of ex-nihilo creation (a suggested solution), created a male gamete with which to impregnate Mary. A single cell is like a universe unto itself (the other option is that God took a gamete from Joseph's body). In either case, the child had the exact characteristics that God desired him to have, and I think that in the kindness of God, he resembled Joseph: "Is he not the carpenter's son"[75] (Matt. 13:55, NIV)?

Jesus, after his spectacular birth, led a quiet life until age thirty, obedient to his parents in Nazareth. He followed the Jewish faith, and no one suspected that he was the Second Person of the Trinity nor did they suspect that Mary was full of grace.[76] John appeared and turned the hearts of fathers to their children and children to their fathers (Malachi 4:6) through his baptism of repentance in preparation for the Messiah and was not killed.[77] Jesus' public ministry began and proceeded without resistance. As my Helmrich Law of Theology states, God does everything twice, and this was the second stage in the teaching of mankind, the first being that to the Jewish people through the prophets.

As Jesus entered his public ministry, one can ask two questions: What was Jesus' work in a world without sin? And what did his Passion and Death look like? How could they even make sense, in a world without sin?

---

[74] Mary is called the Virgin; perhaps in a world without sin, Jesus, Mary, and Joseph (and John the Baptist) would have been the only virgins.

[75] One sees the exactness with which God constructs the Temple in the Hebrew Scriptures. This new Temple, the Body of Jesus, must have been constructed even more exactly.

[76] Another example of the Helmrich Law of Theology that there are two ways for a human being to be totally united to God: the hypostatic union of Jesus; the full of grace of Mary.

[77] Though he could have fallen asleep in death.

First, let's list a few things Jesus said he did, which he could have done even in a world without sin:

- "I came into the world, to testify to the truth" (John 18:37).
- "I came so that they might have life and have it more abundantly" (John 10:10).
- "You are Peter, and upon this rock I will build my church" (Matt. 16:18).
- "I pray...so that they may all be one" (John 17:20–21).
- "Whoever eats my flesh and drinks my blood has eternal life" (John 6:54).
- "Whoever eats my flesh and drinks my blood remains in me and I in him" (John 6:56).
- "I will announce what has lain hidden from the foundation [of the world]" (Matt. 13:35).
- "When I am lifted up from the earth I will draw everyone to myself" (John 12:32).
- "I came not to abolish but to fulfill [the Law and the Prophets]" (Matt. 5:17).
- "[He] became poor although he was rich, so that...[we] might become rich" (2 Cor. 8:9).
- Jesus would have said that a disciple must "deny himself, take up his cross, and follow me" (Matt. 16:24), but the cross would have meant the work God had planned for that person, and to deny one's self would not have meant going against a nature inclined to sin but just acting to put the other first.
- He expanded the Jewish faith to the whole world (Christianity). His first sermon pointed to this expansion, but the reaction in a world without sin would have been different (cf. Luke 4:28–9).
- He preached the Beatitudes, completing the Law given on Sinai.[78]

---

[78] One wonders why, in a country occupied by the Romans and by a religious authority, Jesus would preach a sermon about meekness, forgiving your enemies,

- In a world without sin, Jesus would have healed injuries, wounds, and accidental deaths.
- He made us the adopted sons and daughters of God; he shared with us his mother; he revealed the Father as Abba.
- He revealed his divinity at the Transfiguration.
- He revealed the Trinity and showed how these Persons interacted, understandings that could not be reached by reason.
- He established the everlasting and final covenant between God and man.
- He gave birth to the Church, the Ecclesia, called out from the world, and established the Sacraments.
- The Luminous Mysteries are five of the major things Jesus would have done, even in a world without sin: the Baptism; the miracle at Cana; the preaching of the kingdom of God; the transfiguration; the institution of the Blessed Sacrament.[79]
- Falling asleep in death would have allowed Jesus to reveal not only the Resurrection and the final state of man but his full Divinity.
- "[He broke] the bonds of death [to] manifest the resurrection."[80] Man had to be rescued from death, even death as falling asleep.
- He opened heaven to those who had died and was the first to enter heaven.

That was the first question: What would Jesus' work have been in a world without sin (w/w/sin)? And it seems he still would have had a large percentage of his work to do.

---

etc. From this point of view, it was preached because Jesus was always intended to preach it in God's plan; the world situation was secondary.

[79] One could speculate that in addition, the joyful mysteries bring Jesus to adulthood but did not involve the pain they did involve; the sorrowful mysteries established Jesus as king of this world and Mary the queen (which wouldn't have involved suffering); the glorious mysteries established Jesus as the king of heaven, and Mary the queen.

[80] "The Sixth Common Preface" *Daily Roman Missal* (Woodridge, Illinois: Midwest Theological Union, 2011), p. 762.

The second question is: What would Jesus' Passion and Death have looked like in a w/w/sin? Next, we have to sketch the Passion and Death, indeed all of Holy Week as it would have taken place in a world without sin.[81] Of course, it began with Jesus entering his city on a donkey (as Mary had traveled by donkey to visit Elizabeth).[82] The crowds welcomed him, the religious leaders accepted him and accepted that he was introducing something which they had prepared for but which they would not lead.[83] He would have taught for the first days of Holy Week, preparing for the Passover of that year.[84]

The Passover took place on Tuesday or on Thursday night, Jesus' definitive Passover, which was here not a saving from sin but a Passover from this world to the world of heaven and in itself an act of thanksgiving, praise, and worship. Jesus instituted the Eucharist and provided an example by washing the feet of the disciples. Lucifer, not fallen, moved Judas to lead Jesus to the authorities and to bring him to the Temple.[85]

One notes that the cross, the symbol of God, is too perfect a symbol to not have had its place even in a w/w/sin. The vertical bar indicates love for God; the horizontal bar indicates love for neighbor.

One asks why Jesus had to die on the cross when any shedding of his blood would have sufficed to save the whole world. Perhaps it was because in God's plan that was his work, to die on the cross, even in a

---

[81] God created the world in six days, and his Son brought it to completion in the six days of Holy Week.

[82] Another example of the Helmrich Law of Theology that God does everything twice. In Revelation 19:11, Jesus enters on a white horse symbolizing conquest, but the donkey symbolizes peace.

[83] Twelve leaders of Israel, twelve Apostles multiplied gives 144, the number of hours of creation as seen from the Big Bang. See earlier footnote.

[84] One sees the resemblance between Holy Week and the Mass: in the first part of Holy Week and in the first part of the Mass, the Lord teaches his people.

[85] We have terrible trouble trying to identify the moral culpability of Judas. Since if he did not betray Jesus, Jesus would have not had the opportunity to offer himself to the Father. But this offers one way out: it was always Judas's role to bring Jesus to the authorities while at the same time, he was guilty in a fallen world of shedding innocent blood.

world without sin. In our world of sin, his dying, which would have been a falling asleep, became far more difficult.

We need to work out the details of how it might have been meant to be.

What would Jesus' Passion and death have looked like? In an earlier essay, I concluded that in a world without sin, death would have been a falling asleep[86] and that Jesus would have work to do, but it would become more difficult as a result of sin. One way to approach this question is to look at the Stations of the Cross in a world without sin:[87]

Station 1:   The Sanhedrin confirms that Jesus' task will end in falling asleep (death).

Station 2:   Jesus asks for a cross of wood to carry.

Station 3:   Jesus stops, perhaps kneels, and kisses the earth. Station 4: Jesus speaks with Mary.

Station 5:   Simon and others help Jesus carry his cross.

Station 6:   Veronica approaches Jesus, and he leaves his image on her veil.

Station 7:   Jesus stops, perhaps kneels. and kisses the earth. Station 8: Jesus speaks to the women.

Station 9:   Jesus stops, perhaps kneels, and kisses the earth. Station 10: Jesus removes his outer garments.

Station 11: Jesus is tied to the cross at his request with a pedestal to stand on.

Station 12: The cross is lifted, and as he is lifted up, all the world is drawn to him; all recognize who he is (cf. John 12:32). After saying his last words, he falls asleep in death.

---

[86] Death is often referred to as falling asleep in the New Testament. For example, see Paul (1 Cor. 15:6 or Matt. 9:24 or Acts 7:60). In John 6:50, Jesus says that anyone who eats this bread will never die—or in 6:51, anyone who believes in him will never die—yet they clearly died physically, so it must refer to a different death, the second death, the death of the soul.

[87] The symbol of the cross is embedded in our biology which precedes our falling into sin, one argument that it always would have been God's symbol.

Station 13: His body is placed in the arms of Mary. Station 14: His body is placed in the tomb.[88]

Now let us go through the Passion and Death as the Gospels present them in a narrative format. At the start of the Passion (a word which in itself implies love but not necessarily suffering), Jesus went out to the Mount of Olives to pray to his Father, followed by a night alone in preparation. He was taken to the High Priest,[89] to the Sanhedrin, to Herod. They would have wondered at the mystery of what he was preparing to do and encouraged him, but that the Messiah would die mystified them. Instead of blows, he would have had commendations from the people. And he had, instead of a crown of thorns, an old cloak and a reed: a royal diadem, a robe of purple, and a scepter. Finally, he disrobed and mounted the cross but without suffering.

His work here was to reveal the love and goodness of God by showing his complete trust in God and to offer the definitive offering of thanksgiving to the Father. He was not nailed to the cross[90] but stood up against it, perhaps tied to it with ropes at his request, and standing on a pedestal.[91] Then Jesus prayed, spoke his last words, offered his life to the Father, and fell asleep in death. He offered the Sacrifice prefigured by the willingness to die offered by Adam at the start of the human race and of Isaac. And Mary, like Eve with Adam, offered the Sacrifice with him.

---

[88] In this w/w/sin, everyone died and was buried in the ground but did not decay.

[89] There were two high priests, Anais and Caiaphas. Today, we in a sense have two popes—Francis and Benedict. And both situations have only happened once in the history of Judaism and Catholicism respectively.

[90] I am intent on keeping the cross as the symbol of God and that it was God's chosen symbol from the beginning. It is the perfect symbol pointing to man's love for God and of man's love for each other. There are proteins called Laminins that work to keep cells together, and they have the form of the cross. See https://answersingenesis.org/biology/microbiology/laminin-and-the-cross/. And they would have existed in a world without sin.

[91] For a convincing argument that Jesus stood on a pedestal, see Frederick T. Zugibe, *The Crucifixion of Jesus: A Forensic Inquiry* (New York: M. Evans and Company, Inc., 2005).

There is one act in the real Passion and Death of Jesus which does not involve the kind of sin that Jesus' Passion and Death involved: it is the thrusting of the spear into the side of the dead Jesus. Indeed, this is disrespect to the Body of Christ, but he is already dead. So it seems that in a world without sin, the soldier, inspired by the Spirit or by the angels, with Christ on the cross, would have pierced his side with a spear, and out of his side, blood and water would have flowed to give birth to the Church and the Sacraments: "[A]nd immediately, blood and water flowed out" (John 19:34). And this action would still have been required to show that he had indeed fallen asleep in death.[92]

Jesus, like all people up until that time, was buried in the earth, in his case after being cleansed according to the Jewish Law. He descended to those who had died previously and who waited for him to open the gates of heaven. Then Jesus rose from the dead, revealing the Resurrection and the form of the glorified body, the final form of the human person. This was his central work. He rose from the dead and raised many with him (Matt. 27:52). He had been buried as everyone was buried and had not decayed as no one decayed. Then he rose, the central event of human history. He showed man the solution to the mystery that had faced man since the time of Adam: death, even without suffering or decay.[93] And he also gave man a glimpse into the nature of the next life.[94]

Jesus showed himself to those the Father had chosen from the beginning and during forty days he taught his disciples, finally ascending to his place in heaven. He and the Father sent the Holy Spirit on Pentecost, to the apostles and to Mary, giving full birth to the Church, and bringing the Pascal Mystery to a conclusion.

After the Resurrection, the angels had a greater presence in the world, and since the angels and man had not fallen, they all assisted

---

[92] Covenants require that blood be shed, even in a sinless world.

[93] Perhaps Mary's death, a falling asleep without suffering, was the only time death was seen as it was meant to be. And the incorruptible, blessed, and saints did not decay after death.

[94] The resurrection was also (with the Assumption of Mary) the beginning of the revelation of God's plan for all of creation at the end of time.

man in growing to full stature both as human beings and in Christ. Jesus returned to his Father, leaving us himself in the Eucharist and the Holy Spirit in the Church. Man, now with Christ, still had the two original tasks to continue to fulfill: to fill the earth before Jesus could return and to continue to develop culture, civilization, and all the arts and sciences. Now man had the further task of growing to the full stature of Christ as individuals and as a Church (Ephesians 4:13) that "gathered into one body by the Holy Spirit, they may truly become a living sacrifice in Christ to the praise of [God's] glory."[95]

So during that time. the Spirit, with the cooperation of the Church, revealed to man what Christ had done, formed the deposit of faith, and then penetrated into the internal meanings of his words and actions.

Fortified by the Spirit and by the presence of Jesus in person for a time and now in the Eucharist, the apostles, the second religious leaders but with the support of the first religious leaders, spread the Good News of the Messiah to all of Israel, and then they and Israel spread it to the rest of the world. The Church grew, first in Jerusalem, then in Samaria, and then in all the world. The Jewish religious leaders accepted Jesus and assisted the apostles, the preeminent messengers of the Gospel, throughout the world. The religions of the world, having no element of evil in them and each different, accepted the Gospel as it reached them, bringing their own insights and emphases to allow different aspects of the Gospel to be interpreted and understood more deeply in different places.[96] And in time, the Church grew to the full stature of Christ with the assistance of the Spirit, both individually and as a community.

In a w/w/sin, the developments in the natural world would assist the Church, and developments in the Church would help the world. Faith and reason would not clash but help each other in a friendship-like interaction. And when cultures clashed, for example, the Europeans and

---

[95] "Eucharistic Prayer IV," *Daily Roman Missal* (Woodridge, Illinois: Midwest Theological Union, 2011), p. 807.

[96] As an example, Fr. Bede Griffiths wrote, having served in India, "Hinduism brought out aspects of Catholicism that otherwise would have been difficult if not impossible to see." Fr. Bede Griffiths, *Christ as Common Ground* (Duquesne, 1990).

the Native Americans, they would not clash but would live in mutual respect, even self-sacrifice for the other. And at times "the earth was harvested" (Rev. 14:16), where souls were required of great numbers of people according to God's plan, in our fallen world, they take the form of battles.

Perhaps at this point, the marriage of God and man having begun in Christ, man would have permission to eat of the tree of knowledge, meaning that man would know the location of the Tree of Life and could live endlessly in this world (until the return of the Lord).[97]

Perhaps each person would have St. Paul's choice "[To] go on living in the flesh...[or] to depart this life and be with Christ" (Phil. 1:22–23).

One corollary of the theory that God always intended to become man is that the date of his advent, the date of his death, and the date of his return were fixed by the Father from the start. In his video, *Star of Bethlehem*, Frederick Larson describes the arrangement of the constellations at the time of Jesus' birth and at the time of his death, an arrangement also described in the Gospels. But this arrangement of the planets was set when the stars took shape eons ago. That the stars also have a particular arrangement at his death, an arrangement fixed from the start of time by the laws of physics, supports the idea that the time of Jesus' Passion and Death was set long before man or the sin of man, arguing that in some form, it was always God's plan. The Bride of Christ would be prepared for the Bridegroom, which had to happen before Jesus could return. The Church would develop and would still have seven sacraments. They could have been:

1. Baptism—entry into the kingdom of God.
2. Confession—perhaps Consultation—the opportunity through the person of the priest to discuss issues with God and to receive

---

[97] "What if he...reaches out his hand to take from the Tree of Life, and eats of it and lives forever" (Gen. 3:22)? Apparently. there would have been two kinds of living forever in this world: through the Tree of Life and through one's progeny. The first was lost with sin. But why would God create a tree "good for food and pleasing to the eyes" if it was never meant to be eaten (Gen. 3:6)?

    spiritual guidance and to receive a blessing and the chance to start new if mistakes (not sins) had been made.

3. Confirmation—the receiving of the gifts of the Holy Spirit.
4. Eucharist—the union of God with man.
5. Marriage—the Church would witness and bless marriages.
6. Orders—the Church would ordain priests and Bishops.
7. Sacrament of the Sick—still a Sacrament to prepare those who know they would die or fall asleep soon to make "the great leap from time to eternity."[98]

Throughout this time, in the Eucharist and at the end of time, both the Spirit and the Bride, the Church, would say "Come" (Rev. 22:17). Before the end, the unfallen Lucifer would have brought all the Jewish people back from around the world where they had gone to preach and build, and he would have brought the nations together around Jerusalem where Christ would return.[99]

Finally, at a time appointed at the beginning, Jesus would return as king and ruler to his kingdom. And creation, the new heaven and the new earth, the wedding feast of the Lamb, would begin. Jesus and Mary had accomplished the work they had been given. The way it did occur, Jesus and Mary still accomplished the work they had been given, though it was made more difficult by sin, and some free beings chose to be lost. They earned additional titles or titles with added meanings. We see that God's plan for his creation,[100] perfectly carried out in a world without the fall of the angels or of man, is still being carried out.

If God is in full control, why would he allow the world to be like this? Considering the above, we can see at least three reasons. First, he

---

[98] Our Lady of Good Success, Accessed 9/29/2019, https://www.tfp.org/prophecies-of-our-lady-of-good-success-about-our-times/.

[99] This provides another example of the Helmrich Law of Theology that God does everything twice: the Jewish people would have gone throughout the world, which they did, and the Christians would have gone throughout the world, which they did.

[100] The path that creation takes is in the plan of God: fate. The next world is not governed by fate but is pure freedom.

would not allow his original plan for creation to be changed except for the changes made by misuse of their free will by some of his creatures, even if it could be changed. Second, it does not cause us to lose anything eternally as St. Paul writes, "For this momentary light affliction is producing for us an eternal weight of glory beyond all comparison" (2 Cor 4:17).[101] Third, a definitive reason was recently given by Pope Francis:

When we read about Creation in Genesis, we run the risk of imagining God as a magician, with a magic wand able to do everything. But that is not so…[God] created human beings and let them develop according to the internal laws that he gave to each one so they would reach their fulfillment.[102]

He could not have done it any other way.[103]

Two questions immediately come to mind about the world without sin: What would the mass have looked like? And why did Jesus have to die? The mass, unexpectedly, needs only a few changes to adjust to a world without sin. The mass becomes an action of praise and thanksgiving, a sacrificial offering of thanksgiving, but not a sacrificial offering for sin. And the word *mercy* would be replaced by *love* as in "show us your love" rather than "show us your mercy." In the appendix is one suggestion, a piece titled "The Mass and the Rosary in a World without Sin," one would only have to adjust about 3 percent of the fixed words of the Mass, a very small percentage.

Jesus had to die as we have to die because that is God's plan as we move from this world to the next, though the transitions now involve pain where death would have been only a falling asleep, and our work would not have included suffering. There would still be three locations of human life—the womb, this world, and heaven. Louis Bouyer writes,

---

[101] Infinite quantities provide a model for this—if one adds a finite quantity to an infinite quantity, the size of the infinite quantity is not changed. The suffering of this world takes nothing away from the happiness in the world to come.

[102] Pope Francis, Addressing to the Plenary Assembly of the Pontifical Academy of Sciences, "Evolving Concepts of Nature," October 27, 2014.

[103] And we can now see that the problem of evil was not caused by God at all but by some of his free creatures who freely chose to rebel and to destroy.

"Since the death of Jesus, reality itself is wholly transfigured."[104] And this could have happened even in a world without sin.[105]

Also, this world will end, perhaps exactly when it would have ended if the fallen angels had not rebelled and man had not fallen. Perhaps this is part of what Jesus meant when he said, "It is not for you to know the times or dates the Father has set by his own authority" (Acts 1:7); i.e., that it is part of the Father's plan for this world and is set.

One can say then that the suffering in the world was not part of God's original plan at all, and while it can be traced to the sins of man, it is primarily traced to the sin of the fallen angels and their resulting effect on creation. And the suffering and decay might not have been a punishment of God but in part a direct consequence of man's sin that God just pointed out or an unavoidable remedy. Creation is proceeding according to God's original plan but in a damaged way. As Fr. Benedict Groeschel liked to say, "Something worth doing is worth doing badly." Perhaps we can apply that to all of creation. But the end in heaven is not changed.

Why was Jesus crucified then in this world with sin? He enduring the crucifixion to show God's love for man to have the greatest number of people decide of their own free will to love him, in spite of our sinful inclination to avoid God. Second, to pay a debt to the evil one—he didn't have to, but God is perfectly just, and Satan had won mankind, so the deal could have been that Satan give up the whole human race if he were allowed to torture God in his human nature as much as a human being could suffer. And the preceding suggests a third reason—to carry out the original plan of God in spite of sin.

---

[104] Louis Bouyer, *The Pascal Mystery: Meditations on the Last Three Days of Holy Week* (Chicago: Regnery, 1952), p. 38.

[105] That the relationship of the Son to the Father is "Eucharistic" in eternity before man or sin or sacrifice: "the eternal state of this Son is basically Eucharistic. Without the least suggestion of immolation, without "sacrifice," an entire and unceasing act of thanksgiving, the final achievement of his filial possession of the whole paternal being. Ibid., p. 74, "The Word's Eternal, Beatific State of Oblation," Ibid. p. 75, "Even in a world without sin, the Son would have given all he had to the Father in obedience and thanksgiving."

Four Theological Essays 2—Preface

Catholicism is so rich that to get a full picture of it or to participate fully, one has to plumb the depths of many different elements, not to mention how they relate and interact. We are looking at a few of the central ones here. Heresies usually don't argue for what is not true, but they take one part of the richness of the Church and cut off other parts, they stress one aspect or idea, and neglect other parts of aspects. What they have left is attractive because the Church is so rich they don't notice what is missing. If Catholicism has a fault, it's that it's too rich, infinitely rich. Of course, any theological opinions expressed here are under the authority of the Church as "the pillar and foundation of the truth" (1 Tim. 3:15).

The Mass

1. General ideas.
2. A brief walk through the Mass.
3. The Gloria.
4. The Mass as authorized by Christ.
5. The Mass in three images.
    a. As a mountain.
    b. As a furnace of love.
    c. As a bridal chamber.
6. The Mass as a dance of prayer.
7. The Mass as a dance of the different and the same.
8. The Mass echoes all the sacraments.
9. The Mass's parts have a three-part structure.
10. The Mass as a bridge.
11. The Mass as a rainbow.
12. The Mass as an outline of the Christian life.
13. The Mass as a biography of Jesus, relived.
14. The Mass as a history of Salvation.
15. The Mass has six parts (plus greeting and dismissal).
    i. Six parts of the Mass.
    ii. Six parts ci of the Mass.
    iii. "666" in the Apocalypse.
    iv. Six days of Creation.
    v. Six days of Holy Week.
    vi. Six parts of the Song of Songs.
    vii. Six extinctions of Elizabeth Kolbert.
16. The Mass and The Apocalypse
17. The Mass and Holy Week
18. What is the Mass?
19. The Eucharist
20. The name "Mass"

1. General ideas

I remember years ago going to an opera and sitting in the nosebleed seats. At that height, there was extra space for opera aficionados to place the whole score on tables and to follow each note as the three-hour Mozart opera progressed, which several people did.

The Mass is the biography of Jesus Christ written by the Holy Spirit with the assistance of the Church. While the Mass had the essential elements from the first days after Pentecost, the Holy Spirit has shaped it and refined it for two thousand years. One might argue that the symphony and other musical forms and some poetry takes its shape from the Mass. Doesn't its structure deserve as much attention as a beautiful symphony?

In the briefest sense, in the Mass, Jesus Christ lives again his earthly life. But he does it in such a way that he can share it with us that we can participate in it with him.

The structure of the Mass, both the Sunday Mass and the weekday Mass, stands up to the idea that each part and even the tiniest part is carefully and purposely chosen and fits into the whole. This independent study has been an unalloyed joy for me. Every question the Mass posed it answered, and every time one element implied the presence of another element in another part of the Mass, it was there. It is, in my view and I claim in reality, the most perfect work of art, including all categories of art, even performance art, and at the same time is simple and understandable. Great symphonies have been written along the lines of the structure of the Mass, and great poems ("The Waste Land," for example) have done the same thing. In Sonnet 23, lines five and six, Shakespeare writes: "So I, for fear of trust, forget to say The perfect ceremony of love's rite," and I think he is referring to the Mass (the Mass is a rite that is "said").

To start, we have to make a few general statements about the Mass. First, it is the primary means by which God defeats evil in the world (Vagaggini). He did defeat evil once and for all on the cross, but he managed to arrange to defeat it at different times and in different places over and over again.[1] God's victory is complete. Every time the Mass is said, evil is defeated.

There are two understandings of the Mass, both of which, it seems to me, are valid. The first understanding is that at Mass, we are truly united in a mystical way to the sacrifice of the cross. We are taken, to a degree, out of time and space, and the fruits of Christ's Passion and Death and his victory of obedience are applied to us and to our time and place. The second understanding is that the Mass is a new offering done by Christ and the Church and of equal value to the Passion and Death of Christ[2] (but at the same time not increasing the value of Christ's sacrifice). In either case, we attend Mass daily to conquer evil, within ourselves and in the world, to receive the graces offered, to grow in virtue and in holiness and in wisdom. Since we begin and end the Mass with the sign of the Cross, Jesus might have been referring to the Mass when he said, "Take up your cross every day" (Luke 9:23 CEV).

The Mass has had roughly the same structure from the earliest days of the Church[3] and has similar parts across the twenty-seven different Catholic rites. A full Sunday Mass, as I count it, has seventy-three parts, and the Bible has seventy-three books. "The Mass is the Bible in action,"[4] as Scott Hahn writes. And not only are most of the words of the Mass taken from the Bible, but the Bible finds its home in the Mass.[5] As to power, Padre Pio wrote that "It would be easier for the world to survive without the sun than to do without Holy Mass." And as we see God constructing the form of the sacrifices in the Old Testament, the Jewish Scriptures, we know that God himself constructed the Mass with just as much care.

---

[1]   8 Of course, each Mass affects the whole world, but it reminds me of a compact covering in topology, each Mass creating a circle of some radius around itself, the collection of which covers the whole world.

[2]   "[O]n the altar of the cross is contained and offered in an unbloody manner [in the Mass]," Council of Trent (1562): Doctrina de ss. Missae sacrificio, c. 2: DS 1743.

[3]   cf. *The Didache.*

[4]   Scott Hahn, *What Every Catholic Needs to Know about the Bible,* DVD (Casscom Media, 2013).

[5]   Pope Benedict.

2.A brief walk through the Mass

The end to which the Mass points is union with God, involving all parts of our being: intellect, emotion, feelings, imagination, body, and soul. This takes place most particularly in listening to the Gospel and in receiving Communion.

With that in mind, the Mass begins with the people singing, inviting God's presence (it's notable that the Mass begins with the people's action and request as the second half begins with the people's bringing forward gifts for consecration and the church's and God's response). After the greeting, a showing of mutual respect, we acknowledge our sinful condition and sins and ask forgiveness, also asking Mary and all the angels to saints to pray for us and for God to remember his mercy. Each of the three options of this section includes three parts: sorrow for our sins; a request for prayers; and an expression of confidence in God's mercy. We ask God to bring us to eternal life, which means life with God after death but also means in this Mass to be able to hear the Word of God (cf. John 5:24) and to receive the Eucharist (cf. John 6:53). Confident that our prayers are answered, that we are forgiven, though not forgetting our sinful state, we sing the "Gloria" to God who has now forgiven our sins.

Restored to God's family, we listen to the readings, homily, and Creed in order to be taught by God, our Father, and the Church, our mother, about this family, i.e., how to act, what is true. This listening is a form of communion with Christ. Then, knowing that God is present where two or three are gathered in his name, there he is (cf. Matthew 18:20) and that he answers all our prayers. We pray for the general needs of our world (cf. John 14:13). Our prayer for the world is our response to the readings, the sermon, and the Creed.

The second half begins as the first with the laity asking for God's presence, hereby bringing the gifts to the altar, gifts which we have received from God which will be transformed and offered to God and which will then feed us. The aim of the second half of the Mass is to bring us to the Eucharist. But it also finds its basis in the words of Jesus in the Eucharistic Prayer: "Do this in memory of me." So the gifts are prepared and surrounded by a garden of prayers, which are also instructive. Before the consecration, we pray that the gifts might be accepted, which is not so much that they be accepted in themselves but that we might be considered worthy to offer them. After the consecration, we pray in union with Mary and all the angels and saints whose prayers have carried us through the Mass from the beginning.

In the Words of Institution, the priest says in one Eucharistic Prayer that Jesus "took the bread and, giving thanks, broke it and gave it to his disciples." These four actions stretch over the second half of the Mass: the priest takes the bread in the offertory; he gives thanks in the preface; he breaks the bread in the fraction rite; he gives it to his disciples in Communion.[6]

At the end of the Words of Institution, the priest quotes Jesus' words, "Do this in memory of me" (Luke 22:19). The whole Mass is a fulfillment of this comment. Then the priest says or sings "The Mystery of Faith," which is another phrase for the Eucharist;[7] he declares in awe at what is before him on the altar. The people respond with the brief recounting of Jesus' Pascal action in one of the three three-part responses. Then the priest follows with his fulfilment of the command, "Do this in memory of me," with the anamnesis.

The Mystery of Faith, it seems to me, can be read in two different ways. If it's said and not sung, it is a brief dialogue between the people and the priest, the priest saying "The Mystery of Faith," and the people responding with the content of the mystery of faith in three verses. If it is sung, it is more an expression of amazement at the Eucharist before him (the priest had prayed for this at the end of the Confiteor, "May God...bring us to everlasting life," which is the Eucharist).

The post-institution part of the Eucharistic Prayer involves intercessions through which many receive grace. It is mirrored in John's account of the washing of the feet at the Last Supper (cf. John 13:14),

---

[6] To connect the spiritual and the physical, there are four verbs, four fundamental forces in physics, four Gospels, all perhaps reflecting the four living creatures before the throne of God (Apocalypse 4:6–8).

[7] 14 Suzie Andres, *Something New with St. Therese: Her Eucharistic Miracle* (Unpublished Manuscript) p. 88.

where people are cared for. If we only had the other three accounts, we would not know about this action.

The Doxology, the elevation of the bread and wine offered to the Father, is like the lifting up of the cross. If the Doxology marks Jesus offering himself to the Father and dying on the cross, the great amen then marks the end of Jesus' earthly Life, and our standing up indicates the Resurrection. Right after the Doxology and the offering of Christ to the Father, reconciled to God by Christ, restored, reconciled, we immediately refer to Jesus as Savior and immediately address God as Our Father (we could not address Jesus as Savior unless he had risen; see 1 Corinthians 15:17). We address the Father then the Son directly and offer peace which is the presence of the Holy Spirit. In this section, "peace" is mentioned seven times, all a result of the offering that was just made.

There is then the fraction rite, which makes perfect sense as preceding Communion but which in itself requires thought. It seems that this brief rite, including the phrase "Behold the Lamb of God," the breaking of the Host and a small piece being placed in the chalice, and the phrase "Who takes away the sins of the world," taken together seem to form a reprise of the Mass, a brief summation of the Mass.[8]

Indeed, we receive Communion to complete the Sacrifice, and the bread and wine are a symbol but not only a symbol: they are what they symbolize. And so we have received all the gifts promised to the faithful churches in the first three books of Revelation, including the fruit from the Tree of Life (Rev. 2:7). After this complete union with God, we return to the world of time, so we are asked to pray and say the post-Communion prayer, we give thanks, and then we are dismissed to go into the world to spread the Good News.

3. The Gloria

The Gloria, as it stands now, has three main stanzas, introduced by a brief couplet at the start. Unlike the Creed, which moves by stanza

---

[8]   If so, it is the second one since the three-verse Mystery of Faith spoken by the congregation during the Eucharistic Prayer is also a summary of the Mass.

from the Father to the Son to the Holy Spirit, the Gloria has ambiguity. The introductory couplet is addressed to the one God, as a whole, of course. Then first stanza begins:

"We praise you, We bless you," etc.

At once, this applies to the one God addressed in the opening couplet and to the Father only, who at the end of the first stanza is called "Lord God, Heavenly King, O God, Almighty Father." The last word, *Father*, is ambiguous; at once, it is the Father, the first Person of the Trinity, and the whole godhead. The praise, having both meanings, gives the first stanza a double-layered effect.

The second stanza is not double-layered: it refers to Jesus Christ alone, beginning with his relationship to the Father, and ending with his relationship to mankind.

The third stanza is again ambiguous, beginning with the first three words: "For you alone." At first, it looks like it refers clearly to the Son from the previous stanza, and that is one reading. In that case, the praise and description of Jesus Christ continues through the first four verses of this third stanza:

For you alone are the Holy One,
You alone are the Lord,
You alone are the Most High,
Jesus Christ.

But there is a second reading. The first three verses of the above can be read as going back to addressing the Trinity as a whole, which would be quite fitting. In that case, the last three verses describe the internal relationship of the Persons of the Trinity.[9]

Jesus Christ,
With the Holy Spirit,
In the Glory of God the Father. Amen.

---

[9] Only found again in the Doxology.

We can then say that the first and third stanzas have two readings while the second stanza has one. In this way, the Gloria, as simple as it seems, takes on the shape of a butterfly, and is quite complex:

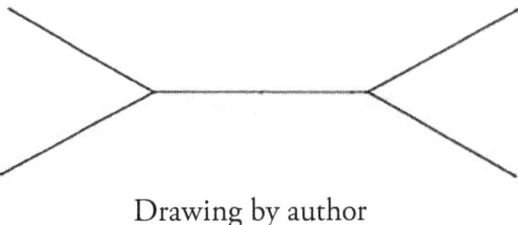

Drawing by author

Preceding the Gloria is the Kyrie, which also has this butterfly structure. The Kyrie begins with "Lord, have mercy," where Lord can mean Jesus or the whole Trinity. And it ends with "Lord, have mercy," where Lord again can have either meaning. But in the middle is the verse "Christ, have mercy," which is directed only to Christ.

4. The Mass as authorized by Jesus

The Mass is clear that the Church does not want to do anything not authorized by Christ, and in the Mass, she makes it clear that Jesus does authorize it. We offer prayers of intercession because Jesus said, "You may ask me for anything in my name, and I will do it" (John 14:14, NIV). Right after the words of Consecration, the priest quotes Jesus, "Do this in memory of me." In other words, what we have just done the priest did only on the authority of Jesus. He told us to do it; otherwise, we wouldn't dare. At the Our Father, the priest says "At the savior's command," i.e., Jesus told us to pray this prayer. Finally, Jesus' words in the words of institution: "Eat of it," "Drink from it." We have the courage to participate in Communion because Jesus told us to do so.

5. *Three images of the Mass*

There are several images of the Mass in Scripture; we'll consider three. The first speaks of mountains: "Who may ascend the mountain of the Lord" (Psalms 24:3, NIV)? Or "May the mountains bring prosperity to the people, the hills the fruit of righteousness" (Psalms 72:3, NIV). I would suggest that these now refer to the Mass. And the structure of the Mass, which is Temple-like, can be seen as a mountain which we climb when we attend Mass. Probably the most convincing quote from Scripture is Hebrews 12:22, NIV, "[Y]ou have come to Mount Zion, to the city of the living God, the heavenly Jerusalem." One scholar spoke of reading great poetry as similar to climbing mountains;[10] in addition, we can see the Mass as the climbing of a mountain.

A second image and reality is the Mass as a furnace of God's love.[11] John tells us that "God is love" (1 John 4:8), and God is wholly present at the Mass, spiritually and physically. In Daniel 3:23 (NIV), we are told "these three (Shadrach, Meshach, and Abednego) men, firmly tied, fell into the blazing furnace," though while there, they felt a cool breeze, were not harmed or touched by the smoke, did not even smell of smoke, and a fourth man appeared with them (Dan. 3:23ff.) This gives us an image of the Mass, what we enter when we attend Mass. At Mass, we experience and are surrounded by the fire of God's love.

The Mass, of course, is the primary interface between God and man. It is the central place, instituted by God, where man has intimacy with God. The image here is the Mass as a bridal chamber. Throughout the Bible, God is spoken of as a bridegroom, and the Church, both corporately and individually, is spoken of as his bride. John the Baptist gives us a very clear statement in John 3:29, NIV: "The bride belongs to the bridegroom. The friend who attends the bridegroom waits and

---

[10] A. Bartlett Giamatti.

[11] Of course, to experience this, one has to have gone to Confession; otherwise, one can't see clearly as Isaiah in the Temple (Isaiah 6:5–8) who couldn't hear clearly until he had been cleansed of his sin.

listens for him."[12] And at Mass, each of us takes God into our being, into our body. To speak the language of our generation, one might say that Mass is sex with God, except to understand that the Mass was not constructed from the image of sex but that sex is a weaker reflection, in the physical order, of the intimacy of the Mass. Finally, if we see the Apocalypse as the outline of the Mass.[13] We can read Revelation 21:2 (NIV), "I saw the Holy City, the new Jerusalem, coming down out of heaven from God, prepared as a bride beautifully dressed for her husband" as the consummation of love found in Communion at the Mass.

6. The Mass as a dance of prayer

One can see the Mass as a dance of prayer between the priest and the people with the priest leading in the sense that we see the priest's prayers and those of the people in all sorts of combinations. The Mass begins with a kind of introduction of the partners, expressing their mutual respect and mutual action to come. The priest says, "The Lord be with you." And the people respond, "And with your spirit." In part, this means may the Lord be with you so you can fulfill your part from one partner to the other, and it occurs at the start of each major section. It's similar to dance partners bowing to each other.

The most common form of dialogue in the Mass is where the priest offers a prayer to God, and the people respond amen as in the priest's presidential prayers. The people listen to the prayer and respond by saying, "Amen." In the offertory, the people's response, twice, is different: "Blessed be God forever."

Sometimes the priest and the people offer a prayer to God together in unison. One sees this in the Confiteor, in the Gloria, the Creed, the

---

[12] Bishop Jan Liesen, *The Voice of the Bridegroom* (EWTN, 2018). In his series, he tells us that even John the Baptist's quote in John 1:27 (NIV), "He is the one who comes after me, the straps of whose sandals I am not worthy to untie," refers to a verse in the Torah concerning the groom and the bridegroom.

[13] "Apocalypse" including the connotation of "unveiling" done by the bride at the marriage ceremony.

Sanctus, the Our Father, the Lamb of God, and the "Lord, I am not worthy" just before Communion. While the priest prays for us, he also prays with us for much of the Mass.

Probably the most intimate prayer between the priest and the people is at the conclusion of the offertory where the priest relies on the people to pray to God that God will accept the gifts offered at the priest's hands. It's intimate because the people's prayer is followed immediately by the priest's prayer. The people conclude the dialogue with "Amen." This section also expresses the unity of the priest's prayers and those of the people, almost like a duet in an opera.

In the Mystery of Faith, the priest and people have joint prayers expressing awe of the Eucharist, side by side. The priest's exclamation is only one line: "The mystery of faith," the people's expression, not a response to the priest but an exclamation of their own, is a three-line phrase of which there are three options. In a way, the people's three-line exclamation is their own minor Eucharistic prayer in that it sums up the action of the Mass.

The priest offers the prayer of the doxology at the end of the Eucharistic Prayer, and the people affirm it with "Amen." But the people offer their own doxology or prayer of praise after the Our Father: "For the kingdom, the power, and the glory are yours now and forever."

Here is a list of the different combinations of prayer, with an example of each:

- The priest says a prayer by himself, the people respond, "Amen."
    - The three priestly prayers, including the Collect.
- The priest recites a prayer, the people give a more elaborate response.
    - "Lord have mercy"; response: "Lord have mercy."
    - "The word of the Lord"; response: "Thanks be to God."
    - At the offertory twice, "Blessed by God forever."
- The priest and people pray together:
    - The Confiteor
    - The Gloria
    - The Creed

- The Our Father
- The priest and the people share a prayer since the priest starts it, so the people know which of the three prayers is being used, and then the people finish it: The Mystery of Faith.
- In one instance, the people say a prayer, and the priest echoes it: in the offertory, the people end the dialogue with, "It is right and just"; and the priest begins, "It is truly right and just."
- The people pray by themselves:
  - The Alleluia verse to accompany the priest to the pulpit.
  - The Mystery of Faith, a summary of the Mass.
  - The small doxology, following the Our Father.

7. The Mass as a dance of the different and the same

A motto for the Mass could be taken from the movie *The Matrix Reloaded*: "Some things never change…some things do." The Mass is accused of being the same, but it changes a lot from Mass to Mass. From the start of the Mass until the Doxology,[14] the bulk of the prayers either have options (the Greeting, the Confiteor, the Readings, the Alleluia verse, the Gospel, the Preface, the Eucharistic Prayer) or are free-form (the Sermon, the Prayer of the Faithful). The only parts of the Mass from the start to the doxology that do not change are the Sign of the Cross, the Gloria, the Alleluia, the Creed, the offertory dialogue, the Words of Institution (not even the Institution narrative, the words surrounding the Words of Institution), and the Doxology.

But interestingly, once the Doxology is complete, the Mass—putting aside the brief post-Communion prayer and dismissal—is the same. If one takes the Mass as a sketch of salvation history, and if one takes the Doxology as the offering of Jesus to the Father, the diversity before the Doxology expresses the diversity of prayer in the world before Christ, and the uniformity after the Doxology and Jesus' offering to the Father expresses the idea that after the death of Jesus, all worship is meant to be one in unity through Jesus.

---

14   It used to be the same from the Offertory dialogue to the end, the whole second half of the Mass.

Of course, one could still argue that each Mass is different; since the congregation is different, each person is different on a different day, the situation is different, often the occasion is different.[15]

8. The Mass echoes all the Sacraments

The Mass in a way contains all the other six sacraments. "Eucharist" itself means an offering of thanksgiving. Here is the list:

- Baptism—We bless ourselves with holy water on entering Church.
- Confirmation—The Creed where we freely state our belief.
- Penance—The Confiteor or Lord have mercy section.
- Sacrament of the Sick—The general intercessions for the sick and the dead.
- Marriage—Communion.
- Orders—The Words of Institution: "Do this in memory of Me."

In addition, we have the teaching of Jesus, which takes place in the readings and the Sermon.

In Revelation 1:4, we see "seven spirits before his throne [the throne of God]," yet they have a unity. If we identify the seven sacraments with the seven spirits, we see their unity in the Mass, which forms a summary of the sacraments. Of course, this does not mean that all seven sacraments are not needed, but that they form aspects of one action of God toward man.[16]

---

[15] "No man ever steps in the same river twice, for it's not the same river and he's not the same man." —Heraclitus.

[16] We can go farther and say that the Eucharist, in a sense, contains the effects of all seven sacraments since the Eucharist is Christ and Christ effects all the sacraments (this seven yet one reality mirrors that of the Trinity, the three and one).

9. The sections of the Mass have a three-part structure[17]

Having made some general statements about the Mass, and having looked at several real images of the Mass, we can proceed to look at the structure of the Mass, going from the least dramatic to the most dramatic. Each part of the Mass seems to have a three-part structure, reflecting the Trinity, and the Mass is an action of the Trinity. Sometimes the structure is three parts, each of which itself has three parts—it reminds one of the patterns in the Celtic manuscripts, the whirls within whirls.

For example, there are three main readings. The Kyrie has three statements in dialogue. The Gloria has three parts, as does the Creed (the Father, the Son, the Spirit). The Eucharistic Prayer, to which the Doxology is a separate piece, kind of the peak of the mountain, has three parts: the pre-Institution, the Mystery of Faith, the post-Institution. The Our Father section has the Our Father plus two embolisms. The Lamb of God is recited three times before Communion. The preface has three parts: the thanksgiving, the action of God for which we specifically give thanks in this Mass, the "Holy, Holy, Holy" said with the angels. The second doxology names three things belonging to God—the kingdom, the power, and the glory. The Mystery of Faith has three verses. And the offertory has three parts, each of which contains a prayer of the priest, a response by the people, and a silent prayer by the priest.

Even each of the priest's prayers—the collect, the prayer over the gifts, and the prayer after Communion—has three parts: the prayer itself, the conclusion "Through Christ our Lord,"[18] and "Amen." And there are three priests' prayers. Also, there are three long recitations, very different among themselves: the Gloria, the Creed, and the Our Father.

The priest, having just consecrated the bread and the wine, says in awe, "The Mystery of Faith," and the people respond with three phrases

---

[17] And the Mass involves all three aspects of time: past, present, and future.

[18] Which at the same time means we offer the prayer to God through Christ and that we receive the response to the prayer through Christ, like a ladder that goes up and down.

of awe. Each of the three choices for the Mystery of Faith response has three parts: the cross and Passion, the Resurrection, the Second Coming (the third option ends with "you have set us free," indicating that when Jesus comes again, we will be free).

There are three offerings of the Eucharist: This is my Body (to us); this is my Blood (to us); and the Doxology (to the Father).

The Eucharistic Prayer begins with a five-verse statement (the Holy, Holy, Holy), and ends with a five-verse statement (the Doxology). They are like two pillars. Or they are like two Stars of David in that they are each made up of five separate statements, and the Star of David is made up of five lines in different directions. It's very fitting that there is a Star of David at the beginning and the end of the Eucharistic Prayer.

The doxology makes the third five-verse prayer:

Through him and with him and in him,
Oh God, Almighty Father,
In the Unity of the Holy Spirit,
All glory and honor is yours,
Forever and ever.

It has five verses, but the first line ("Through him and with him and in him") has three parts, giving it a three-by-five structure. We can see the number five as indicating the presence of the Jewish background of the Mass since five is a symbol of the Jewish people;[19] and three as indicating the Trinity, the Christian revelation.

In the Words of Institution in the Eucharistic Prayer, the same at every Mass in the Roman Rite, is made up of two prayers. The first has three verses:

Take this, all of you, and eat of it,
for this is my Body,
which will be given up for you.

And the second has five verses:

---

[19]   The people of the five books of Moses.

Take this, all of you, and drink from it,
for this is the chalice of my Blood,
the Blood of the new and eternal covenant,
which will be poured out for you and for many for the forgiveness
of sins.
Do this in memory of me.

The conclusion of the Collect, "Through our Lord Jesus Christ, your Son, who lives and reigns with you in the unity of the Holy Spirit, one God, forever and ever" also has three lines and five phrases. One can even say that the Mass as a whole has three sections: the Liturgy of the Word, the Liturgy of the Eucharist, and the silence between the two. The Mass also has three antiphons the entrance antiphon, the alleluia verse, and the Communion antiphon.

10. The Mass as a rainbow

1. Penitential Rite/Gloria
2. Readings
3. Sermon/Creed/Prayer of the Faithful
4. Offertory/Preface
5. Eucharistic Prayer/Doxology
6. Our Father/Peace
7. Lamb of God/Communion.

1	2	3	4	5	6	7

Drawing by author

Each part of the Mass is, of course, important in its own right (or rite) but also contributes to the whole. Leaving out the greeting and the dismissal, we can divide the Mass into seven pieces which are internally similar but different from the others, each one important in itself. In this way, the structure of the Mass can be seen as a rainbow. Placed together, the colors of the rainbow form, of course, normal white light, and Jesus said he is the light of the world. As the rainbow was the sign of peace and of God's covenant with man and a sign of hope, so is the Mass.

11. The Mass as a bridge

It is clear that the Mass is a reliving of the Last Supper and of Jesus' Passion and Death in a bloodless manner. The Eucharistic Prayer calls it a memorial—it is a memorial, but it is what it memorializes.[20] At the same time, it is an anticipation of Jesus' Second Coming. And both really take place in the Mass. In this way, another form for the Mass is that of a cable strung between the two pillars where the pillars are Jesus' First and Second Comings, like a bridge. Or the Mass is the focus of two waves, one from the past and one from the future, one coming forward in time and one coming backward in time. We always see the Passover and Holy Week in the Mass correctly, but perhaps we can see also his Second Coming in the Mass just as much.

This eschatological idea presents itself first in the Confiteor: "May the Almighty and merciful God…bring us to everlasting life." Everlasting life here surely means life after we die, but it also means to bring us to Communion in this Mass,[21] so there is an identification between these two events. The Second Coming presents itself again in the Mystery of Faith; for example, "When we eat this bread and drink this cup, we proclaim your death, O Lord, until you come again." The words "come again" point to the final Second Coming, but they could also point to his coming again to each of us in Communion. One says that in the Mass the Passion and Death of Jesus are relived, that Jesus is offered to the Father in a blood-less manner,[22] and that evil is defeated; one might have to go just as far and say that in every Mass, Jesus' Second Coming

---

[20] Scott Hahn, EWTN.

[21] See John 6:24 (NIV): "Whoever eats my flesh and drinks my blood has eternal life, and I will raise them up at the last day." The verb is *has*, not *will have*.

[22] Of course, Jesus cannot die again, but he offers his body as it was at his death to the Father.

is accomplished as well. In the Mass, Jesus' birth, ministry, Passion, and Death take place, but looking back, the Second Coming takes place but in anticipation.[23]

12. The Mass as an outline of the Christian life

In the Mass, we can see the structure of the Christian's life. We begin the Christian life by entering the family at baptism (holy water). We first learn humility through seeing our own sinfulness and learn to ask for God's mercy (Confiteor). Then we spend years learning about God and salvation history (the readings and the sermon). We are then ready to make our own profession of faith (the Creed). Then we enter some kind of work or service and offer it to God (the Offertory), and we learn that God is not only the good and the true but holy (the Sanctus). We learn to give thanks. We lay down our lives for another(s) in marriage, priesthood, religious life, or in another way (Jesus does this in the Eucharistic Prayer). We learn to offer ourselves to God (the Doxology). While this action is the basis of our lives, we keep doing this work, the taking up of the cross day after day, continuing to ask for mercy and to pray (the Our Father and embolisms). Finally, we die ("Behold the Lamb of God" prayer since we meet Jesus at death), and (we hope) enter into God's presence and rest, perhaps after a time in purgatory (Communion).

In addition, Fr. Benedict Groeschel in *Spiritual Passages* (New York: Crossroad, 1983) elaborates on the classic progression in the spiritual life from the Purgative Way to the Illuminative Way to the Unitive Way, though one experiences pieces of the other two at any point in the journey. This progression, found in particular in St. Augustine (Fr.

---

[23] This solves another problem. It seems reasonable that the presence of Christ in the world would always increase and never decrease with time, beginning with the prediction of his advent. It seems that Jesus left us and is less here until he returns. But if the Mass is as described above, then Jesus is indeed more present to us after his Death, Resurrection, and Ascension than while he walked the earth (it also makes sense of John 14:28, "If you loved me, you would rejoice that I'm going to the Father," since among other reasons, Jesus would now be even more present to us).

Benedict Groeschel's favorite), can be seen in the Mass as we confess our sins (Purgative Way); learn about God and the spiritual life (Illuminative Way); and live in union with God in Communion (Unitive Way). The Mass then not only contains the path or way of man and woman's progress in the Sacraments and over time but also in terms of interior spiritual growth.

13. The Mass as a biography of Jesus

The Mass also sketches the Life of Christ. It is a biography of Christ written by the Holy Spirit (and the Church), and more than a biography, Christ relives it each time Mass is said. The Holy Water font marks the Presentation, the entrance into the spiritual life for a Jewish person. We confess our sinfulness, which of course Jesus didn't have to do, but it matches his hidden life of obedience in Nazareth and the baptism of John, which was one of repentance. Then the readings and sermon parallel Jesus' teaching during the three years of his ministry, which is summed up by the Creed.

Then begins the Liturgy of the Eucharist, which parallels the Passion of Christ, starting with the thanksgiving of the Preface, and the praise of God. The Eucharistic Prayer lines up with the Last Supper, including Jesus' priestly prayer, here said by the priest in the name of the Church, and the words of institution confect the Sacrament.[24] At the Doxology, Jesus dies on the cross; as a matter of fact, the words of the Doxology could be exactly the words Jesus said as he died on the Cross. The pall is placed on the chalice, symbolizing the tomb. Our standing up after the Doxology symbolizes the Resurrection. Right after that, man reconciled with the Father, the Mass has the Our Father and then quotes what Jesus said right in the Upper Room after his Resurrection: "Peace be with you."

---

[24] According to St. Thomas. Though now it seems the view that the whole Eucharistic Prayer confects the Sacrament (historically, there is one Eucharistic Prayer that has the epiclesis after the words of institution; cf. Mazza, *The Eucharistic Prayers of the Roman Rite*).

The congregation's Doxology, "For thine is the kingdom," indicates that the Ascension has taken place since the Father has given the kingdom to the Son. Then Jesus walks with us and assists us as we make our way trying to do his will in this life. And then Jesus comes to us in Communion as a Second Coming.

The Fathers made this parallel in great detail, this small sketch just brings it back to mind. Also, we note that in the Mass, Jesus' earthly life is not only told but, in reality, relived by Jesus before our very eyes. On one occasion, a priest said, "How wonderful it must have been to be at Calvary," by which he meant to be present at the crucial event in human history. But we are present at this event at every Mass.

And the Church, and every priest in particular, out of love retells/reenacts/relives/participates in the reliving of the life of Christ each day. One pictures an army of lives of Christ in each Mass spreading throughout the world from the one in Jerusalem and the Last Supper.

14. The Mass as a history of salvation

The Mass, wonderful that it holds all these contexts, is also a sketch of the history of Salvation. The Mass does not begin with the sign of the cross but with the entrance antiphon—the people crying out for God. Then comes the sign of the cross, God's sign,[25] and is God's response which is the source of the grace that fuels all of salvation history. We confess our sins in the Confiteor—mankind lived without law for many centuries, then the Law made the Jewish people aware of their sinfulness so it could be forgiven and corrected. The human race, from the beginning, praised God, which we see in the Gloria. And mankind always asked God for what he or she needed, which we see in the Collect.

The Jewish people were then entrusted with the Word of God, which they revered, and they studied it. We see this stage in the readings from the Old Testament, the Psalms, and the New Testament. Then

---

[25] It is a symbol that visually describes the Commandments Jesus gave us: to love God (the vertical beam) and to love one's neighbor (the horizontal beam), and this is a summary, Jesus tells us, of the whole Law.

Christ is born and grows up and teaches the Jewish people to whom he is sent first and proclaims to them the nearness of the kingdom of God. We see in the proclamation of the Gospel, the sermon, and the creed. Then Jesus readies for his Passion and Death and the Last Supper, which we see in the Offertory and the Eucharistic Prayer. At the elevation of the bread and wine, Jesus is on the cross; at the Doxology, Jesus dies on the cross and offers himself to his Father.[26]

We stand at this point, symbolizing his Resurrection. Jesus has returned us to our original relationship with God our Father and has taken his place at the right hand of the Father as King of heaven and earth. So from that time until the end of time, the Church prays to Jesus for all our needs, spiritual and temporal. We have been commanded by external commands and formed internally. We indicate both by saying, "At the Savior's command and formed by divine teaching," and we say the Our Father first and an embolism. And when we say, "For thine is the kingdom and the power and the glory," we indicate the Ascension.

Then mankind, having done the work assigned to it, helps to bring God's kingdom which includes goodness in all its forms to earth[27] and defeating evil to the end of time. Facing the end of time, mankind again prays for God's mercy, acknowledging him as the one who takes away sins in the "Lamb of God." Then the "Behold the Lamb of God" and the Fraction, which marks the return of Jesus, whole and entire, the reunification of the body and blood of Christ. Then Jesus gives himself to us in Communion, which is mankind entering into God's rest.

---

[26]   An authoritative interpretation is given by Olive Dawson who has lived for twenty years on the Eucharist alone as she spreads the word about a Marian visionary in Dublin. At the elevation of the Host, Jesus is on the cross, looking at us with love; at the elevation of the chalice, Jesus has died, and the centurion's spear pierces his side and fills the chalice with his blood; at the doxology with our amen, the Church offers him to the Father; when we stand, we have the Resurrection. It makes sense for all these events to take place within the Eucharistic Prayer, the heart of the Mass. Olive Dawson's description also makes it clear why water is added to the chalice—to mirror the blood and water that flowed from his side.

[27]   Which includes goodness in all its forms.

15. The Six Parts of the Mass

Putting aside the shorter parts of the greeting and the dismissal, the clearest division of the Mass is into six parts. Each part has its own purpose, feeling, and culmination:

1. The Confiteor, including the Gloria (sung in part for granting us forgiveness).
2. The readings and the Proclamation of the Gospel.
3. The teaching of the Sermon, the Creed, and the Prayer of the Faithful.
4. The Offertory: the preparing of the gifts and of ourselves.
5. The Preface where we offer ourselves to God, the Eucharistic Prayer, and the Doxology where Jesus is Offered to the Father.
6. The Communion Rite, from the Our Father to Communion, where we have been reconciled to the Father and also received the peace of the Holy Spirit in a decision to Communion, as a result of Jesus' Offering.

Not only does the Mass have six parts, but there are three locations where the Mass takes place: the pulpit/ambo, the altar, and the priest's chair. And each place remarkably plays six roles during the Mass. Starting with the altar,[28] proceeding in order, used only in the second half of the Mass:

1. Christ's crib.
2. The Last Supper table.
3. The cross.
4. The tomb.[29]
5. The Upper Room the night of the Resurrection.

---

[28] The altar has three cloths of linen because there were three linens found in the tomb: the Shroud of Turin, the Veil of Manoppello, and the cloth in Spain filled with blood.
[29] After the Great Amen, Jesus is buried in the tomb. The pall is placed on the chalice, representing the stone in front of the tomb.

6. The Communion table (as at Emmaus).

From the priest's chair the priest performs:

1. The greeting.
2. The Confiteor.
3. The Collect.
4. The Creed.
5. The prayer after Communion.
6. The dismissal.

Finally the ambo/pulpit, used only in the first half of the Mass, has these six roles:

1. The prediction of Christ in the first reading.
2. The praise of God in the Psalm.
3. The wisdom of how to live in Christ in the second reading.
4. The proclamation and words of Christ himself.
5. The teaching on what was heard in the sermon.
6. The receiving of what we ask for in the Prayer of the Faithful.

One finds in the Apocalypse the idea that evil doesn't just do bad things, it doesn't just harm things, it also mocks the good, acts like the good in an attempt to replace it. So, for example, in the two beasts plus the third beast, one finds a mockery of the Trinity, and the harlot in the desert (dare I say it!) is a mockery of Mary. We can see from these examples that evil does not just dislike or prefer not to have God; evil hates God. And the number used as a label for evil is, of course, 666, which not only identifies people in history (for example, Nero, whose name adds up to 666) but indicates that there is something identifiable as 666 in God's plan that the beast mocks by taking on this number.

It could be that six is a very important number in God's plan. Genesis describes God as creating the world in six days, though he did two things on the sixth day. So that is the first six. Then Jesus completed—and redeemed, restored—the world in six days, from

Monday of Holy Week through Saturday of Holy Week, which the Church deeply commemorates in detail every year. That is the second six. The third six, since it has six parts and is a continuation and extension of Jesus' work, is the Mass with its six parts.[30] This 666, which forms the very spine of the creation of the natural and spiritual world, could be what is mocked by evil in the Apocalypse (it also shows the importance of the Mass that it stands as the equal third in this sequence[31]).

I would suggest that the Mass in its structure is found most clearly in the Song of Songs and that the Mass could justly be called "the Song of Songs." This book gives the Mass a beautiful name. The Song of Songs has six parts. Each part begins with the woman looking for her beloved, agonizingly, and then finding him at the end of the part, only to begin the next part without him again. And in each part of the Mass, a specific task is begun and brought to completion, and union with the Lord is accomplished in a different sense at the end of each part.[32]

The Mass's ability to hold all these contexts at the same time, in simple words, argues that it is not constructed by man but by God with the Church's help—which is, of course, the case.[33]

---

[30] One might say that the Rosary, having six parts—five mysteries and the beginning prayers—could also be in this group.

[31] If one adds from Elizabeth Kolbert, *The Sixth Extinction* (Henry Holt: 2014) that there are six major extinctions in the development of life of earth, even the span of life on earth has six divisions.

[32] A second similarity between the Song of Songs and the Mass is that each of the six parts of Song begins with the woman searching for her love, and both halves of the Mass begin not with the priest but with the people calling to God: the first part with the entrance antiphon or song and the second half with the procession of the gifts, asking that they be made holy. The Mass earns the title "The Song of Songs."

[33] One could say also that creation itself can be divided into three parts and each divided into two subparts, making six parts in total, created over six days: the spiritual (angels, the human soul); the material (the physical, the emotional); the intellectual (ideas discovered, created).

16. The Mass and the Apocalypse

The Fathers of the Church wrote extensively on the relationship between the Apocalypse and the Mass, suggesting that "apocalypse," meaning "unveiling," described the Mass as seen from heaven. On the basis of this word, they also expressed the idea that the ultimate relation between God and man is that of a marriage as a bride removes her veil after her marriage; the Church is the bride of Christ. This connection is also made by Christ himself in Matthew 16:28:[34] Jesus refers to the end of time but also to something that will happen within the lifetimes of some of those hearing him. What else could he be referring to except his advent in the Mass?

One notes that the Mass is not discussed extensively in the letters of the New Testament, though it is not left out. One surmises that they did not write openly about it in order to protect the Eucharist from its enemies.[35] But the Mass is so central—why was it left out? It could be that in the vision of the Apocalypse, we have a letter devoted to the Mass, which makes up for its absence. And its enemies could never have used this vision to lead them to the Mass. The Lincolnesque Scott Hahn, in his book, *The Lambs Supper*, writes that the Apocalypse relates to the Mass as the menu does to a meal, and he makes a convincing case. His conversion from Protestantism to Catholicism took place at a Mass where he realized he was seeing the book of Revelation in action. Let's try to pin down the points in the Apocalypse that we can easily identify with points in the Mass.[36]

---

[34] "Truly I tell you, some who are standing here will not taste death until they see the Son of Man coming in His kingdom" (BSB).

[35] But what St. Paul was doing in his voyages around the Mediterranean was establishing Churches, i.e., Eucharistic Communities, not just telling people about the Messiah. The only other longish description of the Mass in the Letters is in the Letter to the Hebrews (12:18–24).

[36] It would be an example of God's sense of humor that the Protestants who have been trying to untangle the book of Revelation for centuries couldn't do so because they lacked (through no fault of their own) the main key to its understanding: the Mass.

- Chapter 1: The vision takes places on the Lord's Day, Sunday, the day of Mass.
- Chapter 1: We are given a blessing for listening (1:3), as at the start of Mass.
- Chapter 1: The candles are lit (1:12), the first thing we do at Mass.
- Chapters 1–3: An examination of conscience for the Church's, corresponding to the Penitential Rite.
- Chapters 1–3: What is promised to those who persevere can be applied to life after death, but also apply to what one receives at Mass: "The victor shall not be harmed by the second death" (2:11); "I shall give some of the hidden manna" (2:17); "I shall… give a white amulet upon which is inscribed a new name" (2:17); "I will give authority over the nations" (2:26); "The victor will… be dressed in white…and I will never erase his name from the Book of Life but will acknowledge his name in the presence of my Father and of his angels" (3:5); "The victor I will make into a pillar in the temple of my God and he will never leave it again" (3:12); "the right to sit with me on my throne" (3:21). And some phrases are left out.
- Chapter 4: God is fully present. This takes place after we have confessed; we say the Gloria. The four living creatures, looking like a lion, a calf, the face of a man, and an eagle (4:7)—the symbols used for the four Gospels, which will soon be read— indicates that their source is heaven.
- Chapter 5: The Scroll is opened, and the only one worthy of opening it is the Lamb who was slain.
- Chapters 6–9: The Lamb breaks open the scrolls and the pictures of the future comes forth. The angels play a role in bringing the messages forth.
- Verses 5:7; 8:3: Incense is offered in golden bowls, the prayers of the saints, and the prayer of the faithful.
- Verse 8:1: The silence in heaven—a silence separates the other readings from the Gospel, allowing the people to contemplate the readings.

- Chapter 10: The small Scroll, no doubt the Gospel, is given to John to swallow and to proclaim, to prophesy.
- Chapter 11: The altar and temple are measured (prepared?), and the number of worshippers counted (as we do to know the number of hosts for Communion). The proclamation, sermon, and creed being finished, the two witnesses show that they were willing to give their lives for their teaching.
- Chapter 12: At the end of chapter 11, the Temple of God in heaven in opened, revealing the "ark of his covenant," which is not only the Church but Mary, the woman giving birth to a son destined to rule the nations. Jesus is "born" on the altar, incarnate under the appearances of bread and wine, the second half of Mass and the Eucharistic Prayer.
- Chapters 13–18: Sensing its ultimate defeat, evil increases its efforts to destroy the child and the woman but fails. There is a series of beasts, ending with the harlot of Babylon, which mimic the good.[37] There is a great conflict between God with his angels and evil, interspersed with descriptions of the holy ones and their praises of God. The holy ones seem to be onlookers; the conflict is mainly between the angels and the beasts.[38]
- Chapters 18–20: Evil is defeated, the last being the devil "who had led them astray" (20:10). This victory is the consequence of Jesus' obedience to the Father. This would correspond in the Mass to consequences of the Sacrifice at the Doxology:

---

[37] The three beasts mimic the Trinity, one creating the other and giving it power. The harlot mimics Mary and the Church. Babylon mimics the heavenly Jerusalem of chapters 21 and 22.

[38] In the apocalypse, there is no detailed mention of Jesus' earthly life (the subject of the Gospels). Specifically, the apocalypse does not describe Jesus' Passion and Death. It might be contained in verse 5:6: "Then I saw standing in the midst of the throne and the four living creatures and the elders a Lamb that seemed to have been slain." He is not sacrificed again as his sacrifice is always present before God, but in one sense, it is given to the Church to reoffer or become present to during the Mass. One could also find a brief reference to Jesus' Passion and Death in 19:13: "He wore a cloak that had been dipped in blood."

reconciliation with the Father, peace of the Holy Spirit, Communion with Jesus, defeating evil externally and internally.

- Chapters 21, 22: The New Jerusalem comes down from heaven and is measured and described. In the Mass, this corresponds to Communion and its effect in the soul and in the community.[39]
- Epilogue: John is told that words are not to be added or subtracted from this book (verses 18, 19), and Jesus says he will come soon. But hasn't he just come? This corresponds to the end of Mass where Jesus has just come, but we are dismissed and sent to go out into world, knowing that he will come (again) soon at the next Mass and at the end of time.

With this many points of contact between the Apocalypse and the Mass, it seems justified to say that the Apocalypse, this "prophetic book" (Epilogue 7), is the view of Mass from heaven as one of its two or three main contexts (the other two being the history of the world from the Ascension to the end of time and a picture of the state of the world at any moment from the Ascension to the end of time).

It is also notable that several periods of time are mentioned in the Apocalypse, and they unfold (except for one) to three and a half years, for example "a time, times, and half a time" (Rev. 12:14, ESV). If God created the world in seven days, and if salvation history is divided into two halves, it makes sense that it would occupy three and a half units of time.[40] The two halves are the half before Christ in expectation and the half after the advent of Christ; the Apocalypse describes the second half of salvation history. And the Mass said by the Church exists during the "second half" of salvation history.

---

[39] Coming down from heaven, it seems to meet the earthly city which strains to try to establish justice itself.

[40] It also gives us reason to believe that Jesus' Public Ministry lasted 3½ years, since the creation of the world took seven units of time.

Also, one has to say that in the Mass, one receives all the things that are promised to the faithful churches in Apocalypse 2–3. The next time someone says they get nothing out of the Mass, one can use this list:[41]

- "The right to eat of the Tree of Life that is in the garden of God" (2:7).
- "Shall not be harmed by the second death" (2:11).
- "I shall give some of the hidden manna" (2:17).
- "I shall give a white amulet upon which is inscribed a new name, which no one knows except the one who receives it" (2:17).
- "I will give authority over the nations" (2:26).
- "The victor will be dressed in white" (3:5).
- "I will never erase his name from the Book of Life" (3:5).
- "[I] will acknowledge his name in the presence of my father and of his angels" (3:5).
- "I will make [him or her] a pillar in the temple of my God" (3:12).
- "He will never leave it [this temple] again" (3:12).
- "On him [or her] I will inscribe the name of my God and the name of the city of my God, which comes down from heaven from my God, as well as my new name" (3:12).
- "I will enter his house and dine with him, and he with me" (3:20).
- "I will give him [or her] the right to sit with me on my throne, as I myself first won the victory and sit with my Father on his throne."[42]

17. The Mass and Holy Week

It could be that each time the Mass is celebrated, we reenact, and Christ actually relives Holy Week.

---

41   "The victor" spoken of no doubt is one who lived his or her life according to God's will for him or her, but also the one who is prepared for Mass and perseveres to the end of the Mass.

42   Probably the source of the Santa Claus tradition.

- The alleluia before the Gospel parallels the welcome of Palm Sunday.
- The readings and the sermon parallel the teaching of Jesus in the Temple in the first half of Holy Week.
- The offertory parallels the preparations for the Last Supper.
- The Eucharistic Prayer parallels the Last Supper: Holy Thursday.
- The Doxology parallels the Death on the Cross: Good Friday.
- The silence after the Doxology, though odd to have silence at the high point of the Mass: Holy Saturday, the king is asleep.
- We stand: the Resurrection.
- "Peace be with you:" Easter Sunday evening in the Upper Room.
- Communion: the event on the road to Emmaus, where the two disciples no doubt consumed the Eucharist Jesus left with them.

18. What is the Mass?

To summarize what the Mass is, one can start with common ideas about the Mass and take them one step further:

1. The Mass is a collection of recollections about Jesus' words and deeds and a discussion of them. Yes, but it is more.[43]
2. The Mass is an ordered collection of recollections, beginning at the start of Jesus' earthly life and ending at his death. Yes, but it is more.
3. The Mass is a retelling of the Life of Jesus from birth to death. Yes, but it is more.
4. The Mass is a retelling of the earthly Life of Jesus told by an ordained minister, someone close to Christ, and so better able to tell it. Yes, but it is more.
5. The Mass is a reliving of the earthly Life of Jesus by an ordained minister, who not only retells it but relives it as an alter Christus (another Christ). Yes, but it is more.

---

[43] The Protestant service.

6. The Mass is a reliving of the earthly Life of Jesus by an ordained minister under the direction of the Church and of Jesus himself. Yes, but it more.

7. The Mass a reliving of the earthly life of Jesus by Jesus himself, under signs and symbols, through the efficient cause of the priest. Before our eyes Jesus relives his earthly life—his birth, life, preaching, suffering, death, offering to the Father, resurrection, ascension, reigning from heaven, and return in glory.

19. The Eucharist[44]

Jesus states that he is "the light of the world" (John 8:12) and so invites us to study light to find characteristics of Jesus by analogy. One, of course, is that nothing travels faster than light, making light and Jesus unique and of the highest excellence. In Newtonian physics, time and mass and length are absolute quantities. But in Einstein's physics of relativity, these are not absolutes; instead, there is just one constant: the speed of light. Length, time, and mass all adjust themselves so that no matter what the relative speed of the observer, light is always measured by anyone moving in any direction at any speed or acceleration as going at the same speed "Jesus is the same yesterday and today" (Hebrews 13:8). In addition, as everything is related to light, all is related to Jesus.

As a particle travels at speeds close to the speed of light, three things happen: its mass gets larger, its clocks go slower, and it decreases in size, and the equations describe to what extent these things happen at a given speed. There is the interesting question, what would happen to the earth if, though it is now travelling at a good speed, it were travelling close to the speed of light? First, its mass would increase and would tend to infinite mass as the speed of the earth got closer to that of light. Second,

---

[44] It is wonderful that the Eucharist is in two species—wine, which allows even infants or the sick to receive; and bread that can be broken into smaller pieces if there are not enough Hosts.

its measure of time would get slower and slower, tending toward zero[45] (which is an analogy for Christ in the Eucharist since Jesus in heaven is outside of time). Third, its size decreases; in fact, it would be the size of a wafer. The size of a Host.

In summary, one can say that in receiving the Eucharist, one is receiving something of infinite importance and power, something from outside of time and of the size of a wafer. One is by analogy receiving the earth traveling at the speed of light.

20. "The Mass"

There are at least three names of the Mass: the Pascal Mystery (stressing its basis in Judaism and the Passion of Christ); the Eucharist (stressing that it is the Thanksgiving Offering); and the Mass. The third name is unusual. In the early persecuted and hidden church, it could have been used as a word to conceal the Mass, a word that hadn't been used before. The word comes close to the word *Messiah*, in French, *Messie*, from the Hebrew *Messiach*; so that might be its source: the Mass is the coming of the Messiah. Perhaps the original ending of the Mass was "Go, the Messiah [his work] is finished," and it was shortened to "Go, the Mass is finished" for security reasons.[46] But when we go to Mass, we are going to see the Messiah.

Another meaning of the name Mass comes from its reflection in physics. In physics, "mass" is a primitive concept, in a way an undefined concept. It might be considered as measurable by the force it takes to change the direction or velocity of an object. But mass is not weight; the weight is how much force the object exerts as a result of the gravitational field it finds itself in. So we weigh so much on earth but

---

[45] As it gets more massive, it takes more and more energy to increase the speed of the earth. It would require an infinite amount of energy to accelerate it to the speed of light. But the increase of mass would be a parallel to an increase in power or force.

[46] But this is just a speculation, if "Mass" is a new word not used before in this context. That the word "Mass" comes from "Messiach" or "Messiah" would mean that the early Church, as we do now, recognized that the principal celebrant at the Mass and its first cause is Christ Himself.

less on the moon. In a similar way, the Mass is of differing weight to the different people who attend or don't attend. On one end are those who don't attend and don't value the Mass; it might be as light as a feather to them. But to those who attend seriously, it is the most powerful or weighty thing in their lives.

Lastly, in view of the infinite mass mentioned above, "the Mass" might refer to the objectively infinite power of the Mass, reminiscent of the rock Daniel saw hewn from the mountain without human hands.

The Rosary

Writing an essay on the comparison of the rosary and the Mass is a joy and pleasure, a labor of love. Mary told us in introducing the first Saturday devotion that we are to receive Communion, go to Confession, say the rosary, and spend fifteen minutes in addition to saying the rosary, meditating on the rosary in general. The only reason for this meditation must be that the form of the rosary itself has meaning and that it's not simply a random collection of prayers. The following reflections are thoughts from my fifteen-minute monthly reflections, and they follow five lines of thought:

1. A comparison of the Rosary and the Mass.
2. The rosary as a Life of Christ, a fifth Gospel.
3. The Hail Mary as a life of Mary.
4. The whole rosary as a life of Mary.
5. The rosary as a sketch of salvation history.

1. If we make a comparison between the rosary and the Mass or to claim that the rosary is Mary's Mass, we have to show that each major part of the Mass can be found in the rosary and vice versa.

The Mass	The Rosary
Sign of the Cross	Sign of the Cross
Penitential rite	Three Hail Marys asking for faith,
hope and charity	
Gloria	The Glory Be at the end of each mystery
Readings	Meditation on the individual mysteries
Sermon	Our thoughts on the mysteries, led by Mary
Creed	Said at the start of the rosary

Universal prayer	Intentions stated at the start of the rosary
Offertory	Our attention, devotion, and detachment
Eucharistic prayer	Prayers for the pope and the Church at the end
Words of Institution	Each time we say the name Jesus He enters world
Doxology	Each mention of Jesus offers Him to the Father
Our Father	Said at the start of each mystery
Peace/Holy Spirit	The Glory Be includes the Holy Spirit
Communion	Each time we say the name *Jesus*, we receive Him
Sign of the Cross	Sign of the Cross

Also, we note that the rosary, if we add to the rosary the Fatima prayers as requested, has seventy-three prayers as the Mass in the smallest division has seventy-three distinct parts.[47]

The Mass is the life of Christ written by the Holy Spirit with the help of the Church; the rosary is the life of Christ written by Mary through her eyes. If they are two very different Masses, they are complimentary: the rosary we can say anywhere; the rosary can be said by anyone; the rosary has the parts of the Mass in different places and in different frequencies; their structures are very different. For example, in the Mass, Jesus is received fully once, where in the rosary, Jesus is received spiritually fifty times.

One notes that the main actions in the Mass are that Jesus comes into the world; Jesus is offered to the Father; we receive Jesus in Communion. These events occur at different places in the Mass and once only. But in line with the chart above, they

---

[47] And the Bible has seventy-three books.

all take place together in the rosary each time we say the name Jesus. He enters the world; He is offered to the Father by us; we receive Him in (spiritual) Communion.

2. The second idea is that the rosary is a life of Christ, a fifth Gospel, and this idea is pretty obvious. The twenty mysteries—note that *mystery* is an older word for *sacrament*— start with the Conception of Jesus at the Annunciation and conclude after His Ascension and enthronement in heaven. There is a structural difference: there are four Gospels, and they each span the whole life of Christ, but the rosary spans the whole life of Christ once over four sets of mysteries (Pope St. John Paul II said all twenty decades every day).

    Another difference is whereas the Gospels tell a continuous account, the rosary is an account of the life of Christ by major episode. Perhaps the difference reflects the difference between the male and the female outlook (also perhaps T. S. Eliot had Mary and the rosary in mind when he described the woman as "the lady of situations"[48]). Jesus tells us to "take up your cross every day" (Luke 9:23), and we start the Mass and the rosary with the cross. In terms of major events in the life of Christ, perhaps the only mystery missing is the Second Coming, which would be the twenty-first mystery.

3. Next we have to show that the Hail Mary can be seen as a life of Mary. Another list is necessary, line by line. On the left side is the Hail Mary, on the right is the event in Mary's life:

Hail Mary	The coming advent of Mary
Full of Grace	Her Immaculate Conception
The Lord is with you	She lives with God completely
Blessed are you among women	She will be the unique mother of the Messiah
And blessed the fruit of your womb, Jesus	She gives birth to Jesus

---

[48] T. S. Eliot, "The Waste Land," line 50.

Holy Mary	She continues to live perfect holiness
Mother of God	She and St. Joseph raise Jesus to adulthood
Pray for us sinners, now and at the hour of our death.	Her role as intercessor with after her death.

It's a comforting thought that in the rosary, we recount the life of Mary fifty-three times.

4. For number 4, we take the rosary as a whole. The introductory prayers with the Hail Holy Queen (which is passed in silence) can be seen as the hidden life of Mary as she developed in wisdom and virtue. Then is the first mystery, the Annunciation, and her whole life with Jesus follows, the last two mysteries celebrating her being given her place in heaven. Then we say the Hail Holy Queen because she has carried out God's plan for her life perfectly. Then the final prayers for the Church ask for her help in her new role as primary intercessor. The rosary started with the cross, which is the source of all grace, and ends with the cross also, the sign of God. We see here, of course, the intertwining of the life of Mary with the life of Christ. Although she doesn't appear on some of the mysteries (the sorrowful mysteries), she is always there.

5. Lastly, we can see the Rosary as a sketch of Salvation history:
   i. The Cross: the center and source, from all eternity the sign of God.
   ii. The first Our Father: God acts, the creation of the world.
   iii. The three Hail Mary's: the three-part genealogy of Jesus in Matthew's Gospel, i.e., the history of Judaism. The development of virtue and worship in Judaism, and even in the pagan nations in other ways at the same time.[49]

---

[49] In a world without sin, the pagan religions would not have had demonic influences.

iv. The second Our Father: God acts again, the saving of Mary from Original Sin, the hidden life of Mary. It is also the first prayer of the first mystery.

v. We pass the Hail Holy Queen bead without saying a prayer: it reminds us that we are looking at the Life of Christ with Mary. But Mary hasn't done anything yet.

vi. The twenty mysteries: the life of Christ, from Conception to Death to Resurrection and Ascension and his bringing Mary to heaven.

vii. The Hail, Holy Queen: Mary has accomplished her task and has been assumed into heaven and crowned Queen of Heaven and earth. She is also the Mother of the Church and our mother.

viii. The Our Father reminds us that Jesus' life was and is from and directed to the Father.

ix. The three Hail Mary's: these are prayers for the pope, the leader of the Church through time, surrounded by Jesus and the prayer he gave us to say. The three might represent the three ages of the Church as in Revelation to the year 500; the 1000-year reign; then the period after Satan was released again for a short time until the end of time.[50]

x. The Our Father: the Second Coming, God is victorious.

xi. The sign of the Cross, the eternal sign of God, which will appear at the end of time.

Of course, these four contexts or schemes are all present at the same time and overlap. We can even add the Holy Spirit and the Father since we pray to them also in the background of the rosary prayer.

Finally, Olive Dawson, who has lived on the Eucharist alone for twenty years and who spreads the message of Mary given to a visionary in Dublin since 1988 around the world, has recently introduced the "Pearl Rosary" from the visionary. In addition to the image, the book, and the blue scapular given by Mary, Mary told the visionary that this

---

[50] cf. Revelation 20.

rosary and scapular are the fulfillment of her promise to St. Dominic that she would save the world through the rosary and the scapular, which I take to mean that this is their final form. The book has a short paragraph for each day on the right-hand page and a "pearl," a short phrase from Mary, on the left-hand page.

The book is meant to be Mary speaking to one personally. If one has a question or difficulty, one says a prayer to Mary and then opens the book and reads a pearl; this is Mary speaking to the person at that moment. I tested this claim the other day. I was at Adoration, and I opened the book, and the pearl was "It's time to pray." The messages are very simple and direct, and they do make one aware that Mary is right with us and hears our tiniest prayers, like a mother with a small child.[51] A clue that it is a real vision is that this rosary, in which we say the Memorare and meditate on a saying of Mary from her book (a "pearl") at each decade instead of meditating on a Mystery of Christ is not meant to replace the usual rosary but is to be said in addition to it.

The image of Mary in the picture—the twelve stars, the garment like the sun, the cherubim like a cloud at her feet, a miraculous image which has to be kept behind glass—is very reminiscent of the image of Our Lady of Guadalupe (it's almost as if Mary wanted to bookmark her apparitions, beginning with the Apparition at Guadalupe with another very similar image). Mary described the image to the visionary and said that its meaning is Mary as the Mediatrix of all graces, which is the fifth Marian dogma all hope to see declared as soon as possible. She has under her left arm a stain of blood which runs down to a Host and into a chalice, meaning that the graces from Christ's Passion and Death are with her to distribute, for where would one hold a tool if one's hands were together in prayer? Under one's left arm so one's right hand is free. And the rosary that hangs from her hands with the Crucifix at the bottom has only fifteen decades because the image was given before Pope St. John Paul II added five more decades in 2002. This image might be in a way a bookend to the image of Our Lady of Guadalupe,

---

[51] Jesus tells us we need to "become as little children" (Matt. 18:3 KJV), and little children have their mothers at their side.

the first given at the start of Christianity in the Americas, and this one at the end.

In summary, one might conclude that the rosary is as powerful as the Mass, just in a different way, not through power directly but through intercession. And while the first Mass had the same power as any other Mass, and the form of the Mass quickly took shape and is essentially unchanged, the rosary developed over the centuries.[52]

---

[52] For an excellent description of the history of the Rosary by Fr. Don Calloway, see https://www.youtube.com/watch?v=dwVdYXyxln0&feature=youtu.be.

The Apocalypse[53]

John the Apostle, being given the care of Mary, had become the bishop of Ephesus and eventually had seven Churches for which he was responsible. Today we would call him the metropolitan archbishop of Ephesus with suffragan dioceses. On the Lord's Day,[54] Sunday, when he would have celebrated Mass surrounded by his priests and people, he had this vision. The meaning of the word *apocalypse* is unveiling, specifically the kind of unveiling that happens at a wedding when the bride removes her veil after the vows are given, and the couple, having gone through a year of engagement or betrothal, are united. One interesting note is that the life of Jesus really does not appear in the Apocalypse nor does his Passion and Death.[55] If one can say that in the Gospels, we see Jesus, the Suffering Servant, one can say that in the Apocalypse, we see Jesus, the conquering warrior. And Judaism expected both kinds of Messiah and weren't sure if they would be one person or two (cf. Roy Schoeman, *What Is Judaism?*).

One overall interpretative structure of the Apocalypse is that it reveals the history of mankind and of the world from the start of the Church until the end of time. At the start, Jesus speaks to John from heaven, so it is clearly after the Ascension. In this view, we can use the

---

[53] I use the titles "Apocalypse" and "Revelation" interchangeably (we might weep as John does in 5:4 that there is no one to open or interpret the book for us; but as the Lion of Judah unseals the book in 5:5, so the Church interprets the Apocalypse).

[54] The parallel, of course, that James Joyce mocked in creating Bloom's day in *Ulysses*.

[55] The only implied reference could be Apocalypse 12:5-6 (BSB): "And she gave birth to a son, a male child, who will rule all the nations with an iron scepter; and her child was caught up to God and to His throne. And the woman fled into the wilderness where God had prepared a place for her to be nourished for 1,260 days." It's the briefest life of Christ, from Birth to Ascension, with the rest of the life of Mary attached. Using a 360-day year, 1,260 days is exactly three and a half, which suggests the beautiful idea that Mary's mission after the Ascension of Christ in some sense lasted the same length in time as the public ministry of Jesus.

Apocalypse to try to determine the shape of what will happen in the world over time. A second overall interpretation is that the Apocalypse describes the situation of the world at any given time after the Ascension of Christ.

In that view, given any year or generation, we can try to identify who in the world is playing each role. Since both are true at once, the Apocalypse has a kind of cross-like structure, one reading extending along the lines of time, the other extending at any given time to the ends of the world. In both views, the history is told from the view of the Church with the Church and Christ at its center.

The first view of the Apocalypse, it is the story of the Church and the world, more specifically from the death of the apostles to the end of time.[56] It begins with Jesus giving a status report to John about the churches in his responsibility. Jesus has already ascended into heaven and has sent the Holy Spirit into the world. And clearly, the Apocalypse ends with the return of Jesus, the vanquishing of evil, the descent of the heavenly city to earth in a spousal sense, and the end of time. So the Apocalypse seems to span the time from the end of the Apostolic Age and the Deposit of Faith, which closed at the death of the last apostle, to the end of this age or the end of time.

In this view, a brief summary of the Apocalypse might be:

- Chapter 1: The Apocalypse begins on the Lord's Day, Sunday on the Island of Patmos, near the end of the life of St. John. John receives the first vision, and he turns around and sees a lampstand with one like the son of man. He turns around: this is behind him, the whole of Jewish history and the advent, passion, and death of the Jewish Messiah who is now speaking to him.

- Chapters 2–3: John is told about the state of the Churches in Asia of which he is the bishop or metropolitan. They are his

---

[56] John was martyred by tradition by being placed in boiling oil, but it was not allowed to hurt him, so he was exiled to the Island of Patmos where he wrote the Apocalypse. So it was written through an apostle, but like God speaking to Moses, it speaks of what would happen after John, the last apostle.

responsibility. It focuses on the internal strengths and weaknesses of the Churches and makes no mention of the external persecution that is taking place. The gifts given by Christ to those who remain faithful are intended for those at that time (through the Mass and the other Sacraments) and for them after death.

- Chapters 4–18: The struggle between the early Church, the Roman Empire, and other adversaries as the persecution continues. The faithful praise of God throughout. The terrible disasters seem to come from God, and to target the enemies of the Church, some of whom repent, though most do not. The death of the two witnesses in Apocalypse 11 correspond to the preaching and death of Peter and Paul in Rome. The number 666 in Apocalypse 13:18 is acknowledged to point to Nero.

- The appearance of the Ark of the Covenant in Apocalypse would point to the addition of new members to the Church, birthed spiritually by the Church with the help of Mary.[57] The first beast would be the Roman Empire, the second beast would be the Jewish religious authorities, and the harlot would describe the luxury and sin at the heart of the end of the Roman Empire (Babylon), which finally falls.[58] Note that the beasts, etc., are destroyed, but not the dragon, the devil, who remains.

- Chapter 19 begins with another vision of God in heaven (as in chapter 4); a victory song is sung, and the books are opened. Then the king arrives, and at first it seems that this is Jesus, but he is not named. I suggest that this person is united with Jesus but that—he wears several diadems— is the pope, and the

---

[57] The woman who appears in Apocalypse 11 looks a lot like Mary at Guadalupe (Mexico City, 1532).

[58] Some Protestant authors, understandably to a degree in the face of the corruption in the Church at the time, saw the "seven hills" in Revelation 17:9 as the Catholic Church since Rome has seven hills. The Roman Empire, as I claim is the harlot, is of course also centered in Rome. For the other view, see, for example, Emanuel Swedenborg, *The Apocalypse Revealed* (New York: American Swedenborg Printing and Publishing Society, 1909), vol. 1–2.

Roman Empire is conquered by the Church and its head. The conquest of the Church is so complete that there is the first resurrection of those who were martyred during those 500 years.

- Chapter 20 (1): The dragon or Satan (Apocalypse 20:2) is chained, and for a thousand years, this king reigns (the popes). The thousand years in the vision matches history because Rome fell in 476 AD, and the Protestant Reformation fractured the Church in 1517.
- Chapter 20 (2): After the 1,000 years, the devil is unchained and causes havoc, "He will go out to deceive the nations at the four corners of the earth, Gog and Magog, to gather them for battle... They invaded the breadth of the earth and surrounded the camp of the holy ones and the beloved city" (Apoc. 20:8–9). The camp of the saints would be Rome and the beloved city, Jerusalem, the first mention of Jerusalem in the Apocalypse.
- Chapter 20 (3): The devil is defeated and removed. The throne of judgment appears, and the Book of Life is opened, and the judgment takes place.
- Chapter 21: The new heavens and the new earth descend from heaven, including the heavenly Jerusalem,[59] which is measured and described and which echoes the Garden of Eden but is of a higher dimension. And at its center is the Lamb who gives it light. It is notable that this takes place in a three-step process: the new heavens and new earth, the heavenly Jerusalem with all its attributes and dimensions, and Jesus himself.
- Chapter 22: John's epilogue where he asks that the Holy Spirit and the Church both pray that this vision, which will take place, will take place soon.

In the second view, forming if we take the time of John as an example, Nero can be identified as the person whose name is symbolized by 666 since the letters of his name, taken as symbols, add up to 666.

---

[59] As opposed to the terrestrial Jerusalem.

The two witnesses, whom Nero had killed, would be Peter and Paul. The woman in the desert would be the Church, giving birth to new members in spite of the danger (with Mary's help). And the first beast would no doubt be the Roman Empire that was trying to destroy the Church and of which Nero was the head. The second beast could be the Jewish religious establishment at the time, which was also trying to destroy the Church. And the harlot would be the immoral practices of the Romans. The arrival of the destroyer of evil and the descent of the heavenly Jerusalem takes place at every Mass that was celebrated during this time.

Having looked at two historically connected contexts of the Apocalypse, there is a third nonhistorical overall interpretative structure of the Apocalypse. Thanks to Scott Hahn (*The Lamb's Supper*), and to the Fathers of the Church, it is that the Apocalypse is the Mass seen from heaven. In every Mass, Jesus offers himself to the Father for the redemption of the world, evil is destroyed, and the rest of the Apocalypse is fulfilled. Scott Hahn proceeds to point out many similarities between the Apocalypse and the Mass which need to be detailed and which seem to make the Mass the primary interpretive structure of the Apocalypse. Scott Hahn suggests that the Apocalypse is the menu to the Mass which is the meal: that's how closely they are related. I would also suggest that in addition, it is the menu and the Mass seen from the perspective of the priest saying Mass. In that case, as John sees these disasters unleashed on the world, it's the result of the reading of the Scriptures and of bringing Christ to earth that unleashes the disasters on the evil in the world. Here is a speculative comparison:

Chapter	Revelation	The Mass
1	Greeting	Greeting
1–3	Examination of the Churches[60]	Penitential Rite
4	Vision of God[61]	The Gloria
5	Scroll opened by the Lion of Judah (Christ)	1st Reading, Psalm, 2nd Reading
6–9	The unleashed disasters that attack evil[62]	1st Reading, Psalm, 2nd Reading
10	Small scroll	Gospel
11	Two witnesses	Sermon/Creed
12	The woman and the dragon	Mary and the whole church is present at the Eucharist; the consecration, evil, threatened, is drawn out into the open

---

[60] We see some evil, the Nicolaitans, within the Church.

[61] "Stood a Lamb as though it had been slain" (Rev. 5:6, NKJV) shows that the passion and death of Jesus and the ascension of Jesus has already taken place.

[62] The words of the Scriptures, the proclamation of the Gospel, dispel evil. These disasters on the evil in the world are seen again in the disasters unleashed on evil in the second half of the book. The disasters do seem to have two sides, like the two-edged sword: they cut, but if allowed, they also heal. They destroy evil and leave people with the choice of cursing God or repenting and praising God. And there are three groups of people on earth who seem to be on the move: those who praise God, those who repent, and those who refuse to repent and who curse God for the disasters.

13	The 2 beasts. Evil, threatened, isdrawn out and imitates the Trinity in its interactions[63]	The preface
14	The Lamb's companions	The saints and martyrs are all present at the Eucharist
15	The 7 plagues, the Temple of Preparation for the Eucharist	God in heaven is opened
16	The 7 bowls of God's fury[64]	The Eucharistic prayer, incense
17	The harlot riding on the beast, imitating Mary and the Trinity	Mary is present at the Consecration
18	In reverse order of appearance, the harlot is destroyed, then the 2nd beast, then the 1st beast	The Offering of Christ to the Father, the doxology
19	Praise of God in heaven	Man is reconciled with the Father
20	Appearance of the rider of the white Christ on the white horse of the Hosthorse	
20	The defeat of the dragon and of death, the Judgment	Peace given, shared

---

[63] The imitation of the Trinity by evil is remarkable: the dragon gives power to the first beast who shares power with the second beast, imitating the Father, sending the Son and the Holy Spirit. Then the harlot, drunk with the blood of the saints, riding on the beast, imitates Mary who lives on the Eucharist and "rides" on the Trinity. The mark of the beast on the forehead and hand mocks the rite of baptism in which the cross, the sign of God, are placed on the forehead and the hands (this section can inform us as to how the Persons of the Trinity interact since it is a mocked by evil; the dragon, Satan, evil, tries to do what God does).

[64] As in other places, the disasters have the militant aspect of attacking the evil on the earth, which has been won by Satan, an attack which the acts and words of the Mass cause and carry out. From the priest's point of view, the actions of the Mass go out into the world and destroy evil.

21	New Jerusalem comes out of heaven	Communion
22	The life-giving water	Communion
Epilogue	Dismissal	

The reading of the Apocalypse as the Mass means that one can say that the Mass can be used to interpret the Apocalypse, and the Apocalypse can be used to interpret the Mass. The connection between the Apocalypse and the Mass also makes sense because oddly, the Mass is spoken of very sporadically and briefly in the earlier letters of the New Testament, perhaps in order to protect the Eucharist from its enemies. But the Mass gets full treatment here.

Finally, we have to see if we can say anything about the placement of the Apocalypse in the Bible and if it tells us anything about what might happen soon. First, the Apocalypse, with the book of Genesis, form bookends that begin and end the Bible, bookends that structurally can be seen as mirror images of each other (if physicists use arguments from symmetry and find them fruitful, they should also appear in theology). Genesis and the Apocalypse are international books, not limited to the Jewish people: the former starting before the Jewish people existed, the latter taking place after the Gentiles joined them in the Church.[65] In between these two books, one has the history of Israel from Moses at the start of Exodus through the acts and letters of the apostles, through their deaths. Between these two books, the Bible is the history of the Jewish people, the occasional brief appearance of a non-Jewish person in the history only supports this point. "Salvation is from the Jews" (John 4:22), i.e., God uniquely used the Jewish people to bring salvation to the world.

---

[65] Some other mirror image notes include: Genesis ends with the death of Joseph, the last living son of Jacob; the Apocalypse begins after the attempted martyrdom by boiling in oil of John, the last apostle, and his exile to Patmos. At the start of Genesis, there is a judgment by God when Adam and Eve fell; there is a judgment on the whole human race when the Book of Life is opened near the end of the Apocalypse. Genesis starts with the ex-nihilo creation; the Apocalypse ends with the new heavens and the new earth.

One might say that the Bible has the general structure, looking like a temple:

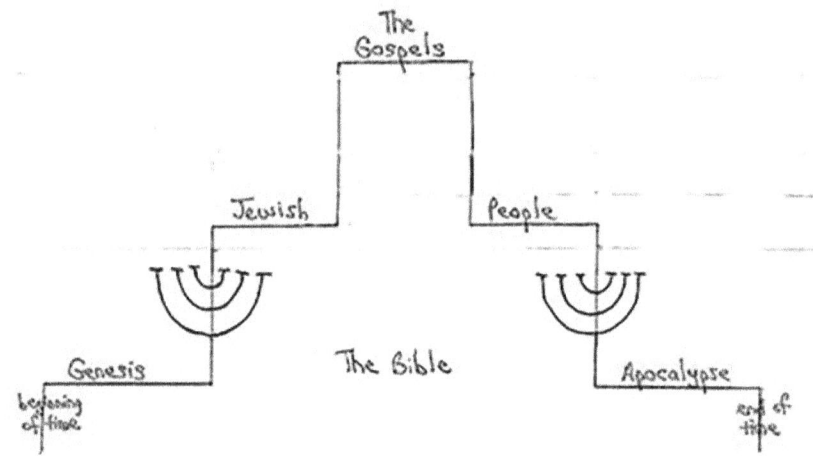

Drawing by author

This diagram suggests the beautiful structure of Genesis and the Apocalypse as bookends of the Bible and to argue that we can consider the span of time in the Apocalypse not as the whole of human history but reaching from the death of St. John and the closing of the Deposit of Faith to the end of time (note also the three levels; also, one sees the three-in-five pattern).

Finally, can we see anything in the Apocalypse that would tell us if we are near the end of time? In Apocalypse 20:1ff,[66] we are told that Satan would be bound for 1,000 years and then released for "a short time." If, as in the first view, the Apocalypse is a prediction of the conquering of the Roman Empire (which was not always evil but became so over time), this short section tells what would happen from the fall of the Roman Empire to the end of time. The thousand-year reign would correspond to the reign of the Church during the Middle Ages

---

[66]   In a way, this paragraph gives a summary of the Apocalypse. If we compare the Apocalypse to the Mass, this section would parallel the Lamb of God section right before Communion: in that section, we are taken from the "Behold the Lamb of God," the words of John at the start of Jesus' Ministry, to the sending of the Holy Spirit at the end of his ministry: it is a reprise of the Mass.

and then the agony of the Church following the year 1500 or so. Thinking in terms of symmetry, the Roman Empire ending in AD 476 or roughly AD 500, it would imply that the time from the end of the thousand-year reign to the end of time might last a little more than 500 years. This last observation suggests that we might be near the end of time, though every time seems to say this.

In a connected observation, if we say that the first part of the Apocalypse describes the world until roughly AD 500, and then there is a period of 1,000 years, and by symmetry, one would expect the final period to last another 500 years, and considering that the years in the Bible date Adam (in Bible years) to 4004 BC, adding the two thousand years after Christ, this makes six thousand years of creation. And we are told God created the world in six "days," so it makes sense that he would complete it in six "days." And climactic things do seem to happen every 500 years.[67]

But that is very speculative. Are there other indications, other signs of the times (cf. Matt. 16:3) that point to the idea that the end of this age is near? I've been able to find these:

- In Genesis, God told Adam and Eve, before the fall, to multiply and fill the earth (Genesis 1:28). It seems that now for the first time, we consider that the earth might have reached the number of people it can support (though some disagree).
- In the Catholic Catechism, it states that a number of the Jewish people must be converted to Christianity by God before the end can come. And we are seeing today a number of the Jewish people converting to Christianity.
- In the Apocalypse, the only mention of the beloved city, Jerusalem, appears near the end of time, when it is encircled by

---

[67] Roughly 2000 BC, Abraham; 1500 BC, Moses; 1000 BC, David and Solomon; 500 BC, the Exile and Return; the year 0, the Advent of Christ; AD 500, the conquest of the Church; AD 1000, the conversion of pagan Europe (see James Reston, *The Last Apocalypse: Europe at the Year 1000 AD* [New York: Doubleday, 1988]) and the split with the Orthodox; AD 1500, the Reformation.

enemies. The city of Jerusalem has been reestablished and is now surrounded.

- In our current discussions about gender ("He created them male and female" [Gen. 5:2]), in our concern for the environment (God put man "in the Garden of Eden to work it and take care of it" [Gen. 2:15, NIV]), and in the Church the desire to get back to the forms of early Christianity, it seems we are back to where we started from.

- Patriarchy, which is a result of the fall (Gen. 3:16, NIV: "And he will rule over you.") is now the subject of criticism and is coming to an end.

- In Mark 9:12 "Elijah will indeed come first," and Jesus identifies Elijah as John the Baptist. But as Jonathan Cahn in *The Paradigm* (Lake Mary, Florida: FrontLine, 2017), the circumstances of Elijah might have returned in our recent history: Elijah, Ahab, Jezebel, child sacrifice to the Baals, and Jehu the restorer; the Clintons, President Obama, abortion, and Trump the restorer. And he argues that we who protest abortion, etc., are the Elijahs of this comparison.

- Jesus was convicted and handed over by the Jewish leaders and put to death by the Romans who represented the whole world. In a deep mysterious way of justice, a large part of the Jewish people was killed and in a very similar way during the Holocaust. Next, if logic holds, is that the whole world has to suffer in this way, and as we look around the world, it looks like this disaster might possibly be at hand.

This is only to suggest that whether we are near the end of time, the return of the Messiah or not, we need to be ready.

Addendum 1

The Apocalypse itself contains three books: the books of the seven seals (chapter 5), the small scroll (chapter 10), the Book of Life (Chapter 20), and it is a vision or a series of visions and not an ordinary book. Yet it is a "book" of the Bible. The first book can be identified with the Old Testament (or Hebrew Scriptures). Jesus, the Lion of Judah, is the only one found worthy to break open the seals (Chapter 5). And the things that "come forth" seem to be the fate of the sinful world. The second book can be identified with the New Testament; John is asked to eat it and then to prophesy, so it is a combination of the New Testament and the Eucharist. And John eats it because he "must prophesy again about many peoples, nations, tongues, and kings" (Rev. 10:11), showing that it is meant for the whole world. But the Apocalypse is part of the New Testament, so this is a recursive situation.[68] So the Apocalypse contains the Bible in which it resides. In addition, as we have seen, the Apocalypse is a sketch of the structure of the Mass. Why would this be?

The Deposit of Faith is the Old and New Testaments: the Inspired Word of God. It began with the books of Moses and ended with the death of the last apostle, St. John, around the year AD 95. But one puzzling question: "Why would the Deposit of Faith end?" If God is coming more and more into the world as time moves forward, why would prophecy end? One argument is that the Bible contains all that is needed for salvation: all had been said. And the Bible is indeed the basis of theology. Any valid dogmas of the Church must have roots in the Bible or, as a result of logic, applied to the truths of the Bible. But why would it have ended? The Mormons address this problem by allowing prophecy to continue: their current president can change dogma, even overturn dogma, since revelation in their view did not end with the death of St. John.

Perhaps the written Bible did end with the death of St. John, but that prophecy did not: it was transformed into something else, an even fuller form in which the Bible took a foundational part. Instead of the written and inspired Word of God, we have the Living Word, the Word of God himself, Jesus, and every baptized person is baptized—priest, prophet, and king—and priests in particular. We can see the Apocalypse then as a transition from the books of the Bible to the Mass. And that

---

[68] 75 Recursion, so important in computer science, takes place when something contains within itself a copy of itself.

is where God speaks to us now, in the Bible readings, but also in the priest, the alter Christus. The Apocalypse is a transition book between the Bible and the Mass which one would expect would be needed.

Addendum 2

There are at least two sources of evil and kinds of evil in the Apocalypse, and they are related to the two books. When the scrolls of the first book are opened, different terrible things "come forth." It's not that the book caused them but almost reported or showed them. And these terrible things happen in a world conquered by sin and evil.

Once John eats the second small books, which will lead him (and presumably others) to prophecy, presumably because the preaching was taking people from the kingdom of evil into the kingdom of God, evil emerges from the pit and kills the two witnesses (we could identify them with Peter and Paul). Then evil returns to the pit but reemerges, giving power to the first and second beast and the harlot. Revelation 20:4–6 speaks of the victory of the martyrs—it could refer to the coming of the Church in the Middle Ages and the victory of the martyrs of the Roman persecutions. If that is the primary reading of 20:4–6, it makes sense that at the end of the book, the Church cries, "Come, Lord Jesus" (Rev. 22:10).

Addendum 3

In terms of the end of the world, the Bible and Salvation history gives us at least two prefigurements of the end of the world. One is the Passover: the ten plagues that freed the Israelites from Egypt and allowed them to seek the promised land prefigures perhaps the disasters that will detach us from our concerns of this world and prepare us to enter heaven. We have seen a first plague in 2020. The other prefigurement is based on the idea that the life of Christ as lived and as reported in the Gospels give us a template for the history of the human race. At the end of the earthly life of Christ, he endures his Passion and Death. If this prefigures what happens at the end of the world, one can say that the Church will suffer dramatically, and so will the whole world.

Addendum 4

It could be stated as a theological axiom that the history of the world, of mankind, and of the Church in particular, must follow the pattern of the Life of Christ. If that is so, one can make a facile comparison between the situation at the death of Christ and the current situation. Christ and his followers faced attacks from the Roman Empire (a pagan empire), from the religious authorities (misguided), and from Herod (who sought pleasure). At this time one could draw a comparison between the Roman Empire and China.[69] One could draw a comparison between the misguided religious authorities and the Islamic terrorists. And one could draw a comparison between the pleasure-seeking Herod and the West. And all three, as in Christ's day, are ready to attack the Church, and the Jewish people also.

Addendum 5

From a Catholic point of view, the ancient Jewish religion[70] culminated with the life of Christ and his three and a half years of public ministry. It might be that the world will end with three and a half years of the reign of the Antichrist in the world, maybe beginning soon.

---

[69] Perhaps Pope Francis's treaty with China, which led to even more martyrdoms of the Church in China, mirrors the persecutions in the Roman Empire.

[70] The Jewish faith which survived was the Judaism of the Pharisees since the Temple had been destroyed and the sacrificial system was no longer possible, and it was reorganized by the rabbis in the first century.

The Mass and the Rosary in a World without Sin[71]

The Mass

Note: Red indicates things changed, brackets [ ] indicate a variable part; parentheses mean a prayer said silently by the priest.

In the name of the Father and of the Son and of the Holy Spirit.
Amen.

The grace of our Lord Jesus Christ,
and the love of God,
and the communion of the Holy Spirit
be with you all.

And with your spirit.

Brethren, let us acknowledge our unworthiness,[72]
and so prepare ourselves to celebrate the sacred mysteries.

I confess to almighty God
and to you, my brothers and sisters,
that I am unworthy,
in my thoughts and in my words,
in what I have done and in what I have failed to do,[73]

---

[71] Note that out of over 2,600 words in the fixed parts of the Mass, only seventy-six words are in red or were changed to adapt the Mass to a world without sin; roughly 3 percent changes shown in red. How little has to be changed. At roughly 2,600 words, using the lengthy First Eucharistic Prayer, adding in the variable parts of the readings, responsorial psalm, the Gospel, the sermon and the prayer of the faithful, the prayer over the gifts, the number of words in the full Sunday Mass stands around 3,000, and in Scripture, 3,000 always indicates an act of God. St. Thomas tells us that as sinners, we experience God's love as mercy, so I replaced the word *mercy* with *love*.

[72] Because we are finite, and God is infinite, independent of sin.

[73] This could refer to failures without being sins.

I am unworthy,
I am unworthy,
I am unworthy;
therefore I ask blessed Mary ever-Virgin,
all the Angels and Saints,
and you, my brothers and sisters,
to pray for me to the Lord our God.

May almighty God remember his love for us,
overlook our unworthiness,
and bring us to everlasting life.
Amen.

Lord, remember your love for us.
Lord, remember your love for us.
Christ, remember your love for us.
Christ, remember your love for us.
Lord, remember your love for us.
Lord, remember your love for us.

Glory to God in the highest,
and on earth peace to people of good will.

We praise you,
we bless you,
we adore you,
we glorify you,
we give you thanks for your great glory,
Lord God, heavenly King,
O God, almighty Father.

Lord Jesus Christ, Only Begotten Son,
Lord God, Lamb of God, Son of the Father,
you take away the unworthiness of the world,
have mercy on us;

you take away the unworthiness of the world,
receive our prayer;
you are seated at the right hand of the Father,
have mercy on us.

For you alone are the Holy One,
you alone are the Lord,
you alone are the Most High,
Jesus Christ,
with the Holy Spirit,
in the glory of God the Father.

Amen.

Let us pray.

[Collect]

Amen.

A reading from the Book of [Daniel]

[First Reading]

The word of the Lord.

Thanks be to God.

[Responsorial Psalm]

A reading from the [First Letter of St. Paul to the Corinthians]

[Second Reading]

The word of the Lord.

Thanks be to God.

Alleluia, Alleluia, Alleluia.

Alleluia, Alleluia, Alleluia.

[Alleluia verse]

Alleluia, Alleluia, Alleluia.

The Lord be with you.

And with your spirit.

A reading from the holy Gospel according to [Matthew]

[The Gospel]

Glory to you, O Lord.

The Gospel of the Lord.

Praise to you, Lord Jesus Christ.

[The sermon]

I believe in one God,
the Father almighty,
maker of heaven and earth,
of all things visible and invisible.

I believe in one Lord Jesus Christ,
the Only Begotten Son of God,
born of the Father before all ages.
God from God,
light from Light,

true God from true God,
begotten, not made, consubstantial with the Father; through him all
things were made.
For us men and for our salvation he came down from heaven,
and by the Holy Spirit was incarnate of the Virgin Mary,
and became man.
For our sake he was crucified[74] under Pontius Pilate,
he fell asleep in death and was buried,
and rose again on the third day
in accordance with the Scriptures.
He ascended into heaven
and is seated at the right hand of the Father.

He will come again in glory
to judge[75] the living and the dead
and his kingdom will have no end.

I believe in the Holy Spirit, the Lord, the giver of life,
who proceeds from the Father and the Son,
who with the Father and the Son is adored and glorified,
who has spoken through the prophets.
I believe in one, holy, catholic and apostolic Church.
I confess one Baptism for entry into the Church,
and I look forward to the resurrection of the dead
and the life of the world to come. Amen.

[The Prayer of the Faithful]

Hear our prayer.

[Concluding prayer]

---

[74] Crucified means would mean attached to the cross with painless ropes, standing on a pedestal.

[75] Apparently, the word *judge* also means *save*.

Blessed are you, Lord God of all creation,
for through your goodness we have received
the bread we offer you:
fruit of the earth and work of human hands,
it will become for us the bread of life.

Blessed be God for ever.

(By the mystery of this water and wine may we come to share in the
divinity of Christ who humbled himself to share in our humanity.)

Blessed are you, Lord God of all creation,
for through your goodness we have received
the wine we offer you:
fruit of the vine and work of human hands,
it will become our spiritual drink.

Blessed be God forever.

(With humble spirit and contrite heart may we be accepted by you, O
Lord, and may our sacrifice in your sight this day be pleasing to you,
Lord God.)

(Wash me, O Lord, from my failures and cleanse me from my
unworthiness.)

Pray, brethren (brothers and sisters),
that my sacrifice and yours may be acceptable to God,
the almighty Father.

May the Lord accept the sacrifice at your hands
for the praise and glory of his name,
for our good
and the good of all his holy Church.

[Prayer over the gifts.]

Amen.
The Lord be with you.
And with your spirit.

Lift up your hearts.
We lift them up to the Lord.

Let us give thanks to the Lord our God.
It is right and just.

It is truly right and just, our duty and our salvation,
always and everywhere to give you thanks,
Lord, holy Father, almighty and eternal God,
through Christ our Lord.
In him you have been pleased to complete all things,
giving us all a share in his fullness.

For though he was in the form of God, he emptied himself
And by the blood[76] of his Cross brought his peace[77] to all creation.
Therefore he has been exalted above all things,
and to all who obey him,
has become the source of eternal salvation.[78]
And so, with Angels and Archangels,
with Thrones and Dominions,
and with all the hosts and Powers of heaven,
we sing the hymn of your glory,
as without end we acclaim:

---

[76] In a world without sin, the only shedding of blood on the cross would have been the lance in Christ's side after he was dead, which gave birth to the Church.

[77] His peace, which is a higher level of peace than that seen even in the sinless world before Christ. Jesus' words, "Peace I leave you, My peace I give you," point to these two levels of peace. One is peace of this world, even without sin; "His peace" is the Holy Spirit.

[78] Salvation because we still needed to be rescued from the falling asleep of death, even without decay.

Holy, Holy, Holy Lord God of hosts.
Heaven and earth are full of your glory.
Hosanna in the highest.
Blessed is he who comes in the name of the Lord.
Hosanna in the highest.

To you, therefore, most merciful Father,
we make humble prayer and petition
Through Jesus Christ, your Son, our Lord:
that you accept
and bless these gifts, these offerings,
these holy and unblemished sacrifices,
which we offer you firstly
for your holy catholic Church.
Be pleased to grant her peace,
to guard,[79] unite and govern her
throughout the whole world,
together with your servant [Francis] our Pope
and [Timothy] our Bishop,
and all those who, holding to the truth,
hand on the catholic and apostolic faith.

Remember, Lord, your servants [Ed and Marian],
and all gathered here,
whose faith and devotion are known to you.
For them, we offer you this sacrifice of praise
or they offer it for themselves
and all who are dear to them:
for the sanctification of their souls,
in hope of health and well-being,
and paying their homage to you,
the eternal God, living and true.
In communion with those whose memory we venerate,

---

[79] 86 To guard from failure and mistakes or from the influence of the fallen angels
if they had fallen.

especially the glorious ever-Virgin Mary,
Mother of our God and Lord, Jesus Christ,
and blessed Joseph, her Spouse,
your blessed Apostles and Martyrs,
Peter and Paul, Andrew,
James, John,
Thomas, James, Philip,
Bartholomew, Matthew,
Simon and Jude;
Linus, Cletus, Clement, Sixtus,
Cornelius, Cyprian,
Lawrence, Chrysogonus,
John and Paul,
Cosmas and Damian
and all your Saints;
we ask that through their merits and prayers,
in all things we may be defended
by your protecting help.
Through Christ our Lord. Amen.

Therefore, Lord, we pray:
graciously accept this oblation of our service,
that of your whole family;
order our days in your peace,
and command that we be delivered from
eternal separation from you[80]
and counted among the flock of those you have chosen.
Through Christ our Lord. Amen.

Be pleased, O God, we pray,
to bless, acknowledge,
and approve this offering in every respect;
make it spiritual and acceptable,

---

[80] Even without sin, it is God's choice to invite us to heaven, of course.

so that it may become for us
the Body and Blood of your most beloved Son,
our Lord Jesus Christ.

On the day before he was to fall asleep in death,
He took bread in his holy and venerable hands,
and with eyes raised to heaven
to you, O God, his almighty Father,
giving you thanks, he said the blessing,
broke the bread
and gave it to his disciples, saying:

Take this all of you, and eat of it,
For this is my body,
Which will be given up to the Father.[81]

In a similar way, when supper was ended,
He took this precious chalice
in his holy and venerable hands,
and once more giving you thanks, he said the blessing and gave the
chalice to his disciples, saying:

Take this, all of you, and drink from it,
For this is the chalice of my blood,
The blood of the new and eternal covenant,
Which will be poured out for you and for many,
Out of love for the world.

Do this in memory of Me.

The Mystery of Faith.

---

[81] 88 His body and blood were still given to the Father and because entry into heaven was not a right but won for us by Christ, even in a sinless world, and it also allowed Christ to reveal the Resurrection. A sacrifice is the annihilation of something good to acknowledge the sovereignty of God: Jesus' falling asleep in death is still a sacrifice.

We proclaim your Death, O Lord,
and profess your Resurrection
until you come again.

Therefore, O Lord,
as we celebrate the memorial of the blessed Passion,[82]
the Resurrection from the dead,
and the glorious Ascension into heaven
of Christ, your Son, our Lord,
we, your servants and your holy people,
Offer to your glorious majesty
from the gifts that you have given us,
this pure victim,
this holy victim,
this spotless victim,
the holy Bread of eternal life
and the Chalice of everlasting salvation.[83]

Be pleased to look upon these offerings
with a serene and kindly countenance,
and to accept them,
as once you were pleased to accept
the gifts of your servant Abel the just,
the sacrifice of Abraham, our father in faith,
and the offering of your high priest Melchizedek,
a holy sacrifice, a spotless victim.

In humble prayer we ask you, almighty God:
command that these gifts be borne
by the hands of your holy Angel
to your altar on high
in the sight of your divine majesty,

---

[82] Jesus' falling asleep in death done for love of the Father and for us could still be called his Passion.

[83] Salvation from death and burial in the earth (without decay).

so that all of us, who through this participation at the altar
receive the most holy Body and Blood of your Son,
may be filled with every grace and heavenly blessing.
Through Christ our Lord. Amen.

Remember also, Lord, your servants [Ed and Marian],[84]
who have gone before us with the sign of faith
and rest in the sleep of peace.

Grant them, O Lord, we pray,
and all who sleep in Christ,
a place of refreshment, light and peace.
Through Christ our Lord. Amen.

To us, also, your servants, who, though unworthy,
hope in your abundant mercies,
graciously grant some share
and fellowship with your holy Apostles and Martyrs:
with John the Baptist, Stephen,
Matthias, Barnabas,
Ignatius, Alexander,
Marcellinus, Peter,
Felicity, Perpetua,
Agatha, Lucy,
Agnes, Cecilia, Anastasia
And all your Saints;
Admit us, we beseech you,
Into their company,
Not weighing our merits,
But granting us your love,[85]
Through Christ our Lord.

---

[84] My parents.

[85] The original word, *forgiveness*, could be kept, meaning forgiveness for our failings
which are not sins, if any, in a sinless world.

Through whom
you continue to make all these good things, O Lord;
You sanctify them, fill them with life,
bless them, and bestow them upon us.

Through him, and with him, and in him,
O God, almighty Father,
in the unity of the Holy Spirit,
all glory and honor is yours,
for ever and ever.

Amen.

At the Savior's command
and formed by divine teaching, we dare to say:

Our Father, who art in heaven,
hallowed be thy name;
thy kingdom come,
thy will be done
on earth as it is in heaven.
Give us this day our daily bread,
and forgive us our failures,
as we forgive those who fail us;
and lead us not into temptation,
but deliver us from evil.

Deliver us, Lord, we pray, from every failure,[86]
graciously grant peace in our days,
that, by the help of your mercy,
we may be always free from failures
and safe from all distress,
as we await the blessed hope
and the coming of our Savior, Jesus Christ.

---

[86] We would know what failures are but not what evil is.

For the kingdom,
the power and the glory are yours
now and forever.

Lord Jesus Christ,
who said to your Apostles:
Peace I leave you, my peace I give you,
look not on our unworthiness,
but on the faith of your Church,
and graciously grant her peace and unity
in accordance with your will.
Who live and reign for ever and ever.

Amen.

The peace of the Lord be with you always.

And with your spirit.

Let us offer each other the sign of peace.

Lamb of God, you take away the unworthiness of the world,
remember your love for us.
Lamb of God, you take away the unworthiness of the world,
remember your love for us.
Lamb of God, you take away the unworthiness of the world,
grant us peace.

Behold the Lamb of God,
behold him who takes away the unworthiness of the world.
blessed are those called to the supper of the Lamb.

(May the receiving of your Body and Blood, Lord Jesus
Christ, not bring me to judgment and condemnation,
but through your loving mercy be for me protection
in mind and body and a healing remedy.)

Lord, I am not worthy
that you should enter under my roof,
but only say the word and my soul shall be healed.

May the Body of Christ keep me safe for eternal life.

May the Blood of Christ keep me safe for eternal life.

The Body of Christ.

Amen.

The Blood of Christ.

Amen.

Let us pray.

[Post-Communion Prayer]

Amen.

The Lord be with you.
And with your spirit.
May almighty God bless you,
the Father, and the Son, and the Holy Spirit.
Amen.

Go in peace, glorifying the Lord by your life.
Thanks be to God.

The Rosary

(Red indicates things changed)

❖ The Joyful Mysteries

- The Annunciation.
- The Visitation.
- The Nativity.
- The Presentation in the Temple.
- The Finding in the Temple.

❖ The Luminous Mysteries
- The Baptism of Jesus.
- The Miracle at Cana.
- The preaching of the kingdom of God.
- The Transfiguration.
- The Institution of the Eucharist.

❖ The Sorrowful Mysteries
- Jesus prays silently in preparation for his great act (The Agony in the Garden).
- Jesus' Body is anointed with oil in preparation for his burial (The Scourging).
- Jesus is crowned with a gold crown (The Crowning with Thorns).
- Jesus is handed a Cross, the sign of God, which he carries with help (Carrying the Cross).
- Jesus is crucified, standing on a pedestal attached to the cross; after three hours, he falls asleep in death (Crucifixion and Death on the Cross).

❖ The Glorious Mysteries
- Jesus rises from the dead.
- Jesus ascends into heaven.
- Jesus and the Father send the Holy Spirit.
- Mary is assumed body and soul into heaven.
- Mary is crowned queen of heaven.

Three Theology Essays—Preface

The following are three more unrelated theological essays. The first is a suggestion about how physics' understanding of the dimensions of the physical universe might reflect the Trinity in several ways. The second is a list of the major Marian apparitions with a brief explanation of each. The third is a suggestion as to how our suffering, sometimes terrible, is consistent with a loving God.

The Trinity and Dimensionality

Before creation, the Trinity can be pictured as follows:

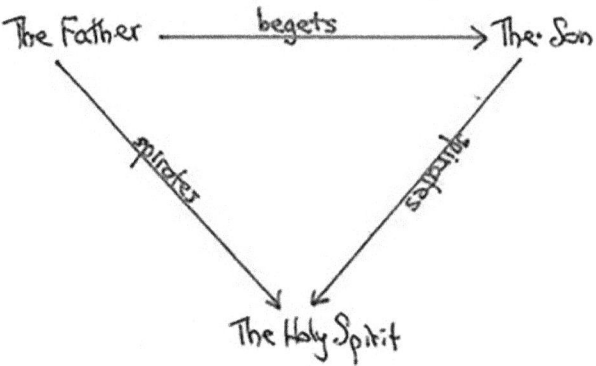

Drawing by author

The Father eternally begets the Son, the Father and the Son eternally generate the Holy Spirit by spiration (their love for each other which is a Person). The Father begets but is not begotten; the Son is begotten and also begets; the Holy Spirit does not beget but is begotten. There are three Persons and three lines of begetting. There is both generation from one Person (Father to Son) and generation from two Persons (Father and Son to the Holy Spirit).[1]

I also like the following diagram which stresses the three different Persons. At the same time that the Father is not the Son and the Son is not the Father and neither is the Holy Spirit, there is also the doctrine of co-extensionality. Where one Person of the Trinity is, the other two

---

[1] Which we see reflected in the two kinds of reproduction we find in nature.

Persons are present also.[2] Along that line, one can say that each Person of the Trinity gives himself to the other two Persons of the Trinity.[3]

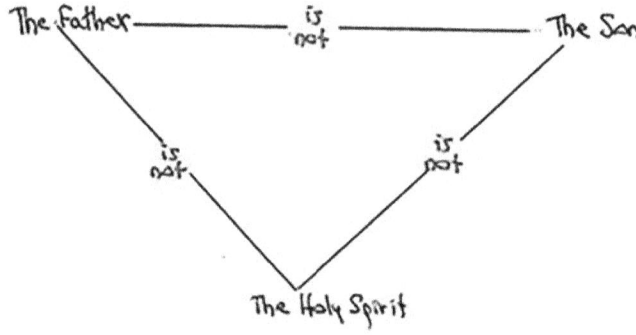

Drawing by author

In considering creation, it makes sense that God would create the physical world in such a way that it would reflect God's being (what else would it reflect?). I would like to suggest that Dr. Pangloss' logic, Voltaire's *Candide* notwithstanding, is unimpeachable. God is all powerful, God is good, therefore God's creation is the best possible creation. For if it were deficient in some way, God would correct that deficiency. But the world, even without sin, might have become more

---

[2] One distinction among the Persons of the Trinity is that the Father is not generated; the Son is eternally begotten by the Father; the Holy Spirit is spiration by the Father and the Son. Another distinction among the Persons of the Trinity is that the Father is not incarnate; the Son is incarnate as man; the Holy Spirit appears as wind, fire, water, and acts through consecrated oil.

[3] The Persons of the Trinity give themselves to each other completely:
The Father gives himself to the Son: "Nor does anyone know the Father except the Son" (Matt. 11:27 BSB).
The Father gives himself to the Holy Spirit: "The Spirit searches all things, even the deep things of God" (1 Cor. 2:10, NIV).
The Son gives himself to the Holy Spirit: "the Spirit drove him out into the wilderness" (Mark 1:12, WEB).
The Son gives himself to the Father: he goes to his Passion and to the Cross. Holy Spirit gives himself to the Son at the Baptism: "the Holy Spirit descended on him in bodily form like a dove" (Luke 3:22).
The Holy Spirit gives himself to the Father by going where the Father wills.

perfect over time, and it does not obviate the possibility that creatures given free will might misuse it.

In discussing the structure of the physical world, Brian Greene (*The Elegant Universe*, p. 283) states that if physicists could show that the structure of the physical world could not be otherwise, that would be a step toward a unified theory. I'm going to try to show not that the structure of the physical world suggested by physicists is inevitable, but I'll try to show that it makes sense as a reflection of the being of God since, of course, God could have made it anyway that was internally logically consistent. Brian Greene suggests that the description of physical reality that he describes in his book is accepted by physicists, though some has to remain unproven for now. But he admits that except for the possibility that the universe cannot be any other way and still exist, which is not known, physicists have no idea why physical reality is constructed in the way it is. Catholic theology gives us at least a suggestion. It seems that there are three sets of dimensions in physical reality, which we will look at separately, going from largest to smallest.

The first is the traditional Newtonian description of physical reality. The physical dimensions are the three extended dimensions of height, width, and breadth, and they form one spatial reality and one spatial experience on the level of our daily experience. In space, one reality with three dimensions is an image of the Trinity.

At the same time, the other dimension is time. But time has three aspects: past, present, and future. Again, one can see here an image of the Trinity: one reality with three dimensions.[4]

In Newtonian physics, the dimensions, including space and time, are independent and do not influence each other. But at the same time, one can say that the two realities of space and time are dependent on each other; without space, time cannot be measured. And without time, space is just a frozen expanse. If one says that the three dimensions of space exist within time, one again sees a three-and-one relationship; if

---

[4] The shamrock is a model of the Trinity attributed to St. Patrick; St. Bonaventure is credited with the phrase "The more I think of the Trinity's three-ness, the more I am aware of its oneness; the more I think of its oneness, the more I see it's three-ness." In any case, it transcends the category of number.

one says that the three parts of time (past, present, and future) each involve space, one again sees this a three-and-one cross relationship between space and time, again reflecting the Trinity's three and one character each time.

This was the framework of Newtonian physics where the dimensions were regarded as completely independent. In Einstein's Relativity, there are these dimensions, but he showed us that they are not independent: they strongly influence and interact with each other, more visibly at the extremes. And this is more accurate in relation to the Persons of the Trinity and the godhead as a whole. Could this largest framework have been made otherwise and still represented the Trinity?

The second largest dimension are other spatial dimensions which are not extended. Putting aside the seventh one, which will come later (this comes from Brian Greene's *The Elegant Universe*), there are six. Physicists have proven that they must form a six-dimensional Calabi-Yau[5] shape. As a picture, though severely distorted in two dimensions, it looks like a dense knot turning in on itself. These balls exist at each point in space since they are spatial dimensions but not extended.

One might say that there are three Persons in the Trinity and three Relations between the three Persons which makes six, so a six-dimensional figure is appropriate. This comparison seems appropriate, each having its own dimension, and would not be extended in order to stress the unity and solidarity of the Trinity: where one Person is, the other two Persons are present also:

---

[5]   Even though they have to meet stringent requirements, this is not one shape but tens of thousands of shapes of a similar six-dimensional form (Green, p. 208).

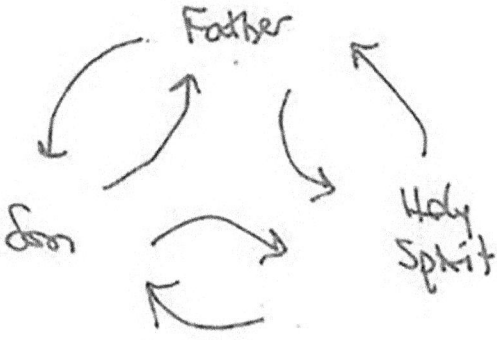

Drawing by author

There is a second interpretation which can be made: we consider not only the Persons of the Trinity but also creation—in particular, man—with whom God and the Persons of God have relationships, in particular the creation of Mary and Joseph and us. In that case, we are left with this diagram in which one line means begets either by one Person or two Persons; two lines mean married; three lines mean the same Persons (or Person via hypostatic union in the case of Jesus):

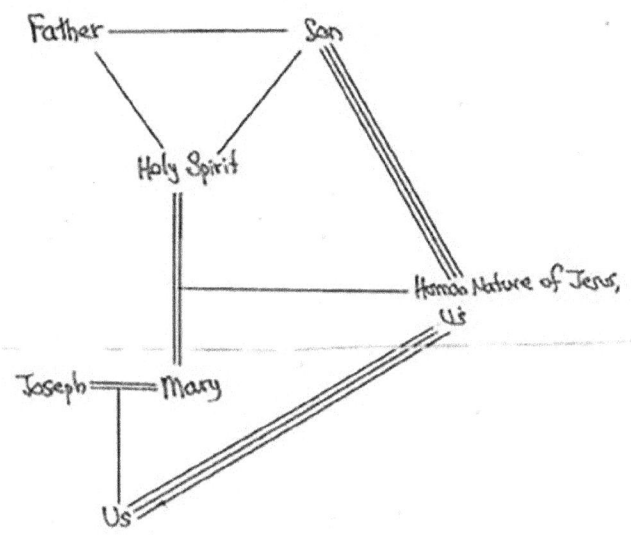

Drawing by author

Counting the Son and the human nature of Jesus as one and counting "us" in two places as one, there are six Persons (or persons) in this picture. If we consider that each of the six Persons (or persons) is critical and can be considered as inhabiting its own dimension, it might be reflected in the non-extended ball of the six-dimensional Calabi-Yau shape.[6] In *The Elegant Universe*, Brian Greene admits that although these six non-extended dimensions do take the shape of a Calabi-Yau six-dimensional shape, he admits that physicists have no idea why there would be a six-dimensional shape here. Perhaps the Trinity gives a rationale for this shape.

In particular, the Father begets but is not begotten; the Son is begotten and then begets; the Holy Spirit is begotten and then begets. Each human being has three sets of parents if not four: our parents, Adam and Eve, Mary and Joseph, the Holy Spirit and Mary (through the Church, spiritually).

So far, we have a total of ten dimensions: three extended spatial dimensions, time, and six non-extended spatial dimensions.

The third and smallest dimension of physical reality in string theory is the string itself or, as Mr. Greene suggests, is better called M-theory. M can be for mystery or membrane since the strings themselves can be more than one dimension, and a string with more than one dimension is called a membrane. Mr. Greene tells us that there were five different but related versions of string theory up until the 1990s. Their equations were approximations. Then it was discovered that what was missing was an additional spatial dimension which allowed these five versions of string theory to be seen as one united theory, M-theory. But he notes that this is the highest number of dimensions the mathematics allows.

At first, the strings were considered as points, then as one-dimensional strings. Then physicists discovered a property of strings called the coupling constant which at first had been kept below one for simplicity but was then allowed to grow beyond one (Greene, pp.

---

[6]   That "us" appears as the result of the love between Mary and Joseph (and of our parents, by extension, physically), of the Holy Spirit, and Mary (spiritually) reflects Jesus' words that one must be born again (John 3:7).

285–287). The different versions of string theory differed in the coupling constant of the strings. If it's small, the quantum variations are less likely (p. 294) to cause the string to temporarily split into several strings; the larger it is, the more likely is this momentary splitting. As it grows, the string itself can develop more dimensions from one to a maximum of nine.[7]

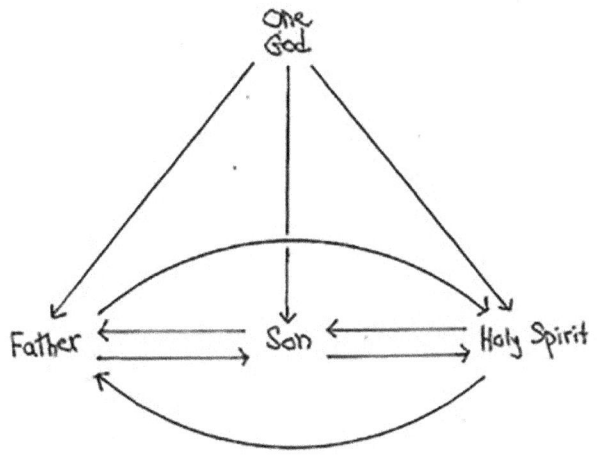

Drawing by author

There is one extra spatial dimension and up to nine other dimensions which are dimensions of the strings or membranes themselves.

If we look at the Trinity before creation, one could say there is one God—the one spatial dimension. Within that, there are three Persons, each having a relationship with the other two Persons of the Trinity and

---

[7]   These are called 1-branes to 9-branes, which in general are referred to as p-branes (p. 316-317).

with the godhead as a whole, making nine total (directed)[8] relationships—the nine possible dimensions of the strings.[9]

Overall, of course, the smaller two groups of dimensions follow from mathematical theories and can't be tested experimentally yet.

In total, then, there are twenty dimensions: eleven spatial dimensions and up to nine other dimensions in three groups. If ten is the number of men needed to worship God, and there are two Testaments, this number makes beautiful sense. These numbers would also have significance to the number of independent physical constants that there are in the physical world (around twenty, depending on how they are counted).[10] And the number of naturally occurring amino acids out of which all proteins are made is also twenty.

And this physical creation is only provisional: the new heavens and the new earth will replace them, though I suspect they will complete them also (cf. 2 Peter 3:10).

---

[8] 10 The Father loving the Son is considered one relationship; the Son loving the Father is considered another relationship as one example. Also, for example, the Son has a relationship with the Father and a relationship with the Holy Spirit and with the Trinity as a whole. An image of this set of relationships is a man in a marriage: the man has a relationship with the woman, the woman has a relationship with the man, and each has a relationship to the marriage, the unity of the two people as a whole.

[9] I've only included the directed relationship of the Trinity as a whole toward each Person of the Trinity to show the subservience of each Person of the Trinity to the whole Trinity.

[10] These are physical constants that are independent of each other. The scientists tell us that if any of them were slightly different from what they are, either the universe as we know it or life on earth would not be possible. If one considers time as having three dimensions—past, present, and future—the number of dimensions rises to twenty-two, which some scientists consider the number of independent physical constants. From another point of view, there is also an argument from two physicists in Brazil (see https://www.nature. com/news/2007/071220/full/news.2007.389.html) that only two of three independent physical constants need to be specified to determine all the others: two of the speed of light, the strength of gravity, and Planck's constant. This view nicely displays the Trinity.

Marian Apparitions[11]

It would be negligent to leave out a few notes on Marian Apparitions, and it's a joy to mention them. Twelve years after Martin Luther posted his theses on the church door at Wittenberg, Mary appeared at Guadalupe in Mexico in 1531. Her appearance sounds just like the appearance of the Woman in Revelation 12:1, KJB:

> And there appeared a great wonder in heaven; a woman clothed with the sun, and the moon under her feet, and upon her head a crown of twelve stars.

Between then and now, Mary has appeared all over the world, in many places and with many messages and warnings, though she had appeared a few times before that. There are eight approved apparitions; there are eleven more apparitions with the approval of the local bishop; there are 386 total Marian apparitions (University of Dayton, https://udayton.edu/imri/mary/a/apparitions-statistics-modern.php). The major Marian apparitions since 1531 follow, though the dominant one for our times is probably Fatima. Often, Mary appeared to suggest ways to avoid a coming disaster, which were often not avoided. I only mention some of the details. I hope that the following will pique the interest of the gentle reader who will search out more details in the many available resources about Mary's words at each of these places:

1. 1531 Mexico, Our Lady of Guadalupe
2. 1594–1634 Ecuador, Our Lady of Good Success (of the Good Event)
3. 1840 Paris, France, the Green Scapular

---

[11] Though I've read this information in other books, some of these brief descriptions come from the site *Wikipedia*, https://en.wikipedia.org/wiki/List_of_Marian_apparitions. These are private revelations that even if approved do not require a person to believe in them since all of the necessary revelations are contained in public revelation. If the Church finds that nothing in the apparition contradicts church teaching, and there are reliable witnesses, they can judge it allowable of veneration or eventually even of supernatural origin.

4. 1846 LaSalette, France, Our Lady of LaSalette, observe the Sabbath; no swearing
5. 1858 Lourdes, France, "Iamthe Immaculate Conception," healings
6. 1871 Pontmain, France, Our Lady of Hope
7. 1879 Knock, Ireland, the Mass
8. 1914 Sept. France, Our Lady of the Marne
9. 1917 Fatima, Portugal, Our Lady of the Rosary
10. 1932 Beauraing, Belgium, Our Lady of the Golden Heart
11. 1933 Banneux, Belgium, Virgin of the Poor
12. 1956 Ohio, Our Lady of America, Purity
13. 1961–1965 Spain, Our Lady of Garabandal, warnings of the end
14. 1968–1970 Egypt, Our Lady of Zeitoun
15. 1973 Japan, Our Lady of Akita Crying over abortion
16. 1994 Rwanda, Our Lady of Kibeho
17. 1981 (to present) Ireland, Our Lady Mediatrix of all Graces
18. 1981 (to present) Medjugorge, Bosnia-Herzegovina, Our Lady of Peace.

In more detail:

1. Our Lady of Guadalupe (1531, Mexico)—Just twelve years after Martin Luther posted his theses on the door in Wittenberg, Mary appeared in Mexico. The Franciscans and Jesuits had not made too much progress with the Aztecs and native Indians. But when Mary appeared, one million Aztecs converted to Catholicism each year for nine years. The Aztecs killed about 20 percent of their children in child sacrifices offered to their gods, and this stopped after Mary appeared, which is why she is the patron of the pro-life movement. The image of Mary (below) is on a tilma, a poncho made of cactus fiber, and should have decayed in twenty years but is still in perfect shape. It's thanks to Our Lady of Guadalupe that Mexico is such a Catholic country. The visionary, Juan Diego, a convert to Catholicism,

was relatively recently canonized for his saintly life after (and before) the apparition. The name Guadalupe comes from a city in Spain.

Mary told Juan Diego[12] the she wanted a church built in her honor at that spot which was a place of child sacrifice. She asked Juan Diego to tell the bishop of her and her request. Of course, the bishop could not believe Juan on his word. On the second or third appearance, Mary told Juan to collect the roses on the hill (which did not grow at that time of year and which were Castilian roses) in his tilma and to bring them to the bishop. When he brought them to the bishop and unfurled his tilma, the image appeared on the tilma.

Of course, scientists have examined the tilma which should have decayed after twenty years. They concluded that the image hovers over the fibers of the tilma and that it is not the result of any paint or dye. Just a few notes about the image: the black tassel around Mary's wrists shows that she is pregnant. The stars on her mantle have been shown to be the configuration of the constellations on the night of December 12 when she appeared to Juan Diego. The figures on her tunic having meanings to the Aztec people; the one over her abdomen means the source of life. Her eyes, when examined in correct optical fashion, show an inverted image of Juan Diego, the bishop, and his assistant at the moment the tilma holding the roses was unrolled. Her loose hair, as an Aztec princess, shows that she is married. She is held up by an angel, a cherub, and under her feet is the moon which is a symbol of the Aztec god, showing them that she and her Son are superior to their gods and that they should accept her and her Son.

Of course, the image reflects Revelation 11: "And there appeared a great wonder in heaven; a woman clothed with the

---

[12] Mary spoke to Juan Diego in his native language, which makes one think that in heaven, one can speak any language at will, something like the learning of Trinity in *The Matrix*.

sun, and the moon under her feet, and upon her head a crown of twelve stars."

On one occasion, a dissenter placed twenty-seven sticks of dynamite in a flower pot in front of the tilma. The explosion bent the heavy crucifix on the altar in front of the tilma, but the tilma was untouched. It was as if Mary was given the task of evangelizing the New World.

Public domain in the United States

2. 1594–1634, Ecuador, Our Lady of Good Success (of the Good Event)—Between these dates, Mary appeared several times to the sister Mariana de Jesús Torres in Quito, Ecuador. Mary told her things about the nineteenth and late twentieth centuries, which sound very familiar: (a) Passion will be unbridled because of the Masonic sects; (b) children will lose innocence; (c) the Sacrament of Matrimony will be attacked and defamed; (d) there will be a scarcity of priestly and religious vocations; (e) the bad behavior of some priests will bring scandal on all priests; (f

) many heresies will be propagated; (g) impurity will saturate the atmosphere; (h) there will be little modesty among women; (i) those who should speak will remain silent.

3. The Green Scapular (France, 1840)—Nine years after the apparitions of Jesus to St. Catherine Laboure which promoted devotion to the Sacred Heart of Jesus, Mary appeared to Sister Justine Bisqueyburu in the same chapel and gave her the green scapular. The promise is that anyone who dies wearing this scapular and having lived a good life will not suffer the pains of hell. Many Catholics wear the green scapular which is a short version of the apron covering the torso, back and front, worn by some orders of monks.

4. Our Lady of LaSalette (1846, France)—At LaSalette, Mary called herself "reconciliation of sinners." Her message was not to work on the Sabbath and to not use the Lord's name in curses. She cried over the state of Europe. She urged conversion. The two children she appeared to were terribly poor. The front of the church at LaSalette has two identical towers, like the church at Medjugorge and like the World Trade Center.

5. Our Lady of Lourdes (1858, France)—A series of eighteen apparitions of Mary to Bernadettte Soubirous. Bernadette was from a poor family. The main message was healing of illness from the spring at Lourdes and the saying of the Rosary. Bernadette became a nun, and her body was discovered incorrupt when it was moved to Navarre. Mary asked that a shrine be built on that spot where people would come in procession. The parish priest asked for the Lady's name. Mary, looking to heaven, said, "I am the Immaculate Conception," always speaking in Bernadette's dialect, which the parish priest took as convincing evidence since the dogma had been declared only four years earlier, and Bernadette had no idea what it meant.[13]

---

[13] Roy Schoeman reminds us that Mary is the spouse of the Holy Spirit and that in a marriage, the two people share everything. Mary was immaculately conceived

By Dennis Jarvis from Halifax, Canada—France-002009—
Our Lady of Lourdes, CC BY-SA 2.0, https://commons.
wikimedia. org/w/index.php?curid=38269784. Author makes
free to use.

6. Our Lady of Pontmain (1871, France)—Only the children could see Mary, not the adults (did Charles Schultz get his idea from here?). Her apparition and action stopped the German troops and led to an armistice in the Franco-Prussian War. The apparition lasted for six hours. In some apparitions, Mary appears, but no words are spoken.

7. Our Lady of Knock (Ireland, 1879)—This is a rare apparition of Mary in that it includes the Eucharist. The apparition took place in 1879 at the end of the terrible hungers in Ireland. As a whole, it is a picture of the Mass. St. John's hand—two fingers

---

(without sin), but the other immaculate conception is the Holy Spirit: here, Mary is expressing the name of her spouse.

together show the two natures of Christ, the three unextended fingers show the oneness of the Trinity (*Knock*, EWTN, 2018).

Mary stands alone and looks up the heaven, only the lamb stands without reference to the other people there: St. Joseph points to Mary and to Jesus; St. John stands between them and also points to them both.

It's as if there are two halves to the apparition: on the left, St. Joseph, Mary, and St. John; and on the right or in the middle, the Lamb on the altar with angels and the cross.

The Lamb on the altar is a picture of Revelation. "Then I saw a Lamb, looking as if it had been slain" (Rev. 5:6, NIV). Perhaps Knock is the first apparition that points to the end of the world.

Jesus is the priest, the lamb, and the altar at Mass— and we see this in the Knock Apparition—St. Joseph, Mary, and St. John (preaching) are on the left side; in the middle, surrounded by angels, is the Lamb standing on the altar, and since it's by itself, one can say that it is the priest as well.

Public Domain, Author: Knock Shrine https://commons. wikimedia. org/wiki/File:Apparition_Chapel_with_Stained_ Window.jpg

8. Our Lady of Fatima (Portugal, 1917)—After the apparition of Our Lady of Guadalupe, probably the most important apparition of Mary is her apparition at Fatima. It appears to be a preparation for the end of the world. One might even suggest that as God created the world in six days, and Jesus restored the world in the six days of Holy Week, it was given to Mary to prepare the world for the return of the Messiah in the six apparitions of Fatima. Each of the six apparitions were very different, ending in the Miracle of the Sun on October 13, 1917, which was reported even in the secular newspapers where 70,000 people saw the sun spin in the sky and seem to hurtle toward the earth (and after which the rain-drenched ground and mud and their wet clothing was completely dry).[14] The apparitions at Fatima took place on the thirteenth of the month between May 13, 1917, and October 13, 1917.[15] The three children in Fatima, Portugal—Lucia, Jacinta, and Francisco[16]—had been visited by the angel of Portugal several times over two years who taught them to pray in preparation for the visit of Mary. Every pope since Pope Pius XI in the 1930s has tried to follow the requests of Mary at Fatima. Most of the popes have visited Fatima, some several times. Pope Saint John Paul II was shot on the feast day of Our Lady of Fatima. Cardinal Ratzinger, later Pope Benedict XVI,

---

[14] Fr. John Boughton, CFR, corrects the usually quoted 70,000 to 75,000. The seventy-five connects it to the era of peace if indeed the era of peace lasted from 1945 to 2020. Fr. Boughton also noted that the Miracle of the Sun was the largest public miracle, seen by more people since the parting of the Red Sea. (Talk [Larchmont, NY], 10/22/2020).

[15] Mary appeared to Jacinta in 1929 on the thirteenth of June. The children were canonized on May 13, 2017. The cause of Lucia is in process.

[16] Francisco and Jacinta died of the Spanish flu around the ages of ten or twelve. Mary had told Jacinta she would go to heaven. They were willing to offer their suffering for poor sinners. Francisco and Jacinto were canonized in 2017. Lucia died in 2005 at age ninety-seven, and her cause is in process.

released the interpretation of the Third Secret of Fatima in 2000, which had been kept hidden to not frighten the faithful.[17]

Pope Francis has said that the message of Fatima is more relevant today than ever. Many books have been written about Fatima. I recommend the one written by Fr. Andrew Apostoli, which is like a Fatima encyclopedia.[18] In each of the following paragraphs, I'll note one fact about the apparitions at Fatima. At Fatima, Mary said that if man did not stop offending God, Russia "would spread her errors abroad." This was the summer of 1917, after the Menshevik Revolution in Russia in February/ March of 1917 but before the Bolshevik Revolution (which was inexplicable in that it actually took over Russia with such a small number of people) in October/ November of 1917. The "errors of Russia" spoken of by Mary at Fatima are contained in Communism, "the sum of all heresies," specifically secularism, materialism, atheism, and the practice of abortion (which was made legal at the start of both Soviet Russia and Nazi Germany). We are struggling mightily with these errors even today. As a result, the popes had Catholics pray for the conversion of Russia at the end of every Mass from that time until Vatican II in 1965. And Mary also said if man did not stop offending God, the Holy Father would have a lot to suffer; Pope Pius XII suffered greatly during World War II, and John Paul II was shot and all but killed.

---

[17] The children had written out the words of Mary and given them to the Holy Father. The third message or third secret described the "bishop in white" who was shot along with many priests, religious, and holy men and women. In 2000, the "bishop in white" was identified as John Paul II who was shot in 1981 so it could be revealed without fear.

[18] Andrea Apostoli, *Fatima for Today: The Urgent Marian Message of Hope* (Ignatius Press, 2010).

Author: Albert Foronda, https://commons.wikimedia. org/
wiki/File:Our_Lady_of_F%C3%A1tima.jpg)

It might be that Mary and the prayers and sacrifices she asked for succeeded. The USSR lasted for seventy-five years (1917–1991). The last day of the USSR was Christmas Day, 1991; the flag over the Kremlin came down at 12:00 midnight of that day. And the next day, the USSR was dissolved (apparently, the leaders of the USSR had no sense of irony). At Fatima, Mary spoke of a period of peace granted to mankind. If Mary meant the period from the end of World War II in 1945 to 2020, that's a period of seventy-five years.[19] The Bible speaks of the length of a man's life as seventy years or eighty years if one is strong (Psalm 90:10). So seventy-five years as an era of time makes sense.

---

[19] The COVID-19 virus became known around the world on 12/31/2019, supporting the idea that we're entering a new stage in history.

The CCP, the Chinese Communist Party, began in 1949. If a third period of seventy-five years is followed, it will end in 2024. Since 1917, every pope has read the messages that Mary gave to the children at Fatima. Popes Pius XI, Pius XII, and St. Pope John XXIII made partial consecrations to the Immaculate Heart of Mary (partial because the bishops of the world could not be united because of war or the Council).

The bishops of Portugal repeatedly consecrated Portugal to the Immaculate Heart of Mary, and World War II and the Spanish Civil War did not cross into Portugal. St. Pope Paul VI was the first pope to visit Fatima. Pope John Paul I only ruled for thirty-three days. St. Pope John Paul II was shot on the Feast of Our Lady of Fatima. In the third message of Fatima, released in the year 2000 to the public, a "bishop in white" is shot as he makes his way up a mountain to a large cross (and many priests, religious, and laypeople are shot with arrows). The bishop in white falls, but the vision does not indicate that he was killed; it is only assumed.

If indeed John Paul II is the bishop indicated in the vision, he was shot but not killed, though it was very close. The assassin couldn't understand it since he said that he did not miss, but John Paul said that the assassin shot accurately, but Mary guided the bullets. The bullet missed his aorta by a tiny fraction of an inch (and John Paul later visited him and forgave him).

In one of the visions, Mary opened her hands and gave the children a vision of hell. They saw souls like embers flying into a large fire and coming back out again. They were terrified. Mary asked them to pray and make sacrifices for poor sinners who have no one to pray and sacrifice for them, a central message of Fatima. On October 13, 1917, the sixth apparition of Mary at Fatima, 70,000 people gathered at Fatima, many to prove that the apparitions were not true.[20] They waited and then saw

---

[20] The name of the town, Fatima, comes from the Muslim occupation of Spain: Fatima was the name of Muhammed's favorite daughter. Muhammad said that

the sun dance in the sky and swirl and appear to fall to the earth: they were terrified. During the Miracle of the Sun, the last apparition at Fatima, the three children saw Mary with the child Jesus and Joseph in several visions while the 70,000 people there saw the sun spin and hurtle toward the earth. If Fatima is a preparation for the Second Coming, and the Miracle of the Sun a template for what will happen at the end of time, perhaps those in God will see God coming while those outside will see disasters. Let's hope that at the end of time, we see Mary and Joseph and Jesus and not the sun hurtling toward the earth.[21]

In the messages to the children at Fatima in 1917, Mary mentions three periods of time: (1) The next and worse war if man did not stop offending God; (2) an era of peace if the world were consecrated to the Immaculate Heart of Mary by the Holy Father in union with the bishops of the world; (3) the end when her Immaculate Heart would triumph.

The war was World War II (preceded by a great light in the sky that Mary said would precede it).[22] The world was consecrated to the Immaculate Heart of Mary on March 25, 1984, by Pope St. John Paul II, thirty-nine years after the end of World War II.[23] The era of peace could be—since there have

---

the only woman who exceeded his daughter, Fatima, in virtue and greatness was Mary. Perhaps one of the unspoken themes of the apparition is the reconciliation of Christianity and Islam.

[21] Because of Mary's stress of praying for poor sinners at Fatima, the following was added to the end of each decade of the Rosary: "My Jesus, forgive us our sins, lead all souls to heaven, especially those most in need of thy mercy."

[22] On January 25, 1938, a large light appeared in the northern sky. Some thought it was the Northern Lights, some thought that Windsor Castle was on fire. One wonders why the light, which Mary said would precede the "next and worse war," appeared in January 1938 when Germany did not invade Poland until September 1939. But Japan invaded Manchuria in 1938, and this can also be considered the start of World War II.

[23] Pope John Paul wanted to do it in 1983 after he got shot on the anniversary of the first apparition of Fatima (May 13), but it didn't happen until 1984. If the era or peace runs from 1945 to 2020, 1983 is the midpoint.

been no worldwide disasters since World War II—the era from 1945 to 2020 (seventy-five years)[24] with the coronavirus being the first worldwide disaster since that time. Perhaps the era of peace is now over. That would leave only the end, during which her Immaculate Heart would triumph.

According to reports, the West was suspicious of a Russian attack in the early 1980s because of Soviet troop movements. We now know that they had identified a weakness in NATO, a weakness in the northern area of Sweden. It makes sense that the Soviet Union would have attempted an attack at this time because after this time, they were too weak to carry it out, and they had to try other strategies. It was their last chance. These areas were not defended directly by NATO but were defended by local forces and not adequately. But then, mysteriously, there was a large explosion at the Soviet Naval Base that would spearhead this attack, the Severomorsk Disaster, reported in the *New York Times*. Several thousand Soviet soldiers died, and the fleet was disabled, and the base was inoperable for several years, making the attack impossible. The clue comes in the date: May 13, 1984, the Feast of Our Lady of Fatima (the day of Mary's first apparition at Fatima).

At Fatima, Mary had asked everyone to pray for the conversion of Russia and had asked for the conversion of the world to her Immaculate Heart by the pope in union with the bishops of the world. Pope St. John Paul II made this consecration on March 25, 1984. It is sometimes argued that this consecration was not done as required (though it was), but one proof that it was accepted by heaven, as Lucia said, was that not even two months later, this unexplained explosion averted World War III (see Roy Schoeman, the last twenty minutes at https://www.youtube.com/watch?v=uImpWVhNy6A).

---

[24] Since the age of a man or woman in Psalms is seventy or eighty years (Psalm 90:10), seventy-five years would be an appropriate period of time for an era. Also, the coronavirus became known to the world on December 30 or 31, 2019, which might indicate that the next year would start a new era.

At Fatima, Mary began to prepare the world for the Second Coming, and she continues at Medjugorje. Adding the apparitions of Medjugorje and the Divine Mercy devotion given to St. Faustyna, Jesus and Mary seem to be preparing the world for the Second Coming.[25]

9. 1914, September, France, Our Lady of the Marne—One wonders why the Germans attacked the French to begin World War I, initiating a period of terrible slaughter. It seems one reason is that they couldn't resist. They had a great military advantage; it was a sure victory. But there is evidence that in September 1914, a month after the war began and with the Germans believing they were two days from reaching Paris, Mary appeared as the Lady of Lourdes and pushed the Germany army back, resulting in the four-year standoff. See https://www.michaeljournal.org/articles/roman-catholic-church/item/our-lady-of-lourdes-and-the-miracle-of-the-marne.

10. Our Lady of Beauraing or Virgin of the Golden Heart (Belgium, 1932–33)—Thirty-three apparitions of Mary. Mary identified herself as the Immaculate Conception and urged people to pray, perhaps in view of the Nazis and the eventual war.

11. Our Lady of Banneux or Our Lady of the Poor (Belgium, 1933)—Eight apparitions of Mary. Mary established a healing spring which was for all nations and which yields about 2,000 gallons of water a day with many healings.

12. Our Lady of America (Indiana, USA, 1956)—Mary pleaded for the US to return to purity, and she stressed the indwelling of the Trinity. Perhaps it was in view of what would happen in the 1960s.

---

[25] The key e-mail of Hunter Biden indicating who would receive what percentage of the money, including Joe Biden, was sent on May 13, 2017, the hundredth anniversary of the first apparition of Mary at Fatima. Pope St. John Paul II was shot and all but killed on May 13, 1981. He immediately asked for the secrets of Fatima (he had been focused on the Divine Mercy) and worked on the consecration of the world to the Immaculate Heart of Mary.

13. Our Lady of Garabandal (Spain, 1961–1965)—Covering the time of Vatican II, Mary appeared many times, perhaps several thousand times, sometimes two to three times a day, to four girls led by a girl named Conchita. There is tape on the Internet of the girls getting an inner call from Mary to come to see her. The girls, often in different places, would run to the spot. If traveling together, they would often run over the rocky ground without looking down and never tripping or falling at speeds and up hills beyond the ability of the onlookers. Sometimes they even travelled backward.

   During the apparitions, they prayed the Rosary with Mary (or to Mary), and those around would give them items for Mary to kiss. Then the girls would return them to their owner without knowing who their rightful owner was. The message of Mary was to repent to prepare for the final days. There would be something in Garabandal at the end that could be photographed but not touched. She mourned over many, even in the hierarchy of the Church who would live in ways not approved by the Church, and teach what the Church does not teach. At one point, Conchita asked Mary when these final events would take place. Mary responded that they would start when "Communism came back." Being 1961, Conchita asked, "Come back? Where is it going?" But we have seen it go and are now seeing it come back.

14. Our Lady of Zeitoun (Cairo, Egypt, 1968–1970)—A silent apparition, Mary appeared at the top of an Orthodox Coptic Church. Perhaps this is where she and Joseph and the child Jesus stayed while they were in Egypt. Muslims have a devotion to Mary.

15. Our Lady of Akita (Japan, 1973)—The weeping statue of Mary brings to mind Mary weeping over the deaths of children in abortion which was becoming legal in the United States. She spoke of the importance and power of praying the Rosary and also predicted, sadly, that evil would infiltrate even the Church with hints that the end is soon and repentance is needed.

Author: SICDAMNOME https://commons.wikimedia. org/
wiki/File:Virgin_Mary_of_Akita_Japan.jpg

16. Our Lady of Kibeho (Rwanda, 1994)—Mary called herself
    "Mother of the Word." She warned the people of Rwanda to
    stop condemning each other, but the genocide occurred when
    the people didn't listen (see Immaculée Ilibagiza).

17. Dublin visionary (Ireland, 1988–present)—Mary has been
    appearing to a **v**isionary in Dublin since the early 1980s. She
    has been told to remain hidden. But a woman in the late 1990s
    was given the task of spreading the messages this woman
    received from Mary. The messages are very like the ones at
    Medjugorje. The woman, Olive Dawson, has travelled around
    the world, speaking of these messages, and giving people the
    rosary, the book of messages, and the miraculous image that
    Mary gave the visionary. To prove that her calling was from
    God, Olive Dawson has not needed to eat or drink (or take
    medicine) since 1999 but lives on the Eucharist. The only liquid
    she gets, for example, is from the Blood of Christ at Communion.

    The miraculous image of Mary given to the visionary looks,
    generally speaking, like the image of Mary at Guadalupe, but its

theme is Mary Mediatrix of all graces: she is all in white, holding the rosary in her joined hands in prayer. Under her left arm is the blood from the Crucifixion which goes down into a chalice above which is a Host. If gotten, as a miraculous image, it must be placed under glass. Mary told the visionary that she wants to perform great miracles through this image if blessed by a priest. The image tells us that the graces of Christ's Passion and Death pass through her hands to the world. The book given to the visionary has "pearls," short sayings Mary gave to the visionary. They echo very much the messages of Medjugorge in style and substance (in a way, it is a companion apparition to Medjugorje.)

18. Our Lady of Medjugorje or Queen of Peace (Croatia, 1981–present)—Still ongoing, now for forty years, Mary stressed saying the Rosary, fasting on Wednesdays and Fridays, attending Mass and Confession, and to read the Bible daily. The Vatican has not made a judgment on this apparition since it is still ongoing with one of the visionaries getting monthly messages. But a recent report from a Vatican investigation argued that the fruits of this apparition are so great—conversions and healings—that it can now be followed freely.

Author: János Korom. https://commons.wikimedia.org/ wiki/ File:Statue_of_Our_Lady_of_Medjugorje.jpg)

Conclusion

Mary in her apparitions takes on the apparel and sometimes the features of the people to whom she is appearing, though she is still recognizable as Mary. One wonders if in heaven we will be able to take on the racial characteristics of different races. If Mary is who the Church tells us she is, one would expect her to have a large role in the end of the world as she does all times since the advent of Christ. And as Mary preceded Jesus in his first advent, she precedes him in his second advent.

The last apparition of Lourdes took place on July 16, the Feast of Our Lady of Mount Carmel, and in the last apparition of Fatima, during the Miracle of the Sun, Mary appeared dressed as Our Lady of Mount Carmel. Not only does this suggest that there might be connections between the different apparitions, but that they find their roots in Our Lady of Carmel which traces back to Mount Carmel where there were communities of prayer back to the time of Elijah.

Of course, there are many other apparitions of Mary. The Church has not had the time or evidence to approve them. One is the Virgin of the Marne who turned back the German armies who were on the verge of victory in World War I (cf. Roy Schoeman, *Salvation if from the Jews* [Radio Maria, Nov. 28, 2020]). There is the apparition of Mary to George Washington, I believe, at Valley Forge (cf. Janice T. Connell, *The Spiritual Journey of George Washington* [Hatherleigh Press, 2007]). And the apparition of Mary in the Philippines in the revolt of 1986 (cf. Roy Schoeman, *Special Election Rosary* [Youtube, Monday 11/23/2020]).[26]

---

[26] 28 A local priest who had not been very familiar with the Marian Apparitions recently studied and did a short series of talks on the four major ones. He said that after his study, he came to one conclusion: they strongly imply that we are near the end of time.

Suffering

In Matthew 8:27, Jesus and the apostles are in the boat, a clear symbol of the future Church, and a storm blows up. The boat is taking on water and is in danger of sinking, and Jesus is asleep in the back of the boat. They are in danger of dying. They wake Jesus, and he calms the sea and the waves. But he reprimands them, not for waking him but for being terrified. "O you of little faith"[27] (Matt. 8:26). He does criticize them, however, for being terrified and for now understanding that he has complete power. On the other hand, he also might have criticized them for being terrified in the face of suffering and death. This pericope might provide an entry into how God wants us to approach suffering and death: with complete trust. I would like to offer a few thoughts on the large subject of suffering. Historically, suffering has probably been the most common reason given for why people rebel

---

[27] 29 That's my tribe, unfortunately, the tribe of little faith.

against God. How can God exist and allow such horrific evil and suffering to take place? Camus left the faith for this reason.[28] And the rebellion against God seems to make its move out of sympathy for people (as if we care more for other people than God does and are more aware of his suffering). More recently, taking Richard Dawkins as an example, the new atheists have brought up the question of why there is suffering at all? Is God a sadist? Does he get joy out of our suffering? How else can we make sense of the reality of suffering and of great suffering? Of course, many Jewish people, in particular, dropped off their trust in God after the tremendous suffering of the Holocaust.

One way to approach the question of suffering is to ask what the world would have been like in a world without sin (w/w/sin)? It's clear that suffering as such was not part of God's plan for the world that suffering, including menial work (and decay after death) were only assigned to man after the fall. Perhaps as a result of the fall, suffering had to be instituted to restore what had been lost to creation. What would have been accomplished without suffering still had to be accomplished, and perhaps suffering was the only way to do it.

The book of Job suggests that this might be the case. At the end, when God appears to Job, God does not simply say to Job, "Who are you to complain? I am God and I will do whatever I want," but gives a rationale. God tells Job, though he does not owe Job an explanation and can do as he wishes, that he is building a world, and by implication, he needs this suffering, Job's suffering, to build this world. In this way, suffering is not a simple punishment but a sad, necessary addition to the world. In that way, the world will get to where it was meant to get, but it will have to do it the hard way.

In addition to what now has to be accomplished through suffering, here are some general observations about suffering:

- In Hebrews 10:5, Jesus is quoted, echoing Psalm 40:6–8, saying, "Sacrifice and offering You did not desire, but a body You prepared for me." Instead of bulls and goats, the definitive

---

[28] 30 But returned before he died as did Sartre.

offering is Jesus' body and blood. By extension, when we suffer, being part of the body of Christ, we can offer our suffering to God also for the salvation of souls. When Mother Angelica was healed of her back injury for which she wore a brace, she felt glad, but then she felt sad because she had nothing to offer to the Lord as a sacrifice. In a w/w/sin, we would have offered works to God, accomplishments and feats, but what we now cannot do or fail to do, owing to ORIGINAL Sin,[29] we make up with suffering as accomplishments and feats.

- The above idea in that we are part of the Body of Christ and our suffering is part of his or that he suffers also in us for the redemption of the world is supported by Paul's statement in Romans 12:1, "[t]o offer (our) bodies as a living sacrifice, holy and pleasing to God." In a w/w/sin, this would not have been necessary nor asked for.

- St. Paul in Romans 8:18 (NIV) gives us perspective on suffering: "Our present sufferings are not worth comparing with the glory that will be revealed in us." St. Paul suggests that, in my words, our suffering is finite but our joy in heaven is infinite and is not comparable.

- St. Paul in 2 Corinthians 4:17 (NIV) gives us another perspective on suffering: "For our light and momentary troubles are achieving for us an eternal glory that far outweighs them all." Which not only reiterates the idea that out suffering is finite while out joy will be infinite but that our suffering works to win for us this eternal joy. In a w/w/sin, God would expect us to work. As a result of sin, we can't do the work he has given to us,

---

[29] Some traditions do not hold for original sin. But it doesn't seem to make much sense that God would create a world with so many problems, even though he created it needing to be perfected, even without sin. G. K. Chesterton said that original sin was the only doctrine that could be proved empirically. In the film *Mother Teresa of Calcutta* (House of Knowledge, 2005), the Hindu doctor called to help a person taken sick says, "I don't know what we're paying for, but we're sure paying for something."

at least not in full, so we have the work of suffering to make up the difference.

- God did not exempt himself from this suffering. It can be argued that he suffered to some degree everything a human being can suffer. So we can't really say suffering is a punishment placed only on us for our sin since, primarily, God paid the price for sin with his suffering and death.

- In several place in the letters of Peter and of Paul, the sacrifice of Jesus is clearly spoken of as a ransom or redemption. In 1 Peter 1:18, Peter speaks of a redemption; in 1 Corinthians 6:20 (ESV), Paul tells us that we were "bought with a price." One asks to whom was this price paid? It's said that God did not have to pay a price to Satan who had conquered us. But I would suggest that God, being perfectly just, voluntarily agreed to pay a price to get us back. And we, as part of the Body of Christ, pay part of this price. If this is the case, our suffering is not the result of God's being bad or evil but of his being too good, too just: he is fair even to the evil.[30]

- Another reason for suffering is to keep us from sin, which would not have been necessary in a w/w/sin, of course, but is necessary since we have a tendency toward sin as a result of original sin. As Paul writes in 2 Corinthians 12:7 (NIV), "In order to keep me from becoming conceited, I was given a thorn in the flesh." One also thinks of the angel injuring Jacob's hip in Genesis 32:25.

- Another reason for suffering is for us to learn obedience. It was obedience that Adam failed, even if it was a severe test, and we became children of disobedience. So we had to be asked to do something which we would not do, would not want to do, and that is suffer.[31] As it says in Hebrews 5:8, speaking of Jesus, "He learned obedience from what he suffered." And God wants

---

[30] "He maketh his sun to rise on the evil and on the good" (Matt. 5:45, KJB).

[31] And dying, though I think dying as falling asleep, would still be present in a w/w/sin.

obedience not because he is a tyrant but because we have to learn obedience on the path to freedom. In addition, obedience has to be present as a factor for the closest of relationships to exist between unequal partners, even one that is eventually friendship.

- Hebrews 2:10 (NIV) even states that Jesus was made "perfect through what he suffered," suggesting that without suffering his human nature, which needed to be trained and educated, we would have lacked something. One sees this in nature in the example often cited of coal becoming a diamond through pressure. Of course, this would not have been necessary in a w/w/sin, and Jesus submitted to this path out of solidarity with us out of love for the Father.

- At Fatima, Mary asked the three children if they were "willing to accept all the suffering heaven sent to them for the conversion of poor sinners," and they said yes. Jacinta, age eleven or so, died alone in a hospital in Madrid of the Spanish flu after having several ribs removed to relieve pressure. Mary had said to them that "many go to hell because there is no one to pray and sacrifice for them." It appears that suffering is one coin in the realm of grace; it's an act we can do for the good of others. It is a form of work. The children had no problem understanding it.

- Along the same lines, our natures were twisted by sin, and it takes suffering to straighten them out again, mostly the grace from Jesus' suffering. This would not have been necessary in a w/w/sin.

- More generally, suffering teaches us all virtues, especially patience.[32] We need to learn virtue as a precursor to becoming holy and we need to become holy so we can exist in the presence of God, and suffering teaches us virtue. Again, in a world without sin, we would not have had to do it this way.

---

[32] In Romans 5:3–5, Paul tells us to rejoice at suffering because it produces endurance and presumably other virtues, and that produces character and then hope—hope that we can face whatever comes to us in this fallen world.

- At the same time, we do have to learn that God has complete and sovereign rights over us. By disobedience, we denied this reality. Suffering, which we don't want to do, definitely teaches us that it is the reality. Suffering teaches us—as does death—the sovereignty of God.

- In a w/w/sin, God would have to find out if we, if man, if men and women, intended to do God's will. In our world, suffering has this function since no one wants to suffer. And we know that all our suffering is known and at least permitted by God.

- The Church, the body of Christ, with Christ as its head, has to carry out the life of Christ as he lived it. Since "No disciple is above his teacher" (Matt. 10:24) and since the bride must be like the bridegroom (St. Faustyna, *Diary*), in our world, this involves suffering, but what we gain is unity with Christ who suffers with us as our head.

- In John 12:24 (ESV), Jesus states that if a grain of wheat die, "it bears much fruit." This no doubt can be applied to suffering as well: it is never wasted. As in Job, God needs it to build the world (but God would not have needed it in a w/w/sin). If suffering were present in a w/w/sin, God would be a sadist.[33]

- In Acts 9:4, Jesus asks Saul (Paul), "Why are you persecuting me?" This reassures us that when we suffer, Jesus is suffering with us, in us, and that he offers our suffering to the Father.

- In Luke 16:25 (NIV), in the parable of Lazarus and the rich man, when the rich man asks that Lazarus relieve his suffering, Abraham says to the rich man: "Son, remember that in your lifetime, you received your good things while Lazarus received bad things," which reassures us that God is aware of everything we suffer.

- When Mary appeared at Guadalupe and Juan Diego was in distress over his sick uncle, Mary said, "Am I not here, I who am your mother?" In other words, Mary (and Joseph and the

---

[33] But since God isn't a sadist, Dawkins is wrong as he is about most everything.

saints) is also with us when we suffer, and we don't need to fear. She then healed Juan Diego's uncle.

- In John 12:28, at the edge of the Passion, Jesus says, "Father, glorify your name!" Suffering, our obedient acceptance of suffering, gives us the most powerful opportunity to glorify God: to say that in spite of what we're enduring, God is good, that "I will see the goodness of the Lord in the land of the living." (Psalm 27:13, NIV) Job's patient suffering clearly glorified God in the face of Satan.
- In Luke 12:50 (NIV), Jesus says in the face of his Passion, "I have a baptism to undergo." So suffering is also a cleansing (not for Jesus but for us) and a passage into eternal life.
- In Genesis 3, God institutes suffering, perhaps not as a punishment but a necessary corrective and the first step in uniting us to Christ who will come. The one who strictly speaking is punished is the snake.[34] It could be that our suffering is the result of the disorder that our sin introduced into the natural and spiritual world.
- In Genesis 3:15 (NIV), God tells the snake, speaking of the offspring of Eve, "You will strike his heel." But this also refers to Mary and her offspring, Jesus. But since we are part of the body of Christ, this also refers to us. So our suffering is inflicted on us by Satan, not by God.[35] (I suspect we have to contribute to the ransom Jesus paid to win us back from evil, a voluntary payment.)
- One way to answer why we suffer, reducing it to the question of why Jesus had to suffer, could be found by looking at the different kinds of offering required by the Israelites in Leviticus since Jesus fulfills all of these sacrifices.
- Leviticus also helps us understand our suffering and death since we become pleasing sacrifices to the Lord. We can always see

---

[34] And as the biologists tell us, snakes have developed shoulders and hip joints, but they've always oddly stopped before developing arms or legs.

[35] Though God allows it to whatever extent it happens.

our suffering as work done that is offered to God to bring about good.[36]

- Finally, suffering gives our life a great nobility and even glory. And when we get to heaven, no matter what else we have done, we can say, "Lord, this is what I have suffered for you"; and the Lord might say, "I did not create you to suffer. Well done, my good and faithful servant" (Cf. Matt. 25:21).

I hope that these are some things we can hold on to when we are suffering. My favorite quote is that of St. Faustyna: "The bride must be like the bridegroom." But it doesn't answer the question as to why we or Christ had to suffer to begin with.

Having established the things that can be accomplished through suffering and perhaps only through suffering, there are three more questions to address. One is why, after Adam fell, did God not restore him to innocence immediately? If he loves us, why has the human race damaged and forced to go through such terrible suffering to reach the goal? Adam and Eve had (St. Thomas) original justice: they had no tendency toward sin; they had to darkness in their intellect; they had no weakness of will; and they had all the grace needed to live with God in this world and to carry out his work (the word *Eden* can mean "place of pleasure," and that's what God intended).

One reason here is that God is outside of creation and outside of time. In a sense, he created all of creation at once, and he can't step in and just stop something; he maintains the integrity of his creation. He gave angels and men (and women) free will, and he would take the consequences. God supports the freedom and responsibility he has instituted.

A second reason is that God is perfect justice and perfectly just. Adam and Eve were fairly tempted, and they fairly fell. To take away the consequences would be to remove the dignity of accepting the consequences of one's actions. This idea does not mean that God would

---

[36] Specifically to make reparation for poor sinners as Mary requested at Fatima.

not help man out of his problem, if he cooperated, but God would not act to undo what man had done and probably couldn't.[37]

A second question is why all mankind had to fall when Adam fell. Adam was and is the head of the human race not only in physical terms but, by God's design, the head of the human family after Christ. If God allowed all the rest of mankind to be free of sin, it would remove Adam from his position as head of the human family; where Adam led, the human family had to follow. And God would not do that.

Finally, why did God allow man to be tempted? Let's assume for the moment that Satan did not just suggest to Adam and Eve that it might be a good idea for them to eat the apple, which they clearly knew was forbidden and which they had every intention of avoiding. Let's assume, with Scott Hahn, that Satan threatened the life of Adam, giving him the choice of being killed (and trusting in God). Adam did not confront Satan and left Eve, undefended, as having little choice but to eat the apple.

But why did God allow Adam to be tempted, to be threatened and confronted with this terrible choice?

One reason is that Adam was intended to be the first priest, the priest of all creation, in God's plan. In order to assume this role, he had to be willing to die, to show complete trust in God. Or at least it was fair that he be tested in this way.[38] If Adam had not been tempted in this way, he would have been tested in another way (one thinks of how Abraham was tested).

But why was Satan allowed to tempt Adam? Satan had decided that he hated God, that he wanted to replace God; why not just exclude him from creation and let creation proceed as planned?

---

[37] Peter Kreeft even suggests that we "fall upwards." As a result of the fall, God's mercy is more clearly seen as is his love for us in not abandoning us but coming to our rescue and earned for God many more titles.

[38] Of course, if the angels had not fallen, Lucifer might have tested Adam, but it would not have been this severe at all.

One reason is that Satan or Lucifer is also a son of God.[39] As in Matthew 5:45 (NIV), "He causes his sun to rise on the evil and the good." One thinks of the deal God made with Satan in Job 1:11 and elsewhere. One thinks of the deal Jesus made with the demons in Mark 5:12 to send them into the swine. And one thinks of the deal that Pope Leo XIII mystically saw Jesus make in 1884 with Satan where Satan asked for a hundred years to have his servants do all they could to destroy Jesus' Church, and Jesus agreed.[40] God even prepared a place for Satan where, since Satan hates God, he would not have to experience God's presence, namely hell, which did not exist in God's original plan. God wants to do him good to the extent he can, even though Satan hates him, or at least to treat him fairly.[41]

Another reason is again that God created all of his creation at once, and Lucifer had a role in that creation. Perhaps he was intended to test Adam and Eve; perhaps he was intended to lead Judas to signal the time for Jesus' falling asleep in death; perhaps he had a role in preparing the world for the Second Coming. But having rebelled against God, when he appeared in these situations, he did not do what God intended but did all he could to damage God and his creation.

So in brief, in rabbinic style, the question "Why do we have to suffer?" can be reduced or replaced by the question "Why did Jesus have to suffer?" If suffering is the only way to recover what was lost and to correct the situation, and if God knew Adam and Eve would fall to temptation, the question "Why did Jesus have to suffer?" can be replaced with "Why did God allow Adam and Eve to be tempted by Satan?" If Satan had not fallen, the only temptation Adam and Eve faced was to

---

[39] One notices that when Jesus speaks to the demons, he describes them accurately but never speaks to them with hatred. Also, Satan could say to God, "I did not ask to exist," giving God another reason for God to deal with Satan justly, though it is not reciprocated at all.

[40] One thinks of David and his rebellious son, Absalom.

[41] 5 It seems that God accedes to some of Satan's requests, if they are reasonable. We see this in Job where Satan makes the case that Job would not praise God if Job were made to suffer, so God allows Satan to make Job suffer. And in Luke 22:31, Jesus tells Peter, "Satan has asked to sift each of you like wheat."

not eat from the Tree of the Knowledge of Good and Evil, and they were fully willing to comply with that command[42] (cf. Gen. 3:3).

The conclusion is that suffering is not a punishment and is not to be blamed on God but on Satan's malice and that God is too good and too just. He makes it rain on the good and on the bad (Matt. 5:45). He would not take away Lucifer's role in creation. And he would not take away his free will or ours.[43]

In conclusion, we might make a list of brief reasons for suffering mentioned above:

- Jesus suffered as an example for us.
- Jesus suffered because of his solidarity with us.
- We suffer because of our solidarity with Jesus.
- We suffer to pay a debt to God's justice—damage had been done.
- Perhaps the Tree of Life was made inaccessible to Adam and Eve not as a punishment but to keep them and any of their progeny (us) from eating of the tree and living until the end of time in a world of suffering.
- If we suffer from the damage done to creation.
- But the other is to satisfy God's justice. God is infinitely good, infinitely beautiful, infinitely good, but also infinitely just. And Adam and Eve freely disobeyed him, no matter what the circumstances.
- We suffer to learn obedience.
- We suffer to learn that God is sovereign, making us do what we would not do.
- We suffer because we can't produce the fruit God intended us to produce, so we suffer to do the work to make up what we lack; it is a form of work.

---

[42] And the command to be fruitful and multiply and the command to guard the garden and to keep it.

[43] Perhaps because in the end, God has all the power, and the damage done can be restored if we desire it.

- We suffer because suffering teaches us virtue, which we would have learned without suffering in a world without sin.
- We suffer because it gives us an opportunity to glorify God, to assert that he is good in spite of our suffering.
- We suffer to do justice to the devil. The devil had won mankind, and the suffering of Christ (and our suffering added) pays a debt (voluntarily) to win us back for God.
- We suffer to reform our inner life, which was twisted by sin.
- We suffer because we were disobedient to God; we are given the opportunity to be obedient through suffering.
- In suffering, we know that God suffers with us, gives us the grace and strength to suffer. In the movie *Quo Vadis*, Peter asks Jesus, "Where are you going, Lord?" And Jesus answers, "To Rome to be crucified again." So Peter turned around and headed back to Rome where he was crucified. Jesus did go to Rome to be crucified again here with Peter. Jesus goes through death with each one of us.
- If pride is the root of all sin, and humility is the ground of all virtue, suffering is an efficient way to teach humility.

For me, though, the most satisfying reason for suffering comes from a different direction. It's not very powerful today to say that we have offended God, so we must suffer to make up for it. God sounds like a punisher, even a sadist, though it is only just. But it is more palatable and understandable these days if we see it in terms of relationship.

In my experience, I committed a grave sin. I confessed the sin, and with the power of the Sacrament of Confession, I know I am forgiven of that sin. But God did better than that for me. He allowed me to suffer terribly for a short time and mildly for a longer time. As a result, when I look back at that sin, I say confidently, "I know I am forgiven of that sin, but more than that, I paid for it." So I know it is not only forgiven but resolved.[44] If anyone now accuses me of that sin, I can say the God

---

[44] Actually, we have evidence that God forgets ours sins once we confess them and do the penance (cf. St. Mary Alacoque).

forgave me, and I paid for it. It's over—done. In a second, in this case a hypothetical example, let's say some-

one takes $100 from me which I needed just at that moment and didn't have. If the person later asks forgiveness, I can forgive him or her. I can even forgive them before they ask in anticipation. But if I tried to have a further relationship with this person, this issue would still exist between us. It actually happened and has to be dealt with. Just as an example for argument's sake, let's say the person suffered ten strokes with a whip (any other punishment would do) for doing this to me, and the person voluntarily submitted to the punishment to restore our unburdened relationship. That would indeed reestablish our unburdened relationship because this issue would be resolved and could be forgotten completely. The person committed this violation, and they paid for it. The purpose of the punishment isn't suffering but relationship, the way to perfect relationship or full relationship.

And it doesn't matter if they returned the money or not because even if they returned the money, the damage of not having it when I needed it was lost.

However, there is another way for my penalty to be paid. Let's say in the above example that the person didn't have the $100 to return, and of course, he or she couldn't restore my lost opportunity or need. But he couldn't handle the ten lashes, so what could be done? What if his friend, out of love for him, said that he would voluntarily take the ten lashes, and the person agreed to accept this act for him, and that I agreed to accept this punishment for his crime, and it was carried out?[45]

In that case, the person who committed the crime could say that he had been forgiven and that his crime had been paid for. To deny that it had been paid for would be to deny the value of his friend's act (it might assume that I have a relationship with this third person as well).

And either or both acts to pay for the crime would allow the crime to be put out of the way and for the desired unhampered relationship

---

[45] An example of this situation is where St. Maximilian Kolbe offered to give his life in place of a family man who was condemned by the Nazis to death in the starvation bunker in the concentration camp.

to be restored. And in a way, it gave both parties or all three parties a chance to show how much they wanted this relationship in the first place.[46]

Of course, these two methods of paying for a crime or offense, which has to be dealt with in order to reestablish relationship, both apply to our sin or offense against God: we suffer, and Christ has suffered for us. But the purpose is not suffering but relationship.

And finally, it is said that the angels, if they could envy, would envy man for two things: for being able to receive Communion bodily and for being able to suffer for God, considering the glory it gives God and the fruits of grace that come from this return of obedience and love.

Addendum 1

In the face of suffering, it seems that the greatest task we have today is to forgive God. We suffer, and the explanation that God did not plan suffering for this world but that it was brought in by our own sin just doesn't seem to satisfy us anymore. We are suffering, and we didn't ask to exist, and why are we suffering? Though we can take this route and might take it without knowing it, it leads us nowhere.

On the other hand, we can do what Mother Angelica did: she had terrible back pain and had to wear a brace because of an accident she had with an industrial floor polishing machine. One day, she had a priest with the gift of healing on her EWTN television program, and he healed her of her back problem. At first, she danced with great joy. But then it occurred to her, "I have nothing to give Jesus." In other words, she gave each pang of suffering to Jesus as a little (or not so little) gift.

Or as Mother Teresa did when she suffered a disappointment or setback or a physical problem, she gave it to God "with a smile." Or we can do as blessed Solanus Casey did, always asking, "What does the good God have in mind?"

---

[46] Here I disagree, of course, with Tom Paine's repeated insistence in *The Age of Reason* that vicarious punishment is never acceptable. I suspect he is looking at the situation juridically and independent of relationship.

But perhaps underneath these actions is the fundamental decision to forgive God: I forgive God for allowing me to suffer. I might well know great joy in the future. I might win grace for myself or others through my suffering. I might learn virtue through my suffering. But that doesn't necessarily solve the problem. I do solve the problem if I choose to forgive God out of love. It's an indifference to suffering in this world—not that it isn't real or is an imagination—out of love as the saints and martyrs and Jesus himself show us.

Addendum 2

Richard Dawkins, the famous atheist/evolutionist, is an extreme example of not forgiving God. When he was young, his mother ran away from England to South Africa with an Anglican clergyman. She died in South Africa, and he, at twelve years of age, had to go to South Africa to bring her body back to England. Instead of forgiving God for allowing this to happen, not easy for sure, he has spent his life attacking God in every possible way.

Three Appendices—Preface

The first essay is meant to support the essay on Cantor. There are sayings from two friends, meant for enjoyment, and then the references.

1. Two Proofs in Cantor's Infinite Arithmetic
2. Jim Lonergan and Fr. Benedict Groeschel Sayings
3. References

Two Proofs in Cantor's Infinite Arithmetic

Cantor's proofs involving the adding of sets of infinite or finite size are easy to understand with a few illustrations, all from Cantor. First, we have to define an infinite number as the size of an infinite set and a finite number as the size of a finite set.

If two non-empty finite sets are added together, where the elements of one are not completely contained in the other, A and B, the result is a new finite set that is greater in size than either of the two original sets. A + B = C, where the size of C is greater than either the size of A or B.[1]

If a set of infinite size A is added to a finite set B, the result is a set with the same size as the infinite set: in terms of size, A + B = A. More generally, if a set of infinite size A is added to another set of infinite size B, the result is a set which has the same size as the larger of the two infinite sets: A + B = A or A + B = B.

As an example, take the infinite set of even natural numbers, set A: A = {2, 4, 6, 8, 10, etc.}

And the infinite set of odd natural numbers, set B: B = {1, 3, 5, 7, 9, 11, etc.}

If we add or join sets A and B, we get set C, the infinite set of all natural numbers:

C = {1, 2, 3, 4, 5, 6, 7, 8, 9, 10, 11, etc.}

Clearly, sets A and set B are proper subsets of set C (they are not equal to C), and sets A and B are not empty. These sets are of infinite size, and we can show that sets A, B, and C all have the same size or number of elements.

To show that the set A and the set C are the same size, consider the mapping n -> 2n from set C to set A. It sends 1 to 2, 2 to 4, 3 to 6, 4 to 8, etc. Clearly, every element in C is sent into A, and every element in A has an element in C sent to it. And no element in A has more than one element sent to it. This is called a one-to-one mapping, like the

---

[1] For example, if A = {1, 2, 3}, and B = {4, 5, 6}, A and B each have three elements, and A + B or A U B = {1, 2, 3, 4, 5, 6} and has six elements, six being greater than the size of A or B. Finite sets follow Aristotle, "The sum is greater than the parts."

rungs of a ladder, and its existence leads to the conclusion is that set C and set A have the same number of elements. A similar mapping n -> 2n-1 from set C to set B shows that the sets C and B have the same number of elements. So all three sets—A, B, and C—have the same size. Stating it more generally, if we add two sets of infinite size, A and B, we get a third set, C, which has the same size as the larger of the two original infinite sets.

If we consider a set D of finite size, for example: D = {0, 2, 4, 8, 10}

Since adding an infinite set to set B did not increase its size at all, adding a smaller finite set, set D, to set A, the result does not increase its size at all either. More generally, if A is an infinite set and B is a finite set, the resulting set A + B has the size of the infinite set A. This piece of the arithmetic of infinite numbers gives a model where adding a finite quantity to an infinite quantity does not change the infinite quantity. Of course, this result is nonintuitive since finite sets don't act this way.

Now let's sketch Cantor's proof that there is no largest infinity. If A is a finite set, we can always form the set of all subsets of A, called A' or the power set, and this set is always strictly larger in size than set

A. Cantor showed that this statement holds even if set A is infinite in size. Then, if A is a set of infinite size, the set of all subsets of A, the power set of A, or A', is infinite and strictly larger than A. If we take the power set of B', namely B'', this set is infinite and strictly larger than B'. Clearly, this process can be continued indefinitely, leaving {B, B', B'', B''', B'''', etc.], where $B_{n+1} > B_n$ in terms of size. The conclusions are that there are different sizes of infinity, at least an infinite number of sizes (1, 2, 3, 4, 5, etc.) and that there is no largest infinite size.

Jim Lonergan and Fr. Benedict Groeschel Sayings

Jim Lonergan (1938–2017)

(Before the politically correct era)

Faithful friends are a sturdy shelter.

—Sirach 6:14

1. [On someone leaving the Catholic Church over some disagreement] "You're leaving the Church? Don't let the door hit you on the ass on the way out."
2. [On what a priest should say to a lector who refused to read a part of the Gospel] "Get out. I have eyes and legs, and I can read it myself. I was just trying to be nice."
3. [On not being able to put salt on food after his heart attack at age forty] "No one told me that salt is what gives food taste."
4. [On not being able to eat food with cholesterol after his heart attack at age forty] "I live Lent all year round."
5. [On someone who promotes evil] "I would make him wish his father never met his mother."
6. [Quoting Stephen Decatur] "My country, right or wrong, but my country."
7. [On de-accessioning books from a small library in Manhattan] "I'm working on the Manhattan project."
8. [On turning away an unwelcome solicitor] "Don't go away mad. Just go away."
9. [On being asked questions over the phone pacifically] "Oh, why would you want to know something as personal as that?"
10. [On all the medicines he had to take] "I rent my body from the drugstore."
11. [On winning small arguments by not responding, using passive aggression] "You can't push a string."

12. [On a new student worker finally understanding a direction] "If you can't bring Mohammad to the mountain, you can bring the mountain to Mohammad."

13. [After a not too successful evening] "It's been real, it's been nice. It hasn't been real nice."

14. [On research for library science classes] "Little known facts by less known people."

15. [On finding an easier way of doing something] "There are more ways to skin a cat than to drop an elephant on it."

16. [A response the saying in computer science, "Garbage in, garbage out"] "The person who put it in was garbage."

17. [On a computer not working] "Wind it up tighter next time."

18. [On a computer not stopping] "You can always pull the plug."

19. [On some women getting angry when a man holds a door for them] "When manners come back, mine won't be among them."

20. [On some politicians] "How did these idiots make it through the birth canal?"

21. [On Ted Kennedy running for president] "Every time he tries to run for president, Mary Jo Kopechne will rise out of that lake."

22. [Of a not too tall man who, in depression, has taken to eating] "He's easier to jump over than to walk around."

23. [In regard to those who stretched the meaning of the Council] "He is Vatican too much."

24. [To a young man who wouldn't follow directions] "I would stick my foot so far up his ass he would see my foot when he brushes his teeth."

25. [Of someone not working too hard] "He thinks the world owes him a living."

26. [On a student worker who has too many suggestions] "If I want your opinion, I'll ask you for it."

27. [On a student worker who has too many suggestions] "If I want your opinion, I'll give it to you."

28. [On Deism] "God gave it a kick and then left it to itself."

29. [On Socialism or Communism] "What's mine is mine, and what's yours is mine too."

30. [Jim's favorite Scripture verse, which he used in certain circumstances] "Scripsi, scripsi."[2]

31. [A favorite person in the history of the Catholic Church] Torquemada.

32. [On Senator Joseph McCarthy] "For all his problems, he turned over some rocks and found some snakes."

33. [On intellectuals] "If you send an intellectual out for a loaf of bread, he'll come back with a quart of milk."

34. [On a priest who tampered with the words of the Mass] "I would parboil him."

35. [On committees] "The mountain groaned and brought forth a mouse."

36. [On someone not putting the Host immediately in his or her mouth] "Eat it or give it back." —Jim

37. [On an unlikely event] "You could count the number of times that has happened on less than one hand."

38. [On a news reporter he didn't like] "He would have to come up to be retarded."

39. [Jim's self-description] "I'm a type-A personality. The shortest path between two points is a straight line."

40. [On seeing someone's nose broken] "His nose was taking a slow walk to his left ear."

41. [On someone about to get a tongue-lashing] "Better put on your asbestos suit."

42. [Of his mother, a very capable RN who made house visits, on what she would do to a slipshod doctor's office] "Half the office staff she would fire, and the other half wouldn't work for her."

43. [Of a "milk toast" or mild preacher] "It's like putting your hand into a pitcher of warm spit."

---

[2]   "What I have written, I have written." —Pilate (John 19:22).

44. [On needing the word *convex*] "I wish I had a confectionary oven."

45. [On someone getting an unfair deal] "I don't like being screwed without taking my pants off."

46. [About a priest who gave a ho-hum sermon] "I've forgotten more theology than he knows."[3]

47. [On the existence of moral truths that hold regardless of one's religion] "I don't care if he's a Hottentot and worships a stick."

48. [About adults' knowledge of their religion] "Many adults, titans of Wall Street, lawyers, doctors, unfortunately, are fifth-graders when it comes to religion."

49. [One of his favorite stories] "When the No Nothings in the 1850s threatened the Catholic Churches, Archbishop Kendrick of Philadelphia decided to pray about it, and four churches burned down. In New York, Archbishop John Carroll said, 'If you burn down a church, I'll turn this into another Moscow' and lost no churches."[4]

50. [On a well-carried out strategy] "Sometimes I don't rattle before I strike."

51. [On how he would reprimand a badly disobedient officer if he were in the army] "When I got through with him, he'd be able to walk out under a closed door."

52. [On firing someone after making a big mistake] "If I were his boss, he would meet himself coming in the front door."

53. [As he got older] "I could swear that my bladder had ears."

54. [On explaining why a leader would make a decision that causes others to suffer, bringing to mind *The Odyssey*] "It depends on whose ox is being gored."

55. [On a bad driver coming in the other direction] "He's taking his half out of the middle."

---

[3] Jim was a simply professed Dominican Brother and an ordained deacon but was denied the priesthood three months before his ordination for psychological reasons.

[4] Napoleon had burned down Moscow about forty years earlier in 1812.

56. [On being accused of not being a good Christian] "That's between me and my confessor."

57. [On an unpredicted snowstorm] "I just shoveled four inches of partly cloudy."

58. [On a news reporter] "He changed his hairstyle to look older… the former style took ten years off his life."

59. [On a poor news reporter] "That brain removal operation was successful."

60. [On compromising to get along] "Be reasonable; do it my way."

61. [At hearing of a priest making a mistake] "Priests put their pants on just like the rest of us, one leg at a time; otherwise, they fall on their butt."

62. [On a revolutionary struck by a policeman] "He saw stars he didn't know existed."

63. [On dealing with an undisciplined youth] "After I got through with him, he'd have a brand-new outlook."

64. [On an unctuous person] "He has all the personality of a tarantula in heat."

65. [On a clever political move] "He has something up his sleeve beside his arm."

66. [After a friendly attempt initial try that did not work] "Well, we tried nice, and it didn't work. Now we'll try ugly."

67. [When someone finally understood something] "'I see,' said the blind man as he picked up his hammer and saw (a triple pun[5]).

68. [When someone didn't get what he or she wanted] "And I want to be pope, but it ain't gonna happen" [sic].

69. [On whether or not a new idea will be accepted] "Run it up the flagpole and see who salutes it."

---

[5] The only other three-word pun I've seen is where the father and three sons were out West to herd cattle: "I called the ranch 'Focus' because that's where the sons raise meat" (Asimov).

70. [On someone getting a life sentence] "He'll spend the rest of his life breaking big rocks into little rocks."

71. [On the time right before a disaster] "I thought God was in his kingdom and all was right with the world."

72. [On inspiration] "If you go out on the street corner and preach Christ, and the Holy Spirit did not send you to do it, you'll find yourself on the street with no money and no clothes."

73. [On returning to work after lunch] "Back to the salt mines."

74. [On someone saying, "That's a good idea"] "That's the only kind I have."

75. [After watching a politician claim that his way was right, only to find it was very wrong as Jim predicted] "A large piece of humble pie, anyone?"

76. [After watching a politician claim that his way was right, only to find it was wrong] "You better speak your words softly. You might have to chew them."

77. [On someone making a dumb statement] "He couldn't spell 'CAT' if you spotted him the 'C' and the 'A.'"

78. [On the lethal nature of the SS] "The SS were so dangerous that if they captured an SS officer, the officer would say, 'Take him to the prison camp and be back in ten minutes.' The problem was that the camp was two hours away [they were shot]. And if an SS officer was captured and traveling on a train, they were told, 'If the SS officer sticks his head out of the window, shoot it off,' and they did. They were so dangerous."

79. [On facing a difficult adolescent] "Bring back the draft."

80. [On disciplining a worker] "I would hand him his head."

81. [When the snake bites the snake-handler in a fundamentalist service] "No one told the snake."

82. [On low pay] "We pretend to work, and they pretend to pay us."

83. [On getting older with increasing health problems] "The game is not worth the candle."

84. [On a public figure caught misbehaving] "Roman hands and Russian fingers."
85. [In a rare pensive moment] "I need a new life."[6]
86. [On it raining with a blue sky and a rare admission] "I never understood that."
87. [Because Jim only saw out of one eye at a time] "I only see out of one eye."[7]
88. [On optics, à la Gracie Allen]

    Jim: "Lightning is scary when seen from a plane twelve miles away."
    Ed: "Why twelve miles?"
    Jim: "Because that's how far the human eye can see." Ed: "But what about seeing the moon?"
    Jim: "That's not measured that way. That's measured in nautical miles."

89. [On cuisine] "I buy stuffed peppers... I take out the stuffing and throw out the peppers... I don't like green peppers."
90. [On Catholics not accepting the teaching of the Church] "If you don't want to play by the rules, you can pick up your marbles and go home."
91. [On Pope Francis, who was a Jesuit, and the sometime discomfort of the Irish with the poverty of the Franciscans] "The pope is a closet Franciscan."
92. [On short flights] "A puddle-hopper."
93. [On liturgists after Vatican II who stretched the bounds of liturgy a little too far] "I would put all the liturgists in a bag and then shoot the bag."
94. [On aging actors becoming less able] "Paul Newman was one of the few actors who survived until the end of his career."

---

[6] Which is exactly what Christ offers us.
[7] He was cross-eyed at birth and had the operation too late to have binocular vision restored.

95. [On James the Greater and James the Lesser] "I think the greater means he was the older brother."[8]

96. [On being accused of changing his position on an issue] "That was then, this is now."

97. [On the theology of salvation] "There is no salvation outside the Catholic Church, unless you mean that people of good will are saved by the cross of Christ no matter what their religion. On the other hand, if I deserve to be condemned, even the Catholic Church can't help me."

98. [On the current presidential candidates] "A group of has-beens and never was-es."

99. [On God] "Keep in mind that God doesn't need us. He is self-sufficient in himself as Trinity."

100. [On saying something unpopular] "Just spell my name right. The worst thing is being on stage and not being noticed."

101. [On silly questions like "What was God doing in the time before creation?"] "Creating hell for people who ask questions like that."[9]

102. [On being disinterested, using Irish exaggeration] "It's like I almost care."

103. [Showing his Jansenist leanings (a heresy that taught that no pleasure was allowed) from a training over which he had no control] "That disgusting Renaissance art."

104. [On the gentle saintly Cardinal Terrence Cooke, d. 1984, getting angry at an unjust criticism] "That was the one occasion Cookie got up on his hind legs."

105. [On enemies of the Catholic Church] "Historically, the greatest enemies of the Catholic Church have been ex-priests. They had it all and they gave it away and they can't get it back."[10]

---

[8] What parents would name two of their sons James?

[9] Actually, it's a good question: it looks like there was no time before creation, it seems now that time was created with physical creation.

[10] An example of this saying, in my opinion, is James Carroll. In *Constantine's Sword* (2001), he argues that because the Church misused power to whatever extent during the Middle Ages, it would have been better if they had never been given

106. [One of Jim's favorite quotes, this one from Henry Kissinger or John Connolly, reputedly, during the riots] "If he lies down in front of my limousine, it will be the last limousine he lies down in front of."

107. [On presenting an obvious solution to a problem that the other person hadn't thought of] "He looked at me as if I had invented the wheel."

108. [On fights in hockey] "If you give a bunch of Neanderthals a bunch of sticks, what do you expect?"

109. [On what he could do to a child who was giving his parents a hard time] "Give me a few hours with him. When the parents get him back, they'll think I gave them back the wrong child."

110. [On a criminal who hurt someone that he needs to feel some pain] "Someone needs to 'splain [sic] it to him."

111. [On abbesses from Europe in the Church before Vatican II who are equal to ruling bishops in canon law] "No bishop with a sense of self-preservation took them on."[11]

112. [On a car not moving at a green light] "It ain't gonna get any greener" [sic].

113. [When a politician suggests a particularly ridiculous idea] "Just pat him on the head and tell him to go away."

---

the freedom from Constantine making the Church legal in the early 300s. But that freedom allowed the Church to fix the contents of the Bible, to fix the Mass and Breviary, to develop Canon Law, to fix the Creed—i.e., to establish its way of life which allowed the Church to rescue Europe after the fall of the Roman Empire, at the very least. Also, at a talk at Iona College (New Rochelle, New York, May 2019), he argued that the division between the Christians and Jews during the first century was the fault of the Christians and that this separation set the pattern for all future conflict between any two groups, even until today. It's unique in my experience that I heard a talk where I disagreed with everything the speaker said. He even suggested that Calhoun College at Yale should not have been named Franklin College because Benjamin Franklin established the University of Pennsylvania—he didn't know that Yale had been working on the Franklin papers for the last forty years.

[11] Rightly or wrongly, he would use the name of (Blessed) Mother Mallinckrodt, the foundress of the Sisters of Charity, because her name sounds harsh.

114. [On teaching] "The secret of teaching is to make them more scared of you than they are of each other or of anything else."

115. [On the treatment of enemies] "When I get through with him, there won't be enough left to bury."

116. [On priests giving a short sermon at the very start or at the very end of Mass] "Of course he had to give us a spiritual nosegay."

117. [On someone making a big mistake] "He really stepped in it."

118. [On a new theological idea that is heretical] "Some heresies are so old they're new again."

119. [On someone writing something heretical] "I wouldn't use it to paper my cat's litterbox. My cat would refuse to use it."

120. [On Church organization] "Every bishop is pope in his own diocese."

121. [On Canon Law] "You can do anything with a rescript."[12]

122. [On revolts] "The first man who rebels, hit him in the face with a shovel. It will give the others pause for thought."[13]

123. [On a worker who finally understood the instructions] "It's always darkest before the dawn."

124. [On caring for his heart trouble compared to his other ailments when cars had carburetors] "If the carburetor doesn't work, it doesn't matter what's going on with the tires."[14]

125. [On a bad politician] "You know what they say. If you don't have less on, you have more on."

126. [On his funeral] "Half will come to mourn. The rest will come to make sure."

127. [On conflicts] "Let's get it on."

128. [On prolific writers] "He's never had an unpublished thought."

129. [On Catholics who hold up their hands during the Our Father] "Raindrop Catholics."

---

[12] A rescript is permission to do something that ordinarily would contradict canon law.

[13] Yet he always remembered, almost with horror, the time he ran over a squirrel that had run in front of his car, leaving him no time to turn away. He had to take a bar out of his trunk to put it out of its misery. He would not hurt a fly.

[14] Showing Jim's limited knowledge of how cars work.

130. [On someone making a risky choice which ends in disaster] "You pays your money and you takes your chances" [sic].

131. [On a priest giving a detailed explanation as to why he wants to leave the priesthood] "Okay, Father, what's her name?"

132. [On counseling a gay person] "Of course I could counsel a gay person as long as he didn't want to sit on my lap."

133. [On not responding when an "enemy" said something inappropriate] "I just let it hang there."

134. [On people in the congregation who make prayerful hand gestures during Mass] "Oratory gestures are reserved to the priest."

135. [On someone being lured into a trap] "'Come into my parlor,' said the spider to the fly."

136. [On an archbishop who wears purple and hopes to be a cardinal, wearing red as if he were a cardinal] "That's the reddest purple I've ever seen."

137. [When he was very sick and was asked about his car] "Don't talk about trivialities."

138. [After someone says something particularly questionable] "It takes all kinds to make a world."

139. [On a proud priest] "He thinks he's another Fulton Sheen."

140. [On the most confused children] "The most messed up kids are the children of child psychologists."

141. [On Darwinism] "Maybe your ancestors were apes."[15]

142. [On getting an argument from a worker] "Because I said so."

143. [On doing something he didn't want to do] "I had to make an explicit act of the will."

144. [On high Anglicanism] "Smells and bells."

145. [On seeing a priest sitting on the ground under a tree praying] "Hey, Siddhartha."

---

[15] Jim, of course, agreed with Catholic doctrine: however man and woman's body evolved, at some point, God intervened and inserted a human soul into this body.

146. [On Cardinal Spellman dealing with his priests] "You could steal a car at high noon, and he would protect you, but if you caught you with a woman, you were finished."

147. [On life in general] "You have to do what you can't get out of."

148. [On World War II] "Our Germans beat your Germans."

149. [When someone relates a terrible experience that is now over] "Besides for the loud noise, how was the play, Mrs. Lincoln?"

150. [Jim's favorite quote about Communism, adjusted from George Orwell's *Animal Farm*] "Some pigs are more equal than others."

151. [On someone assuming he was naïve] "I was born at night, but it wasn't last night."

152. [On his life] "I had the talent of administration but never had a chance to use it."

153. [A favorite harmless dialog] "First Massachusetts woman: 'What did you have for lunch?' Second woman: 'Scrod.' First woman: 'I've never heard it before in the pluperfect.'"

154. [On computers and artificial intelligence] "If it can really think, we'll baptize it."[16]

155. [On deciding not to confront the boss over a disagreement] "You have to decide what hill you want to die on."

156. [One of Jim's favorite stories] "One day, a man broke into a Capuchin Franciscan monastery and killed an elderly friar who probably couldn't hear what the man wanted. He also attacked a nun in another monastery, and then he fled town. The police didn't find him. A few months later, the local head of the Mafia sidled up to the police chief and said, 'Do you remember that case about the nun who was attacked? You can close that case.'"

157. [Another favorite story] "One time on Arthur Avenue in the Bronx, someone stole the crown from the statue of Our Lady of Carmel. The local Mafia in the area let the word get out:

---

[16] In Thomistic terms, if it thinks like a person, it would have to have a human soul created by God, so it should be baptized.

'Either the crown comes back or the hands that took it come back.' The next day, the crown was in a box on the rectory steps."

158. [On being right and someone else wrong as Sylvester catching the bird in his mouth] "What bird? Who, me?"[17]

159. [On poisonous snakes in Texas where the poison has to be sucked out of the bite] "What happens if you get bit on the butt? You find out who your friends are."

160. [On parental duty] "That father was with his son at the library. After a hard day of work, it was the last place he wanted to be. But he was there."

161. [On an obvious point, showing his training in St. Thomas Aquinas' terminology] "That's just simple apprehension."

162. [On getting older] "I'm dying by inches."

163. [On liberals] "They eat their own."

164. [On materialist evolution] "Maybe your ancestors were apes."

165. [Jim was conservative, but on seeing a politician who is more conservative] "He makes me look like Rebecca of Sunnybrook Farm."

166. [On a poor presidential candidate] "The other party could run Donald Duck and win."

167. [On a severe looking archbishop] "If he smiled, his face would crack."

168. [On asking for a favor] "If you want something done, ask the man who is busy."

169. [On a conflict finally breaking out into an open fistfight] 182. "There are two people in history of whom you do not ask "And a good time was had by all.""

170. [On being asked who said something he disagreed with] "Some nonentity."

171. [On someone choosing unattractive clothing or decor] "He has all his taste in his mouth."

172. [On politics] "America is God's last chance to make a world."

---

[17] Jim's favorite cartoon character was Garfield.

173. [On art] "Art never did anything for me."

Fr. Benedict Groeschel (1933–2014)[18]

174. [On acting while one has the chance and that sometimes one only gets one chance to do something] "You will not pass this way again."
175. [On the existence of evil] "People can't be that cruel without help."
176. [On Hugh Hefner] "When he comes to die, he will be as chaste as possible."
177. [On being asked to say a Mass for the intentions of the Blessed Virgin Mary] "I do not have that much courage."
178. [On priestly celibacy] "But I dream in technicolor."
179. [On New York] "If sex is what made people happy, New York would glow."
180. [On the path of his vocation] "In the novitiate, I told my spiritual director that I didn't feel that I had a cross. Then one day, a truck pulled up with crosses of all different colors and sizes, and they were all for me."
181. [On Euthanasia] "They lived badly. They might as well die badly."
182. "There are two people in history of whom you do not ask the question, 'Who is it?' but 'What is it?' Buddha and Jesus."
183. [On the existence of fallen angels] "Man cannot be that bad without help."
184. [On being told that his building of a hospital for the poor in Central America was a large endeavor] "I hate small endeavors."
185. [As he got older] "After saying two Masses, I feel as if I've been run over by a bus."

---

[18] Fr. Benedict Groeschel was Mother Teresa's liaison with the Archdiocese of New York from the 1970s to the 1990s. His great-great-granduncle was the Primate of Ireland. He was a Capuchin Franciscan priest and then started his own reform order, the CFRs.

186. [On getting older] "It feels like Christmas comes around every two weeks."

187. [On advising someone to enter a career different from the person's father's career] "My father was not a priest."

188. [On the mystery of relics] "We don't even have a side table from St. Joseph."

189. [On salvation outside the Church] "God wouldn't leave salvation only in the fumbling hands of the Catholic clergy."

190. [On passing a dilapidated house, echoing a person or the Church] "I hate to see a broken-down house."

191. [On death] "Who wants more of this?"

192. [Responding to praise and that he should have a long life, keeping his humility] "You can't kill a bad thing."

193. [On the work of a priest] "If you want gratitude, buy a dog."

194. [On himself] "I hope to get to purgatory."

195. [On a poor man who kept getting involved in petty crime] "He's doing life on the installment plan."

196. [On preaching] "Sometimes you send your bread on the waters, and all you get back is some soggy bread."

197. [Fr. Benedict spoke to and advised bishops and cardinals and gave retreats to priests from all around the country. A living saint. On being reminded jokingly by the pastor of the parish in which his retreat house resided that the pastor had some authority over him] "Don't let it go to your head."

198. [On the large amount of work God had given him to do] "If there were an easier way to get to heaven, I would have found it."

199. [On his working all the time] "One day, the wheels will fall off."

200. [His response on being asked how he was doing] "It's the worst day of my life."

201. [On heaven] "There must be an easier way to get to heaven."

202. [After saying several Masses and leading a Rosary group] "I was overdosing on piety."

203. [On our broken world] "When one wants to pray, often it is time to work, and when it's time to work, often one wants to pray."

204. [On the existence of heaven] "When you're from Jersey City, you know there just has to be something better."

205. [On someone not accomplishing what he should] "He'll be sweeping up ten years after the apocalypse."

206. [On the Franciscan style of birthday celebrations] "Sickness and death both abound/Death and darkness all around/But happy birthday, happy birthday."

207. [On strategy from his early days as a caddy echoing Pope Francis] "Stay on the fringe."

208. [On coming from Jersey City and receiving an award for serving the poor from the Queen of Denmark] "In Jersey City, we're not too familiar with dealing with royalty."

209. [On God's love for us compared to our love for God] "I'm not impressed with our love for God."

210. [On where he came from] "I'm from Jersey City where most of the mayors end up in jail."

211. [On a not too successful abstract sculpture] "A direct hit on a junkyard."

212. [On giving a universally great man a local honor] "It would be like naming Jesus a monsignor."

213. [On being asked by a very wealthy upper east-side New Yorker for help since she found no meaning in life] "You could fake it."

214. [On Terrence Cooke, his secretary and then auxiliary bishop, succeeding Cardinal Spellman as Archbishop of New York in 1968] "They forgot who was feeding him his Wheaties."[19]

---

[19] A bishop does not have the authority to name his successor, but Cardinal Spellman had so much authority in the American Church that he had great unofficial say as to his successor.

215. [On being born in Jersey City and to be buried in Newark, New Jersey] "I guess going from Jersey City to Newark is a step up."

216. "In the struggle between the East and the West, the East will win because they have the people." Sermon, 11/5/2004 (the West has killed many of its people, sadly).

217. "Judas was sorry." Sermon, 1990.

218. [On being asked to be one of Mother Teresa's spiritual directors] "It's like paddling a canoe next to the Queen Mary."

219. [On how to live life] "Go for the gusto."

220. [On getting tired as he got older] "It's like someone pulled the plug."

221. [His suggestion for his tombstone] "I tried."

222. [On stepping into the middle of the conflict in Lebanon in the 1980s to rescue a hospital of disabled children and being asked about the soldiers] "All I see are children of God."

223. [On being asked about Christopher Hitchens,[20] a vicious and vocal critic of her] "It's not between me and him. It's between him and God."

Mother Teresa of Calcutta – St. Teresa of Kolkata (1910–1997)

224. [With an interviewer and a photographer on being asked the greatest cause of evil in the world] "Me, you, and him."[31]

225. [On a priest contradicting her plans] "Remember, you're just a priest."

226. [When she wanted a piece of property for a convent, and the archbishop argued for another place, ensuring that she would get her wish] "Well, you know, I am just a sick old woman."

227. [On Eucharistic Adoration] "The best time you will spend on earth."

---

[20] Christopher Hitchens was the one who petitioned the Vatican that Mother Teresa not be beatified; he argued that she loved the poor in order to build a kingdom of her own and wanted to keep them poor and sick.

Other

228. [On being criticized by a cardinal and getting defended by Rome] "You have a diocese, I have a television station." —Mother Angelica

229. [On Karl Haas of NPR's "Adventures in Good Music"] "He has a sense of humor, though it's rather elephantine."—Tim Coln32

230. [On the naturalness of man seeking God] "We have a God-detector in us." —Peter Kreeft, Talk (Eastchester, New York, 2018).

231. [On the mercy and goodness of God] "When we fall, we fall upwards." —Peter Kreeft, Conference (Immaculate Conception Parish, Tuckahoe, N., 2018).

232. [On God not overriding our free will] "We are given enough light so that those who seek the truth will or can find it. But we're not given so much that those not interested in the truth have to accept it against their free will." —Peter Kreeft, Conference (Immaculate Conception Parish, Tuckahoe, NY, 2018).

233. [Comment of a Jewish doctor when asked why he was sitting on the right while attending the profession of vows of a Catholic nun, one of his patients] "I'm sitting on the groom's side." —Dr. Arnold Zucker. MD.

234. [Comment of a Jewish doctor on the Israelites crossing the Red Sea, reflection on his patients] "When God brought the Israelites through the Red Sea, Moses brought the crippled and lame also, left no one behind." —Dr. Arnold Zucker, MD.

235. [On peace from a coworker] "I am a Franciscan Sister of Peace, and I'll go to war to prove it." —Sister Georgeanne.

236. "Science is man's attempt to understand the mind of God." —Caprice Adler (à la Einstein).

237. [On only receiving e-mails from the boss which were critical] "Another nastygram." —Michael Sarro

238. "I might not leave this world a better place, but I'll leave it a cleaner place." —Michael Sarro

239. [On temptation] "It's my strongest weakness." —Uncle Frank Lowe

240. [To an unpleasant person] Unpleasant person: "See you tomorrow." Response: "Not if I see you first." —Uncle Frank Lowe

241. [His method of repeating predictable bureaucratic directions] "Yada, yada, yada, woof, woof, woof." —Anthony Mastantuoni

242. [On being told that his rather uninspiring boss was not in because the light in her office was out] "Her light has been out for years." —Anthony Mastantuoni

243. [On death] "You can't get out of this world alive." —Richard Mitchell

244. [On a worker at a country club always asking his boss questions] "Every time I turn around, he's up my nose."—Gori Cesarotti

245. [On working at a country club] "We were born on the wrong side of the fence." —Gori Cesarotti.

246. "What would you do without me? You would do without me." —Vera Turvin

247. [On prayer and fasting] "I haven't managed to pray and fast. All I've managed is to pray and eat." —Saroin Porter

248. [On bad new ideas, including Communism] "Modernism is the sum of all heresies." —Pope Saint Pius X

249. [On China] "Russia was one thing, but when China gets going, look out." —Robert Sandstrom

250. [On Communism] "If I had ten Franciscans, I could have saved Russia." —Lenin.

References

Literature

Alighieri, Dante. *Inferno*. 1913. Boston, New York: Houghton, Mifflin and Co. (Translated by Henry Wadsworth Longfellow.)

—. *Paradiso*. 1913. Boston, New York: Houghton, Mifflin and Co. (Translated by Henry Wadsworth Longfellow.)

—. *Purgatorio*. 1913. Boston, New York: Houghton, Mifflin and Co. (Translated by Henry Wadsworth Longfellow.)

Asimov, Isaac. 1971. *A Treasury of Humor*. Boston: Houghton, Mifflin Company.

Beckett, Samuel. 1957. *Murphy*. New York: Grove Press.

Boethius. 1999. *The Consolation of Philosophy*. New York: Penguin Books.

Carroll, Lewis. 1971. *Alice in Wonderland*. New York: W.W. Norton. Chaucer, Geoffrey. 1977. *The Canterbury Tales*. New York: Penguin Books. (Translated into modern English by Nevill Coghill.) Echevarría, Roberto González. 2009. *Cervantes' "Don Quixote."* Open online class. https://oyc.yale/NODE/256.

Eliot, T. S. 1943. *The Four Quartets*. New York: Harcourt, Brace & World.

—. 1943. *The Waste Land*. New York: Harcourt, Brace & World. Goethe, Johann Wolfgang von. 1908. *Faust: parts I and II*. London:

J. M. Dent & Sons, LTD.; New York: E. P. Dutton & Co., Inc. (Translated by Albert G. Latham.)

Graziano, Vincent. 2018. *The Family Jewels: A Novel*. Larchmont, New York: GGP Publishing, Inc.

Ibsen, Henrik. 1935. "The Wild Duck" in *Eleven Plays of Henrik Ibsen*. New York: B. A. Cerf: D. S. Klopfer: Modern Library.

Joyce, James. 1951. *Exiles: A Play in Three Acts*. New York: Viking Press.

—. 1960. *A Portrait of the Artist as a Young Man*. Harmondsworth, Middlesex: Penguin Books.

—. 1980. *Ulysses*. Middlesex: Penguin Books.

Kruzewski, Debby. 2018. *Precious and Fragile Things*. La Vergne: Covenant Books.

Mann, Thomas. 1936. *Death in Venice: And Seven Other Stories*. New York: Vintage Books. (Translated by H. T. Lowe-Porter.)

Melville, Herman. 1949. *Moby Dick or The White Whale*. Garden City, New York: The Literary Guild of America.

Milton, John. 1957. "Paradise Lost" in *Complete Poems and Major Prose*. New York: The Odyssey Press.

—. 1957. "Paradise Regained" in *Complete Poems and Major Prose*. New York: The Odyssey Press.

—. 1957. "Comus" in *Complete Poems and Major Prose*. New York: The Odyssey Press.

—. 1957. "Sampson Agonistes" in *Complete Poems and Major Prose*. New York: The Odyssey Press.

Murphy, Charles M. 2019. *Mystical Prayer: The Poetic Example of Emily Dickinson*. Collegeville, MN: Liturgical Press.

Mussio, Thomas. 1993. *Models of the Soul and Versions of Conversion in Renaissance Poetry from Dante to Milton*. Michigan: University of Michigan.

Pynchon, Thomas. 2006. *Gravity's Rainbow*. New York, NY: Penguin Books.

Rabelais. 1990. *Gargantua and Pantagruel.* New York: Norton. (Translated by Burton Raffel.)

Rodgers, John. 2008. *John Milton and Paradise Lost.* Open Online Class, https://oyc.yale.edu/NODE/106.

Rostand, Edmund. 1923. *Cyrano de Bergerac.* New York: Modern Library. (Translated by Brian Hooker.)

Shakespeare, William. 1917–1928. "As You Like It" in *The Yale Shakespeare.* New Haven: Yale University Press.

—. 1917–1928. "Hamlet" in *The Yale Shakespeare.* New Haven: Yale University Press.

—. 1917–1928. "Henry IV pts. 1, 2" in *The Yale Shakespeare.* New Haven: Yale University Press.

—. 1917–1928. "Henry V" in *The Yale Shakespeare.* New Haven: Yale University Press.

—. 1917–1928. "Henry VI pts, 1. 2" in *The Yale Shakespeare.* New Haven: Yale University Press.

—. 1917–1928. "King Lear" in *The Yale Shakespeare.* New Haven: Yale University Press.

—. 1917–1928. "Macbeth" in *The Yale Shakespeare.* New Haven: Yale University Press.

—. 1917–1928. "A Midsummer Night's Dream" in *The Yale Shakespeare.* New Haven: Yale University Press.

—. 1917–1928. "Richard II" in *The Yale Shakespeare.* New Haven: Yale University Press.

—. 1917–1928. "The Tempest" in *The Yale Shakespeare.* New Haven: Yale University Press.

—. 1985. "Twelfth Night" in *The New Cambridge Shakespeare.* New York: Cambridge University Press. (Edited by Elizabeth Donno.)

Toole, John Kennedy. 1980. *A Confederation of Dunces.* Baton Rouge: Louisiana State University Press.

Trollope, Anthony. 1867. *The Last Chronicle of Barset,* v. 1–3. Leipzig: Bernhard Tauchnitz.

—. 1940. *The American Senator*. 1940. New York: Random House.

—. 1948. *He Knew He Was Right*. London, New York: Oxford University Press.

—. 1951. *The Eustace Diamonds*. Garden City, NY: Doubleday.

—. 1962. *Barchester Towers*. London: J. M. Dent, New York: E. P. Dutton.

—. 1973. *Mr. Scarborough's Family*. London, New York: Oxford University Press.

—. 1974. *The Belton Estate*. London: Oxford University Press.

—. 1982. *Can You Forgive Her?* New York: Oxford University Press.

—. 1982. *Phineas Finn, the Irish Member*. Oxford, New York: Oxford University Press.

—. 1982. *The Way We Live Now*. Oxford, New York: Oxford University Press.

—. 1983. *Phineas Redux*. Oxford, New York: Oxford University Press.

—. 1983. *The Duke's Children*. New York: Oxford University Press.

—. 1983. *The Prime Minister*. Oxford, New York: Oxford University Press.

—. 1985. *Orley Farm*. Oxford, New York: Oxford University Press.

—. 1989. *Doctor Thorne*. New York: Oxford University Press.

—. 1989. *Framley Parsonage*. New York: Oxford University Press.

—. 1989. *The Small House at Allington*. New York: Oxford University Press.

—. 1989. *The Warden*. New York: Oxford University Press.

—. 1993. *The Fixed Period*. Oxford, New York: Oxford University Press.

Wodehouse, P.G. 1933. *Heavy Weather*. Boston: Little, Brown, and Co.

Science

Ferris, Timothy. 1988. *Coming of Age in the Milky Way*. New York: Morrow.

Gingerich, Owen. 2004. *The Book Nobody Read: Chasing the Revolutions of Nicholas Copernicus*. New York: Walker & Company.

Greene, Brian. 2003. *The Elegant Universe*. New York: Vintage Books. Primack, J. R. 2006. *The View from the Center of the Universe: Discovering Our Extraordinary Place in the Cosmos*. New York: Riverhead Books.

Szpiro, George G. 2003. *Kepler's Conjecture*. Hoboken, NJ: John Wiley & Sons.

Solomon, Robert. 2008. *The Little Book of Mathematical Principles, Theories, & Things*. New York: Metro Books.

Theology

Anonymous. 1961. *The Cloud of Unknowing*. Baltimore: Penguin Books. (Translated by Clifton Wolters.)

Arminjon, Fr. Charles. 1881. *The End of the Present World and the Mysteries of the Future Life*. Manchester, NH: Sophia Institute Press. (Translated by Susan Conroy and Peter McEnerny.)

Badde, Paul. 2010. *The Face of God: The Rediscovery of the True Face of Jesus*. San Francisco: Ignatius Press.

Bergsma, John Sietze. 2019. *Jesus and the Dead Sea Scrolls: Revealing the Jewish Roots of Christianity*. New York: Random House.* Bergson, Henri. 1935. *The Two Sources Of Morality And Religion*. New York: Henry Holt and Company.

Bloch, R. Howard. 2004. *God's Plagiarist: The Fabulous Industry and Irregular Commerce of the Abbe Migne*. Chicago: University of Chicago Press.

Board of Trustees of the Confraternity of Christian Doctrine. 2010. *New American Bible* (revised edition). Philadelphia: American Bible Society.

Bouyer, Louis. 1950 *The Pascal Mystery*. Chicago: Regnery.

Bressel, Jonathan. 2016. *Treasure of Shabbat*. Jerusalem: Living Press.*
Cahn, Jonathan. 2020. *The Night Light* (DVD). Lodi, NJ: Hope of the World.

Calloway, Fr. Donald H., MIC. 2020. *Consecration to St. Joseph, the Wonders of Our Spiritual Father*. Stockbridge, MA: Marian Press.

Carstens, Christopher. 2017. *A Devotional Journey into the Mass*. Manchester, NH: Sophia Press.

Cavins, Jeff. 2011. *The Bible Timeline: The Story of Salvation*. (VHS) West Chester, PA: Ascension Press.

Connell, Janice T. 2013. *The Spiritual Journey of George Washington*. North Charleston, NC: CreateSpace.

Crean, Thomas. 2009. *The Mass and the Saints*. San Francisco: Ignatius Press.

Cruz, Joan Carroll. 1987. *Eucharistic Miracles and Eucharistic Phenomena in the Lives of the Saints*. Rockford, IL: Tan Books.

Davis, Stephen (ed.) 1997. *The Resurrection*. Oxford, New York: Oxford University Press.

De Caussade. 1975. *Self-Abandonment to Divine Providence*, Garden City, NY: Image Books. (Translated by John Beevers.)

De Montfort, Louis. 1985, 1941. *True Devotion to Mary*. Rockford, Ill.: Tan Books. (Translated by Fr. Frederick Faber.)

Dulles, Avery Cardinal, S. J. 2008. *Church and Society*. New York: Fordham University Press.*

Feingold, Lawrence. 2018 *The Eucharist: Mystery of Presence, Sacrifice, and Communion*. Steubenville, OH: Emmaus Academic.*

Gihr, Nicholas, Dr. 1931. *The Holy Sacrifice of the Mass*. (6th ed.) St. Louis, MO: Herder Book Co.

Groeschel, Benedict, Fr. 2010. *I Am with You Always: A Study of the History and Meaning of Personal Devotion to Jesus Christ for Catholic, Orthodox, and Protestant Christians.* San Francisco: Ignatius Press.

Hahn, Scott. 1999. *The Lamb's Supper: The Mass as Heaven on Earth.* New York: Doubleday.

—. 2016. *The Creed: Professing the Faith through the Ages.* Steubenville, Ohio: Emmaus Road Publishing.*

—. 2018. *The Fourth Cup: Unveiling the Mystery of the Last Supper and the Cross.* New York: Image.

Hahn, Scott and Leonard, Matthew. 2020. *Genesis to Jesus* (VHS series) (EWTN).

Hildebrand, Dietrich von. 1962. *In Defense of Purity: An Analysis of the Catholic Ideals of Purity and Virginity.* Baltimore, MD: Helicon.

Jaspers, Karl. 1961. *Nietzsche and Christianity.* Chicago: H. Regnery Co. Jungmann, Joseph. 1976. *The Mass: An Historical, Theological, and Pastoral Survey.* Collegeville, MN: Liturgical Press.

Kowalska, Faustyna, St. 2000. *Diary: Divine Mercy in My Soul* (3rd ed. with revisions). Stockbridge, MA: Marians of the Immaculate Conception.

Larson, Frederick A. 2007. *The Star of Bethlehem: Unlock the Mysteries of the World's Most Famous Star.* Santa Monica: Genius Entertainment.

Mahoney, Tim. 2015. *Patterns of Evidence: Exodus* (DVD). St. Louis Park, MN: Thinking Man Films.

—. 2019. *Patterns of Evidence: The Moses Controversy.* (DVD). New York, NY: Virgil Films.

—. 2020. *Patterns of Evidence: The Red Sea Miracle* (Pts. 1, 2, DVD). St. Louis Park, MN: Thinking Man Films.

Mazza, Enrico. 1986. *The Eucharistic Prayers of the Roman Rite.* New York: Pueblo Publishing Co.

Meier, John P. 1979. *The Vision of Matthew: Christ, Church, and Morality in the First Gospel.* New York: Paulist Press.

Moorman, George J., Fr. 2007. *The Latin Mass Explained.* Rockford, IL: Tan Books.

Noll, Mark. 2005. *Is the Reformation Over? An Evangelical Assessment of Contemporary Roman Catholicism.* Grand Rapids, MI: Baker Academic.

—. 2006. *The Civil War as a Theological Crisis.* Chapel Hill, NC: University of North Carolina Press.

O'Connor, Edwin. 1958. *The Dogma of the Immaculate Conception: History and Significance.* Notre Dame, IN: University of Notre Dame Press.

Ott, Ludwig. 1954. *Fundamentals of Catholic Dogma.* St. Louis, MO: Herder Book Co.

Pacwa, Mitch, 2020. Fr. *Scripture and Tradition.* EWTN series. Paine, Tom. 1974. *The Age of Reason.* Secaucus, NJ: Citadel Press. Paine, Thomas. 1892. *The Complete Religious and Theological Works.* New York: Peter Eckler.

Pelikan, Jaroslav. 2003. *Credo: Historical and Theological Guide to Creeds and Confessions of Faith in the Christian tradition.* New Haven: Yale University Press.*

Richard, R. Thomas. 2004. *The Interior Liturgy of the Our Father.* Beaufort, SC: Fidelis Publications.

Schoeman, Roy. 2020. *What Is Judaism?* Twelve-part Youtube series. Schroeder, Gerald. 1990. *Genesis and the Big Bang: The Discovery of Harmony Between Modern Science and the Bible.* New York, NY: Bantam Books.

Shay, Scott A. 2018. *In Good Faith: Questioning Religion and Atheism.* New York: Post Hill Press.

Sheets, John R., S. J. 1967. *The Theology of Atonement: Readings in Soteriology.* Englewood Cliffs, NJ: Prentice-Hall.

Strobel, Lee. 1998. *The Case for Christ: A Journalist's Personal Investigation of the Evidence for Jesus.* Grand Rapids, MI: Zondervan.

Vagaggini, Dom C. 1976. *Theological Dimensions of the Liturgy: A General Treatise on the Theology of the Liturgy.* Collegeville, MN: Liturgical Press.

Wengier, Francis J. 1955. *The Eucharist–sacrifice.* Milwaukee, WI: Bruce.

Wiese, Bill. 2006. *23 Minutes in Hell.* Lake Mary, FL: Charisma House.

Zugibe, Frederick T. 2005. *The Crucifixion of Jesus: A Forensic Inquiry.* New York: M. Evans and Co.

Miscellaneous

Berger, Joseph. 2014. *The Pious Ones: The World of Hasidim and Their Battles with America.* New York, London: Harper Perennial.

Dwyer, T. Ryle. 1981. *Michael Collins and the Treaty: His Differences with De Valera.* Mercier Press.

Greenblatt, Stephen. 2011. The Swerve: How the World Became Modern. New York: W.W. Norton & Company.

Gregory, Brad S. 2012. The Unintended Reformation: How a Religious Revolution Secularized Society. Cambridge, MA: Harvard University Press.

Netanyahu, Benjamin., Sr. 1995. *The Origins of the Inquisition in Fifteenth Century Spain.* New York: Random House.[21]

Reston, James. 2005. *Dogs of God: Columbus, the Inquisition, and the defeat of the Moors.* New York: Doubleday.

Wilson, Mercedes Arzu. 2006. *Love and Fertility: The Ovulation Method, the Natural Method for Planning Your Family.* Mandeville, LA: BBE.

---

[21] Books not yet read.

We have found the Messiah.

—John 1:41

About the Author

Edward L. Helmrich graduated from Yale in 1983 with a BA in mathematics and courses in philosophy and English literature. He finished one year of graduate mathematics at Fordham University. During a few decades of limited action because of illness and working in the library at Iona College for the (Irish) Christian Brothers, he collected thoughts on faith and literature. Putting together these thoughts and assisted by those presented on EWTN, especially by Scott Hahn, the result was a set of essays and a set of collections of thoughts on different subjects.

He lives in Larchmont, New York, and is a member of the Legion of Mary and the Knights of Columbus and serves as lector, eucharistic minister, altar server, and sacristan at the local Catholic church.

www.ingramcontent.com/pod-product-compliance
Lightning Source LLC
Chambersburg PA
CBHW051139120626
46547CB00012B/874